The Joy and Heartache
of
Our 1960s Music

Also by Mark R. Millikin

Jimmie Foxx: The Pride of Sudlersville

The Glory of the 1966 Orioles and Baltimore

Babe Ruth: Star Pitcher of the 1914 Baltimore Orioles (a booklet)

The Joy and Heartache
of
Our 1960s Music

Mark R. Millikin

ST. JOHANN PRESS

Haworth, New Jersey

ST. JOHANN PRESS

Published in the United States of America
by St. Johann Press
P.O. Box 241
Haworth, NJ 07641
www.stjohannpress.com

Library of Congress Cataloging-in-Publication Data
Millikin, Mark R.
   The joy and heartache of our 1960s music /
Mark R. Millikin
     p. cm.
   Includes bibliographic references and index.
   ISBN 978-0-9914277-1-0 (paperback)
   ISBN 978-1-937943-51-6 (hardcover)
   1. 1960s popular music – History. 2. United States and
   worldwide. 1. Title

The paper used in this publication meets the minimum requirements
of the American National Standard for Information Sciences—
Permanence of Paper for Printed Library Materials,
ANSI/NISO Z39/48-1992

ISBN 978-1-937943-51-6

Manufactured in the United States of America

Dedication

    This book is dedicated to my mother, Rose Marie (Schafer) Millikin and my father Walter Clark Millikin, who gave me and the rest of our family our love for music. They loved popular music and played it often in our home. My mother played the Billboard Hot 100 songs on AM radio in Randolph, Massachusetts from 1957 to 1962, and then in Perry Hall, Maryland, from 1962, onward. Nat King Cole, Frank Sinatra, Sam Cooke, Elvis Presley, Herb Alpert and The Tijuana Brass, and Lou Rawls were just a few of their favorites in the '50s and '60s, and they also embraced some of the Motown hits from the '60s. They played Mitch Miller's Holiday sing-along favorites every Christmas season to make sure we did our share of singing (our family of six and larger groups of friends and relatives who came to our house). Even after mom passed away in 1998 at age 71, dad made it abundantly clear for the next 18 years how much he still enjoyed popular music whether listening to it or singing along with it, examples being Rod Stewart's *American Songbook*, Frank Sinatra, and Big Joe Turner's cover of "Shake, Rattle and Roll." Too, they loved dancing and tried to make sure their daughter and sons did, too. Mom sometimes interviewed me the day after Teen Center dances. Sitting at the kitchen table with me with a grin on her face, she'd ask, "Did you dance much? Was the band good? What songs did they play?"

Contents

Acknowledgments

I THANK MY WIFE, DEBRA MILLIKIN for her love and her constant support and encouragement during this project. She shared many music videos with me reminding me how those singers and bands looked, sang and danced.

It never ceases to amaze me when I listen to popular music, how great so much of it sounds, the pleasure it brings to me and so many people I know. I can't imagine a world without it. I applaud the talent and ingenuity of musicians, vocalists, and producers everywhere. Since the beginning of this project, I've spent thousands of hours listening to music of the late '50s, the '60s and early '70s, mining hundreds of ideas from my memories of those songs when I was a pre-teen, teenager and in my early 20s.

I thank Tom and Bill Douglass, Jabber and Ralph Friesner for all those wonderful listening sessions to new hit records at their houses from 1965 to 1970. Thanks to Tom Nicholson, Mike Applegate, Joe Fitzpatrick and Jerry Weiskopf for all those joyful car rides in Perry Hall listening to our favorite songs from 1968-70. I thank Rick Ofeldt, Bill Van Dyke, Donald Parker, Bart Teems, Kenny Van Dyk and other fraternity brothers for those listening sessions to a wide variety of LPs from 1971-74. Some CDs and books helped me think outside my comfort zone and listen to songs I was not familiar with. Jon Savage's tome, *1966: The Year the Decade Exploded,* and his CD collections of familiar and not so familiar music: *Teenagers & Youth in Music 1951–1960; 1965: The Year the Sixties Ignited; 1966: The Year the Decade Exploded,* and *1967: The Year Pop Divided* were very helpful. It has been a joy for me to become much better acquainted with the music of Bob Dylan; Peter, Paul & Mary, Carole King and country western music of the '60s during this project. Ken Burns' documentary, *The Vietnam War,* made me aware of a broader array of music in the '60s, especially songs that were not hit singles that were on albums only, so they were not played on AM radio. Burns' DVD documentary contains over 100 songs from the '60s and early '70s, and his accompanying CD-set contains 38 of the same songs.

I pored through Joel Whitburn's The Billboard Book of Top 40 Hits: Complete Chart Information About America's Most Popular Songs and Artists, 1955-2009; Joel Whitburn Presents Across the Charts: The 1960s; and Joel Whitburn Presents Top 1000 Hits of the Rock Era: 1955 – 2005, getting reminders about songs I had forgotten about and new information about songs I've always liked, and information about ones I never heard. Mr. Whitburn's books contain information about the first week a hit single was on a chart, how many weeks it stayed on the chart and its peak position on the chart. His books greatly aided me in reconstructing the chronology of various hit singles and different covers of the same song. Whitburn's books were a constant source of fact checking. I note the years that songs first appeared on record charts in this book because song chronology is very important in popular music.

In 2017 and 2018, *Just Right Radio* 104. 7-FM radio broadcasting from Raleigh, NC, gave me many chances to hear songs from the '50s, '60s, and '70s, that I had forgotten about, and some I don't recall ever hearing before.

Three short courses I took at North Carolina State University's Osher Lifelong Learning Institute in 2017-2018, broadened my understanding of music and the relationship between different music genres – (1) *Music of World War I* and (2) *Radio Music of the 1940s* by Dr. Marilyn Lynch and *What In The World Is Music?* By Dr. Jonathan Kramer.

Friends and family have been instrumental in making me aware of TV programs, CDs, DVD documentaries and radio stations that continue to improve my knowledge of '60s music. Jabber told me about *Standing in the Shadows of Motown,* the documentary about Motown's musicians, The Funk Brothers. My cousin Jo Anne Weaver gave me a heads up about the CNN

News' TV documentary series: *The Sixties*. My brother Glenn Millikin reminded me of many songs of the '60s, his favorite era of music. Davis Hays made me aware of the Documentary, *Soundbreaking* that aired on PBS early in 2017. My son Luke plays '50s, '60s, and '70s music for me every time I visit him and his wife Jennifer. My daughter, Melissa Messina and her husband Mike gave me DVD sets and CDs that improved my understanding of '60s music, and my stepdaughter Crystal Sturgill made me aware of concerts related to '60s music in North Carolina. Luke and Melissa took me to see the Beach Boys in concert at the Merriweather Post Pavilion in 2012, during their 50th anniversary tour. Mike Messina and I had many discussions about '60s music especially The Rolling Stones and Bob Dylan. Jesse Sturgill played the *Stingray Music* App, "Jukebox Oldies" for me when we visited him and his wife, Mary Anne.

Many of my high school classmates, cousins and other friends reminded me of what it was like growing up in the '60s, our favorite songs, and the thrill of going to teen center and dancing to live bands playing, current and recent hit songs. Tom Douglass, Ralph Friesner, David Pace, John Bayne, Tommy Nicholson, and Jimmy Ulman were especially helpful recounting our life and music in the '60s. I thank some of my other high school classmates: Jane Nolan Andre, Jeff Barrett, Carolyn Rill Bell, Louise Beyer Bell, Margie Dennis Bender, Robert Brathune, Barbara Canatella, Barbara Webner Carter, Diane Smith Cikanovich, Dawn Elgin Colwell, Bo West Doxanas, Pat Smith Edelmann, Sharon Hewitt, Karen Bragg Hoskins, Gerry Lewis Kuhlman, Monica Bayne Marcum, Debbie Turner Morris, Jennifer Jones Neuhauser, Janet Haebler Penczek, Debbie Tircuit Ryan, Linda Schrenker Natale, Evelyn Wald Sias, Dottie Jones Smith, and Bette Anne Cole Tassone, for sharing some of their memories about Teen Center and our '60s music on *Facebook*. I also thank Carol Cicci, Phil Hoskins (teen center days and its bands) and Peggy Clarke (Herb Alpert's music) for sharing some of their memories of our '60s music with me in person or on *Facebook*. I thank Galen Tromble for starting a discussion on my behalf with some of his trumpet playing friends to discuss the influence Herb Alpert had during their formative years of playing trumpet and listening to music in the '60s.

Thanks to Barb Sullivan and Bruce Sullivan and several members of our Perry Hall High Classes of '69 and '68 for sharing a few memories on *Facebook* about the Beatles concert they attended in Baltimore's Civic Center in September 1964. Barb and Bruce had seats close to the front row.

Musical DVDs that were especially helpful included *Standing in the Shadows of Motown; Get On Up; A Hard Day's Night; The Beatles: The First U. S. Visit; Eight Days A Week: The Touring Years; T. A. M. I. Show; Motown: The DVD: Definitive Performances; Time/Life History of Rock 'N' Roll, The Beatles Anthology;* and *Soundbreaking: Stories from the Cutting Edge of Recorded Music.*

Preface

T HE SEEDS OF THIS BOOK WERE PLANTED IN 1957, when I heard mom and dad play Sam Cooke's "You Send Me" and Patti Page's "Old Cape Cod," and in 1960 and 1962 when I heard their 45-records of Elvis's "Now or Never" and "Return To Sender" and Chubby Checker's "The Twist". It wasn't just the sound of the records playing that impressed me, but their happy faces and their dancing, too.

I was "there" in the '60s (and late '50s and early '70s). I saw Elvis Presley on the *Ed Sullivan Show* in the '50s, and the Beatles' first appearance playing music in America on *Ed Sullivan* in February 1964. I witnessed the British invasion of rock bands in 1964 and 1965, and the U. S. musicians' rebuttal.

In the '60s, living the life of a teenager was thrilling and invigorating because popular music turned us upside down, inside out. When I listened to popular music in the early '60s every day, it was broadcast on AM radio, only. It followed us everywhere we went whether we heard actual playing of it or were just singing a song in our head, or out loud, or humming a tune. The quality of the sound of our hit songs improved with new instrumentation and better technology. New dances abounded. Whenever we went to weekly dances at Teen Center or monthly high school dances at Perry Hall Senior High School, we danced to "Live" bands that ignited us with their stirring covers of current and recent Top 40 hit songs. Their live music fueled an adrenalin rush to go along with teenage levels of sex hormones—a veritable explosion of excitement inside of us.

There were many musicians playing songs in different genres, some of which were new in the mid and late '60s. This gave us a rich variety of themes, rhythms/beats and sounds. We had more alternatives and choices of popular music than our older brothers and sisters and parents ever dreamed of when they were teens. Music of the '60s took over teenagers' lives. It became a part of so much of what we did, often elevating our enjoyment and sometimes our heartache of being that age.

The music we listened to as teens was our catalyst, fueling our emotions, our ups and downs, especially with young love. It was our mood engine. In the absence of covering the love theme and courtship in classes in school, we tried to learn as much as we could about it in '60s through all the songs we listened to. Sometimes this was problematic because songs often oversimplified the topic and were often idealistic, rather than realistic. Still, popular music affected our thinking about the love scene—we were always hearing the lyrics and they grabbed us. Other songs hyped dancing (usually connected with courtship or celebrating the euphoria we felt being together), and some songs addressed social causes, but the love scene and popular music were intertwined most of the time in the '60s, just like it has always been.

When we were pre-teens and teenagers, many of us listened to music with our friends for a half hour or more and talked about why we liked or disliked various songs. How often do you listen to music with a group of friends that way when you are middle-aged or a senior citizen? If we attended college and lived on campus we listened to music by ourselves and with friends in our dorm or fraternity/sorority bedrooms, and at dances and concerts more often than any time later in our life.

We often grow up believing that the music we listened to as teens was the best pop music ever recorded. This is because the music we heard in our "formative years', especially when we were teens, has a special importance to us that stays with us our whole lives. I do not try to make the case in this book that '60s music was the best overall set of popular songs ever recorded and released. However, many music fans and some musicians who grew up in the '60s and became successful recording stars later, believe the '60s were the best era for popular music. Tom Petty said in an interview for the *Soundbreaking* documentary: "All people always think their time, their music, was better. Mine actually was. "Phil Collins wrote in his liner notes for his album, *Essential Going Back* (2016): "I grew up in the '60s and even allowing for the cliché that whatever era you grew up in, "your own" particular era provided the music that was the "best," the '60s were without a doubt the pinnacle of the songwriting, producing and the performing art. Thank God, I grew up in those years. "

We grew up hearing our parents and other adults say things like, "Oh that song brings back memories of when I was with so and so or on my first date or at my first dance. "It was hard to believe that their memory could reach back that far in time or be affected that deeply by a specific song. Now, we baby boomers are experiencing the same thing. Music that we heard when we were pre-teens and teens is often locked in place in our memories just the way our parents said it worked. Our memory that is triggered by a song we hear from that time of our life sometimes reminds us of the first time we heard the song, a person or people we were with or especially a girlfriend or boyfriend we were with when we heard it, a local band that played it or a dance venue where we heard it. Sometimes we remember a specific connection with a song so clearly that we know why we feel a certain way when we hear it; other times we're puzzled why a song spurs a strong emotion in us. My high school classmate Jimmy Ulman recently said it best, "If you are like me all you have to do is hear a certain song and its takes you right back to those times on Ebenezer Road in Perry Hall [at our high school]. While I listen, I can hear voices and see the faces of my classmates. "

Teens often like or even revel in the thought that they can label much of the current popular music "their music" at any one time, and like knowing their parents don't like the same music. In the '60s, our parents did not like garage music or psychedelic music, but many of them liked Motown music and many songs on the adult contemporary (AC) chart. In the mid-'60s the AC chart shared some of the same songs that were on the BB Hot 100. Some songs that both teens and parents liked, appeared on the AC chart, and some songs we both liked were on the BB Hot 100, chart only.

Melissa and Luke liked some of the music from "my" teen listening years. Melissa was playing "Magic Carpet Ride" in her Anne Arundel Hall dorm room at University of Maryland when I arrived there when she was a 19-year old college student, and Luke enjoyed some of Marvin Gaye's later hits from the '70s and the Doors' music when he was 17. I should not have been surprised that they liked some music from the '60s and '70s. After all, I liked some of my parents' music, and Melissa and Luke sang some of the Beach Boys' '60s music with me when they were 10-12 years old and we were driving on our way to Ocean City for a beach vacation. Years later in June 2012, they took me to see the Beach Boys concert at Columbia, MD during the Beach Boys' 50th anniversary tour.

In 2018, we still hear our '60s music more than we ever dreamed we would 50 years after so many of those songs first became hit records. We hear those songs in restaurants, gas stations, travel stops, stores, and original covers of many hit records are played in the background of new TV commercials.

The story of these songs is much more exciting for me to write about than music from another era – they reached their peak popularity when I listened to music most closely and played them more often as a pre-teen and teenager. For many of us in the '60s, music was all-encompassing. We became one with our music. It was that way for me beginning at the age of 11 (1962) and remained that way into my early 20s (1973). I listened to it whenever possible and liked the variety of what I was hearing.

Knowing the chronology of songs and covers of various songs in popular music is key to a better understanding of how recording artists were influenced by music they were listening to, before they wrote or recorded a song. At the risk of being a bit unwieldy, in this book I usually include the year a hit single or album cut was first issued by a recording artist, rather than listing that information in an appendix or not at all. I hope for most readers this is a convenience when they read this book.

Many sections of this book could be expanded as the basis of books of their own. Examples are the sections herein on "How did they make that sound?" and "Musicians competing and learning from each other". These sections in my book provide a brief set of examples, only, for the reader.

Few books exist that explain from the non-musicians' point of view, how popular music affects us and why we love it so much. We're the silent majority in the world of music. We have a harder time talking with musicians and non-musicians about music and explaining why we like certain songs. But we're obviously glad that musicians create and play music and it's a very big part of our lives. Too, we have an important role in deciding what songs become the biggest hit singles and record albums because of our overall buying power.

This book is not just about popular music in the 1960s in the United States. Many of these songs reached widespread popularity in scattered regions, worldwide. Little did I know back in the '60s and early '70s, that countries other than the U. S. , United Kingdom and Canada had their own charts tracking the appeal of current hit songs, many of them being the same ones we were listening to in the U. S. A few random examples follow. Popular music listeners in 1966, made the Beatles' "We Can Work It Out" b/w "Day Tripper" number one in U. K. , U. S. , Australia, and Netherlands; number two in Germany; and number 3 in Belgium. In 1966, "Good Vibrations" reached number one in the U. S. , the U. K. , New Zealand and Malaysia; number 2 in Canada and Norway; number 3 in South Africa, Ireland and Finland; and number 4 in The Netherlands. In early 1969, Tommy James and the Shondells' "Crimson and Clover" peaked at number one on charts in the U. S. , Canada, Germany, New Zealand and Switzerland (but did not appear on the U. K. chart). In 1971, Rod Stewart's hit single, "Maggie May" gained widespread appeal, peaking at number one in Canada, U. S. , U. K. , and Australia, number two in Ireland, number three in New Zealand, number five in Switzerland, and number 11 in Germany. Thus, this book pertains to popular music fans in the U. S. , U. K. , Canada, Germany, Switzerland, Australia, New Zealand, and to some extent Norway, Finland, Denmark, Belgium, and South Africa.

I cover some of the music and musicians of the mid-late '50s, because they formed much of the foundation of music of the 1960s, and I also cover popular music of the early '70s, because it's a direct outgrowth of '60s popular music. I recount the story of life in the '60s and how conditions of the times affected our music and how music affected our lives.

I hope that this book stirs up memories of songs that baby boomers liked that they may have forgotten about. It may prompt some people to revisit forgotten favorites or make them aware of songs they did not know about back then. It should also give people who did not live in the 1960s, a better understanding of that music.

During this project, I kept re-visiting the songs and the moments and people connected to them that have brought so much joy to me. Collectively, all the music I heard in the late '50s, the '60s and early '70s and my family and friends associated with them, inspired me to write this book. Hearing those songs again during this project, kept rejuvenating me to complete this book.

1

Ways we listened to music

♪

FOR MANY OF US, music listening started with the songs our parents or older brothers and sisters played on their phonograph and the radio. My mother loved the current Top 40 playlists on WBZ-AM radio in Boston in the late '50s and early '60s, and WCAO-AM radio in Baltimore from the early '60s, onward. Mom and dad bought 45-records—some Elvis songs, Nat King Cole, Chubby Checker's "The Twist," Sam Cooke, Lou Rawls, and Al Martino. They were happy with their portable Hi Fidelity *Majorette* record player their neighbors and family gave them before we moved from Baltimore, MD to Randolph, Massachusetts in 1957. Their record player had the standard 45-record spindle that held a stack of records on it that automatically released the lowest record for next playing when the current record was finished.

In the '60s, we pre-teens and teenagers across the nation listened to AM music on our desk radio in our bedroom, transistor radios, car and kitchen radios; records on our bedroom phonograph, family room phonograph, our friends' record players; jukeboxes in eateries; and sometimes recording groups on TV. Those 45-records and LPs were vinyl discs stored in paper and cardboard sleeves, but once we put them on a phonograph and turned up the volume, they sent a jolt through us. We heard live music at Teen Center and High School dances and live concerts. In the late '60s, teens started buying 8-track tape players, mostly for their cars.

In my bedroom, that ultimate safe, relaxed environment, I listened to AM radio, records and reel-to-reel tapes for thousands of hours from 1963 through 1969. I played my 45s and record albums (LPs) often because of their ready access (and hoped some of the new 45-records I bought would have good B-sides). Now if I hear those songs they often take me back there. It's strange and a bit eerie sometimes, but still enjoyable to hear them in that context. They evoke various memories of that relaxed atmosphere for music listening, our loving family life, a girl I liked or friends I was with when I heard those songs.

I cannot remember either of my parents ever coming into my bedroom and saying, "Please turn the volume down on that radio or record player, or how many times are you going to play that same record? "We teens were famous for playing a new 45-record or LP over and over, again, and playing it loud, before finally mixing it in with other records we owned and giving it a break before we tired of it too much. My parents had good reasons to come in my room and complain—I just don't remember them doing it. It's amazing to me how patient and tolerant they were.

Teens across the U. S. bombarded their younger brothers and sisters with their music. Sometimes we listened to music together in our house, because my brothers and I shared a room and Nancy's room was just down the short hallway from our room. What were my younger brothers Glenn and Steve and my sister Nancy thinking when they heard my radio, records or reel-to-reel tapes playing? Sometimes they had to be thinking, "that song again? " Or, "I like that song, or I sure don't like this one. "When they hear some of those songs today, it still takes them back to our home on Tammy Road in Perry Hall in the '60s.

Uncle Dick gave dad a reel-to-reel tape player in the mid-'60s and made reel-to-reel tapes for dad that included Herb Alpert, Dionne Warwick, and Bert Kaempfert. Those tapes had a healthy dose of "easy listening/adult contemporary" hit singles playing when my parents had family and friends at our house. Dad and I were excited when he bought a *Sony* stereo receiver/cassette tape player, Garrard 40B turntable and stereo speakers in 1970. Now we had *stereo* for FM radio and records in our family room/den.

Everyone had a different set of songs that we liked best for a whole host of reasons. Each of us have a different personal make up. We heard a similar set of songs compared to our friends. Still, we each heard songs in a different order and number of times based on when we listened to the radio, music our parents played or listened to, and what music our friends played when we saw them and what records we and our siblings owned. Some teens, especially if they lived in more rural areas, heard a heavier dose of country western songs and many black teenagers living in the cities heard mostly soul music on their radios and record players, compared to the mix of songs many suburban white teens listened to. Thanks to my friends during junior high school, high school and college, I heard many more hit songs from their 45s and LPs than I would have heard otherwise.

Our AM radio DJs gave us a few tidbits about our hit songs and hit makers, and some teens bought teen music magazines. Some of the more popular teen magazines in the U. S. in the '60s were *16*, *'Teen* Magazine, *Tiger Beat*, *Flip*, *Fifteen*, and *Teen World*. By the mid and late '60s, more LPs' liner notes told us about the album's songs and its musicians. *Rolling Stone* Magazine started November 9, 1967, and it is still publishing 51 years later.

2

AM Radio

♪

AM RADIO STATIONS were our lifeline to hearing current and new pop, soul and other music and recent oldies from a few years ago, in the 1960s. We dealt with the inherent difficulty of tuning in an AM station (FM stations playing popular music in stereo came later, mostly in the late '60s and '70s) and broadcasts were often plagued by some static. We usually heard songs for the first time on a random basis while listening to AM radio. We also heard some new hit songs for the first time on a 45-rpm record or long-playing record album (record album or LP) at our friend's house.

Beginning in 1963, I listened to popular music on my desk radio in my room on weekends and after school each day in between homework, and all summer. In the summer, before we started working part time or full time, we had plenty of time to listen to music even though we played plenty of sports and made regular trips walking to our shopping center, only a quarter of a mile away. Many of us had as much homework in junior high school as in senior high school, but we still became very familiar with the weekly top forty hits on several radio stations.

There was more anticipation when listening to music on radio in the '60s. We didn't have on-demand playlists that we have now, compliments of iTunes and other MP3 files. Unless you owned the song on a 45-record or record album, it was strictly a matter of luck as to whether you heard one of your favorite songs or a new song that day. If you listened to a station for an entire hour or two, you were likely to hear a top ten hit you were waiting for, but that was hard to do. You could change the dial to other stations, but then it became more of a hit or miss as to whether you heard the songs you liked best over that one or two-hour period. Even musicians had to deal with this limitation when a new hit song they liked was first released. The Beach Boys' Carl Wilson recalled: "When the Beatles' 'I Want To Hold Your Hand' first came out on the radio, I stayed up all night just to hear the song about once every hour. "

Sometimes, when we waited for our favorites to be played on AM radio, it brought out the worst in our lack of patience (and it still does). I had great difficulty letting a song that was not one of my favorites play through and just listen to a mix of favorites along with personal also-rans for 30 minutes in a row. If I heard the beginning of the next song and it was not one of my favorites, I often changed the station searching for a better song and picked one I liked, even if it was half over. Driving down the road in our cars, the car radio was always on, and push buttons or radio dials let us switch back and forth between various stations searching for a good song to put us in a good mood or keep us in a good one.

Because most songs (then as always) had a unique intro, we knew in a few seconds if it was a "don't touch that dial (tuning knob)" song or "it's time to find a better tune." It became a source of pride to recognize a song's beginning in as few notes as possible. Aaron Neville's "Tell It Like It Is" began with about 12 successive piano notes and you knew it was his slow-dance masterpiece within the first few notes. "Summer In The City" started with two successive organ notes and a drum beat, then the same two organ notes and drumbeat and you knew it was that song before John Sebastian started singing, "Hot town, summer in the city…" The Soul Survivors' "Expressway To Your Heart" blurted out two different successive sets of five car horn "notes" that lasted five seconds, so we knew before the drums, guitar or horns even began, that one of our favorite soul songs was under way. Brian Wilson's opening "I-I-I-I-I-I" with the echo and organ sound in the background told us "Good Vibrations" was starting before Brian sang the rest of the Beach Boys' song. Tommy James' lead singing (with an echo): "I-I-I-I… " and six opening lead guitar notes signified that "Crimson And Clover" was playing, before he sang: "Oh, I don't hardly know her." And there were the opening guitar riffs for many songs like "Day Tripper," "Satisfaction," and

"Don't Worry Baby" and the opening orchestral bits for the *Sgt. Peppers* album's intro song and the *Magical Mystery Tour* album's opening song. The opening drum beats for the Temptations' "Ain't Too Proud To Beg" are unmistakable. And the examples are endless.

Transistor radios were small and portable (battery operated), and they gave teenagers and others an easy way to listen to the music and baseball or football games in the late '50s and '60s. They even had a small portal for an earphone plug so teens could listen to them in private or late at night in our bedrooms. I rarely listened to music on a transistor radio in our house because it was hard to tune in stations and they didn't sound very good, even compared to our static-ridden AM stations on desk radios (especially during any thunderstorm).

Still, the transistor radio came in handy if we were outside in our yard or elsewhere. For three summers when I was 13 to 15, I stayed at my Grandmother Mil's (my dad's mother) house in East Baltimore for several days and went to the Oriole games at Memorial Stadium with my step-grandfather, William Mix. When I was there without an AM desk radio, I was grateful I had a portable transistor radio with a fresh battery for three days to hear my favorite music on Baltimore AM radio stations, WCAO, WWIN, WEBB and WSID. We had no air conditioning then, so I sat on Grandmom's and Mr. Will's marble steps at their rowhouse on N. Curley Street in the sweltering heat in July and August. In the last week of August 1964, I daydreamed about driving a car in a few more years when I heard the Beach Boys' "I Get Around" and Jan and Dean's "Dead Man's Curve" and wondered what the Beatles' movie *A Hard Days' Night* was like, hearing their song of the same name. Listening to the Drifters' "Under The Boardwalk" made me daydream about our family summer resort, Ocean City, Maryland. Other songs I heard on those marble steps in August 1964 were: "My Guy," "Rag Doll," "Where Did Our Love Go," "G.T.O.," "House Of The Rising Sun," "Out Of Sight," and the brand new "Dancing In The Street." Some of those young city teen girls on N. Curley Street stopped by to meet me, the new kid on the block. I loved the attention, but sometimes my grandmother came to the door and shooed them away from our steps: "Alright, you girls go home now!" She probably knew they had a rougher edge than what I was used to in the suburbs. Once I was back home, I put the transistor radio away. I was back to listening to our Top 40 songs on my desk radio, turntable and reel-to-reel tape player.

At night, some local or nearby AM radio stations would sign off by 6pm, so that more distant cities' AM stations' signals reached our radio. Radio listeners living in or near Baltimore, could hear popular music from some AM radio stations with strong broadcasting signals from New York, Boston, Philadelphia, Pittsburgh or nearby Washington, D. C., or we listened to that city's baseball announcers broadcast their hometown team's game. It was another form of research even though I didn't look at it that way at the time. It was fun confirming on my own that teens in many other cities along the East Coast were listening to the same music we were listening to in the Baltimore area. The strength of signals from the more distant stations often faded in and out, so the clarity of a song being played, or a baseball broadcast was compromised. Often, it was just a short matter of time before I reverted to our hometown's radio stations.

When the Beach Boys issued their new hit single "That's Why God Made The Radio (2012)" for their 50th anniversary tour, it connected fully with those old feelings we had, listening to AM radio in the '60s (and FM radio in the late '60s and the '70s). They knew what it was like to listen to their hits and other groups' hits on radio in the '60s, and now they were prodding us to take a ride in our cars and do it again.

In 2018, we love having a large on-demand playlist—we feel like we're living in luxury compared with the circumstances we grew up with. Ironically, sometimes there is a certain appeal listening to the Pandora Station or Sirius Radio today and being surprised when one of our favorite songs plays next, maybe one we haven't heard in a while or forgot about. It's also a little bit like listening to radio in the '60s, being surprised when the next song started playing, rather than pre-arranging a list of the next songs to listen to.

3

Watching the top 40 and buying some of our favorite songs

♪

WE PICKED UP THE NEW LIST of Top forty songs the first day it was released each week on bright colored sheets in Michael's TV & Radio in Perry Hall Shopping Center, usually taking it home (like many electronics shops Michaels sold new TVs, phonographs and radios, and repaired old ones; and sold musical equipment, sheet music, 45-records and LPs). We compared how a song was climbing to a better rating closer to number one or losing ground by having a rating closer to number 40 or off the chart, compared to last week. Which hit singles were in the Top Ten and which song was number one? Any new songs on the new Top 40 caught our eyes (and ears), especially if the song was by a group or vocalist we liked. Which top-selling popular music record albums (arranged in order by their current ranking) were still on the right-hand wall in Michaels and which ones were new? When we pored through the record bin of 45-rpm singles at Michaels, we often found that one or more songs we hoped to buy were sold out, with the owner, saying, "I can't keep that single in the store. It's a red-hot seller here." It was a little bit of inside information you heard firsthand from an "expert" that you won't hear about in that manner today, if you just buy an iTunes song or a CD online. "You were conducting research, you just didn't call it that," Stephen Rabin told me in February 2018. Michael's wall of the top 40 selling record albums was on display all the time, so I looked that over for about ten minutes every week. It often gave me a target or goal for the next album to buy. We could only see those albums, hold them, and read their song lists right there in record stores—there was no way to access information about them at home without computers and the inter net (songs of an album might be listed or covered in a teen magazine or *Rolling Stone* starting in 1967, but most of us didn't buy music magazines). Luckily, we had another option for buying 45s and LPs a few doors down in the same shopping center—Woolworth's five and dime also carried them. While the two stores carried mostly the same current hit singles and LPs, some of the ones they carried were different and sometimes one store was sold out of a 45 or LP, but not the other store.

I remember the first few 45-records I bought in Michaels—it was the summer of '64 and I was 13. I bought The 4 Season's "Rag Doll (June)" with its appealing beat and vocal harmony, The Supremes' "Where Did Our Love Go (July)" with its catchy beat and up tempo feel, and Ronny and The Daytonas' "G. T. O. (August)" about Pontiac's new hot-selling car (a worthy contender of Ford's Mustang and Chevrolet's Camaro in the mid and late -'60s). After that, it's a bit of a blur as to what I bought in what order. Many pre-teens and teens have similar memories of their first records. Of course, musicians remember their early records, too. Paul McCartney recalled that his first 45-record was Gene Vincent's "Be-Bop-A-Lula (1956)," and Elton John remembers that one of his earliest records was Presley's "Hound Dog (1956)."

My first couple record albums were gifts from mom and dad—*Beatles '65* and The Beach Boys' *All Summer Long* for Christmas 1964. Then I bought *The Temptations Sing Smokey* and The Rolling Stones' *Out of Our Heads* in 1965, before retreating to the more affordable 45s for a while. It seems like I played each album about one hundred times, playing whole sides of *Beatles '65* and *The Temptations Sing Smokey*, uninterrupted. The excitement of having my first album, *Beatles '65* likely elevated my liking of the LP, but the great quality of those songs also boosted my enjoyment of it. I had legitimate bragging rights to being one of the earliest pop listeners to get a copy of *Beatles '65*. It was released in the U. S. on December 15, 1964, and I saw it in Perry Hall's Woolworth's up the street about a week later. I told my mother about it just days before Christmas and she bought a copy. *Beatles '65* went on to sell more copies in 1965 than any other "non-soundtrack" LP (almost 2 million). Sometimes, I cheated and went straight to playing the LPs' two songs from its hit single, "I Feel Fine" and "She's A Woman." I couldn't get enough of them, especially "I Feel Fine."

Because I took the weekly trip to Michaels during my junior high school and high school days, and I listened to the Top 40 songs on the radio regularly, I kept pace with the new hit songs that were being issued and the length of time some hit singles remained on the Top 40 of different radio stations. Once I was in college, I didn't listen to radio as much, heard LPs played by my friends and dorm mates often, but I no longer had a rigid routine to keep me in touch with the bigger picture, the larger set of hit singles on the charts and larger set of LPs that were the most popular sellers. In other words, I lost my "edge" on knowledge of the bigger set of hit singles and LPs while in college from 1969 to 1973, compared to when I was in junior high and high school from 1963 to 1969. After my days at University of Maryland, my knowledge and exposure to new hit songs on the charts was even more random and scattered with only occasional listening to the radio or a friend's new LP. This was also the case with many other music lovers who were my age.

Walking up the street or visiting someone at their house when we were teens, our conversation often included, "Hey have you heard that new song by the Temptations, Beatles, Beach Boys or that new Motown record? It was a thrill to listen to popular music on AM radio because that was where you often heard a new hit record for the first time or heard the new rankings of hit records, including the new number one song first. When you're a pre-teen or teen, music gets inside you more, seeps into you and feels more a part of you when you hear it and play it by yourself or with friends. Too, the first few times we heard a *new* song we liked that was on its way up the hit chart, it sent ripples of excitement through us. Its newness made us want to hear it again to enjoy it, and "memorize" it so we knew it from beginning to end. We embraced these songs more fully when we were pre-teens and teens who loved popular music. Teens feel the same way today. Tommy James recalled, "There's nothing more exciting on this earth than an exploding [new] smash-hit single because it just happens everywhere at once and it just goes. It's like an atom bomb. "

Because we listened to popular music so often during our teen years we felt qualified to be in the discussion of what song out of the current hits should be number one. We liked hearing what was the new number one song. If it was one of our favorites it was a confirmation that the experts or the bulk of record buyers agreed with us and we had good judgment in what song should be rated the best. If we didn't like the new number one song, we felt incredulous that it was overrated, or we were surprised its sales were so high.

We couldn't afford to buy *all* the records of all the songs we liked the most, but most of us were buying records. A survey in a March 1966 issue of *Newsweek* estimated that 75 percent of boys and 90 percent of girls in the U. S., (ages 13 to 17) owned records, and 50 percent of boys and 72 percent of girls owned record players. Since our spending money limited how many records we could buy compared to the larger number we liked, we depended on all our other co-listeners to help collectively weigh-in and determine which songs sold the most and kept on being played by DJs in our listening area and around the country. I liked three songs I had on a reel-to-reel tape, "Soul Man," "Tell It Like It Is," and "Sweet Soul Music," just as much as three favorites I had on 45-records: "Reach Out, I'll Be There," "Midnight Confessions" and "Hey Jude." With limited spending money to use for records each week, I was content to have some of my favorite songs on any of three media—45s, LPs and reel-to-reel tapes, for my ready access song list. It was always difficult picking what records to buy when a song was still on the hit charts and its record was readily available in stores because there were so many good current songs at any one time. The longer they were off the current hit charts, the tougher it was to find and buy a hit single in a record store. From 1964 through 1969, I bought about forty 45-records and forty LPs.

Other things always competed for our limited weekly spending money, like sub sandwiches and other food, clothes, sport or music magazines or saving to buy a car. Later, when we were driving, gas and money for dating limited how much we could spend on records. The March 1966 *Newsweek* issue said that America's 17. 9 million teenagers had $12 billion spending money for an average of $670 per teen/year, and an article in August 1966 in the Baltimore *Sunday Sun* estimated that U. S. teens had $15 billion yearly for an average $833 per teen. Whole 12-inch sub sandwiches were $2. 50, a tomato and cheese 12-inch pizza was $1. 10, movie tickets were about $1. 25, gas was 33 cents a gallon, a 45-record was 75 to 90 cents and an LP was 3. 50 to $4.

The present-day marvel of iTunes makes it easy to play an old song and "re-connect" in our minds with the times when it was a current hit and part of our younger lives. Any song by any artist can be bought at the click of a few keys on the computer or smartphone keyboard and a few seconds downloading time. Now we can buy a song off iTunes for 99 cents or a $1.29. It's a rare example of avoiding inflation, except you don't have the actual record and record sleeve, but you have the music. A cautionary note is that if you're a stickler like me who enjoys the version of the song you grew up with the most, many songs by an artist have various versions including "re-recorded" ones and it's worth a few minutes of your time to play some of the versions including the "original" version and "single" version if they are available, before you decide which one you should buy.

4

AM radio disc jockeys

♪

MANY AM-RADIO DISC JOCKEYS all over the U. S. were a joy to listen to in the '60s. The excitement DJs felt was palpable to radio listeners when they played a new song by the Beatles or Marvin Gaye or other hitmakers on the radio. The DJs were often pumped up when introducing a song even after it had been a hit record for weeks on the BB Hot Top 40 or a radio station's own Top 40. Dan Ingram on New York's WABC-AM in the '60s could be heard saying, "I shall return with 'Stop In The Name of Love' while a girls chorus sang in the background, "the Dan Ingram Show." A DJ on Cleveland's WHK-AM in 1965, could be heard saying, "Guys, Bobby Dylan comes front and center at WHK with song number six on the survey. It's called 'Like A Rolling Stone'. You're gonna hear the whole six-minute version here." A video exists of the Ronettes' Ronnie Spector sitting and swaying to Marvin Gaye's "Pride and Joy" in Murray the K's (Murray Kaufman) WINS-AM studio in New York, waiting to meet the Beatles in February 1964. AM radio was where it was at, baby!

In Baltimore, we listened to Johnny Dark on WCAO-AM in 1968, introducing "Girl Watcher": "Every time I hear this next record, I can't help but conjure up thoughts of Ocean City [Maryland]. Would you hand me my binoculars, please? Here come the O'Kaysions. "DJs often emceed live concerts in their home city and Dark had the pleasure of introducing The Beatles to the crowds for two shows in Baltimore's Civic Center on Sep-

13

tember 13, 1964. Dark, Bob Bartel, Kerby Scott and Jack Edwards were among the more popular WCAO disc jockeys. Likewise, Bob Eubanks, a DJ from KRLA (1110-AM) in Los Angeles was instrumental in bringing the Beatles to the Hollywood Bowl and introducing them before their show began there in August 1964.

Meanwhile, Baltimore's black disc jockeys cast a spell over listeners of soul music—Maurice 'Hot Rod' Hulbert on WWIN, Fred 'Rockin' Robin' Robinson on WEBB and WWIN, and Paul 'Fat Daddy' Johnson on WSID (often referred to as the station with Soul In Depth) and WWIN. Fat Daddy, the "330-pound King of Soul, his Royal Highness and high priest of rock n' roll," said, "I programmed my show for the Negro originally. Rhythm and blues used to be race music. But Fat Daddy has become such a large character with everybody that now I program my show for white and black, both. Music brings people closer together. On Perry Hall High School's Friday night dance floor, live band soul music brought blacks and whites together in the late '60s. More and more bands picked up on the popularity of soul music as the first choice for dancing, teaming up black soul singers with white musicians in teen bands in Baltimore and elsewhere around the country.

Fat Daddy's intro was: "Hear me now. Up from the very soul of breathing. Up from the orange crates. From the ghetto through the suburban areas comes your leader of rhythm and blues, the expected one—Fat Daddy, the soul boss with the hot sauce. Built for comfort, not for speed. Everyone loves a fat man! The Fat Daddy Show is guaranteed to satisfy momma. I'm gonna go way out on a limb on this one, Baltimore. Fat poppa. Show stoppa. "

I taped Hot Rod's intro when I was a teen: "Hello mommios and daddies, keen teens, ladies and gentlemen. Commander Hot Rod moving and grooving, wheeling and dealing, hop, skipping and jumping in here, there, each and everywhere bringing you the best in music, oyay, the best in songs, the best in jive, the best in helpful information, dedicated to you, the greatest people in the world, my listeners, as we move and groove, wheel and deal, hop, skip, jump here, there and everywhere. I gotta say this is without a doubt the High Priest of Space, not the flower, not the root, but the seed, sometimes called the herb, sometimes called the burner. VOSA (voice of sound advice)!"

Some AM radio DJs gave us advice about our love lives. When Fred "Rockin Robin" Robinson signed off in the mid '60s at WEBB, he said: "The Old Bird [Rockin' Robin] says, "Hang loose and rock easy (his theme song, 'Rockin' Robin' by Bobby Day playing in the background). Just remember my friend, when you're at the crossroads of your love life—when you're at the fork in the road. And you don't know which way to go. That's the time to take the word from the Bird—Remember if it's good to you, goodness news, it's got to be good for you! I really love it!"

White and black stations that played songs on the Top 40 occasionally mixed "golden oldies," "blasts from the past," or "flashbacks" with current hits (there were no oldies stations). On WWIN an echoing DJ's voice announced that a golden oldie was next on the station's playlist: "Going back, Going back! Way back to get this one! A WWIN Golden Oldie blast!" Or a station would feature a "double play" or "twin-spin," two songs in a row by an artist.

It's difficult to imagine anyone loving their work more than these guys. They were playing their favorite music and getting paid for it, "carrying on" in voices that couldn't be happier while narrating and rhyming on their radio shows, interviewing guests, taking song requests by phone and emceeing for local and national (and international) hit-making groups that came to Baltimore to play at local clubs or concerts. Baltimore's Johnny Dark was one of many disc jockeys who liked their job so much that they felt like they "never worked a day of their lives." It was much the same in towns and cities all over the U.S. We listeners were nodding our heads or dancing, humming or singing along, or drum beating on any nearby surface while we listened to our DJs' playlists.

5

Jukeboxes

JUKEBOXES CONTINUED TO BE POPULAR IN THE '60s much the way they were in the '50s. At our local shopping center, we played songs (a dime for one play; three plays for a quarter) directly on the jukebox at our bowling alley and off the Seeburg Wall-O-Matic player selectors in Reads Drugstore (jukeboxes in the '60s used 45-records; today some of them use CDs). Some of our high school's Beta Phi guys played "Heat Wave" and "Rag Doll," and others played some Beatles' and Herman's Hermits songs in the bowling alley. It was loud and had plenty of bass and made you wish you had one at home. At Reads' Drugstore lunch-counter we played the Rip Chords' "Hey Little Cobra;" Jan and Dean's "Surf City," "Dead Man's Curve," and "Little Old Lady Of Pasadena." Others we played included the Beach Boys' "Surfer Girl" b/w "Little Deuce Coupe," and "I Get Around" b/w "Don't Worry Baby;" Elvis Presley songs and Beatles songs. Even if we had no "extra money" to play some songs, we listened to the music other teens played. In Reads we heard tunes playing from the nearby lunch counter while we pored through new issues of magazines in the periodicals racks, or we sat at the lunch counter drinking a vanilla or cherry coke listening to "free" music. Likewise, less than a quarter mile from the shopping center we played music on Berg's Farm Dairy's jukebox and listened to tunes that we or other teens were playing. There we listened to the Miracles' "Going to a

Go-Go," "I Heard It Through The Grapevine" by Marvin Gaye, The Beatles' "Day Tripper" b/w "We Can Work It Out" and other hit singles.

We couldn't believe that in the Fall of '66 at Perry Hall High School we had a jukebox in the cafeteria to listen to hit songs during lunch. Here we were taking a break from classes, eating lunch on one of three "shifts," seeing guys and girls from tenth through twelfth grades and the icing on the cake was listening to some of our favorite hit singles. With several hundred students per lunch shift who were listening to the music, there was usually someone popping coins in the machine often enough that the jukebox seldom stayed quiet very long. That first year of high school, '66-'67, soul songs were often our first choice—hit records by Aretha, The Temptations, Sam and Dave, The Miracles, and The Four Tops. During our senior year of high school (1968-69), two 45-records that were one-hit wonders—"Judy In Disguise (With Glasses)" by John Fred and the Playboys and the Lemon Pipers' "Green Tambourine Man" were played as often on our lunch period jukebox as new hit singles by repeating hit makers—Steppenwolf's "Born To Be Wild," the Doors' "Hello, I Love You," the Beatles' "Hey Jude," The 5th Dimension's "Aquarius/Let the Sunshine In" and Blood, Sweat & Tears' "You've Made Me So Very Happy." Of course, with jukeboxes, it only took one or two people who really liked a song and kept playing it to give you the impression that a song was more widely popular among the lunch shift than it really was.

Now we have *Touch Tunes* in many bars. You can upload the *Touch Tunes* on your smartphone and play music off the bar's *Touch Tunes* hardware (looks a little like a modified jukebox) directly from your phone.

6

TV shows, movies and musicals

S OME TV SHOWS OF THE LATE '50s AND THE '60s spiked record sales and
the popularity of recording artists, just like live concerts did, and still
do. The *Ed Sullivan Show* and Dick Clark's *American Bandstand* pro-
moted many different popular music recording artists' songs with their live
performances in the late 1950s and 1960s. *Bandstand* was the kingpin of all
TV shows featuring popular music groups in the '50s and '60s, because it
featured popular recording artists *and* teens dancing. We liked catching
recording artists doing one or more of their hits and watching other teens
dance because we learned new dance moves.

Clark's "Rate A Record" on *Bandstand* often asked three teens to listen
to three records newly released and rate them between 35 and 98. When
asked why they liked a song, a key factor that made many tunes highly rated
was, "It's got a great beat and you can dance to it." Many records that Clark's
teens rated high became hit singles on the BB Hot 100 and AM radio stations' weekly Top 40s across the U. S.

No one makes the right choices or predictions all the time about a
record's future on the hit single charts, whether they are musicians, record
producers, record company owners or popular music listeners. One future
hit single flopped on *Bandstand's* Rate-A-Record in late '63, when Clark's
three teens of the moment rated The Beatles' "She Loves You" (on Swan
Records) before the group made their first tour in the U. S. Clark's teens

gave the record an average of 73, and they laughed at a picture of the Beatles' "long hair." But no matter, in late January 1964, "She Loves You" hit the BB Hot 100 and became number one for two weeks, beginning March 21.

Clark featured hundreds of teen idol musicians on *Bandstand* singing one or two of their songs. His thoughtful interviews with his guest musicians fascinated TV viewers and his autograph table for his performers was a welcome extra perk for his show's teen dancers. He was an early promoter of the R&B black artists. Johnny Mathis, Little Richard, Chuck Berry, Jerry Butler, Chubby Checker, Little Anthony and the Imperials, Jackie Wilson, Major Lance, The Platters, Dionne Warwick, The Ronettes and The Crystals appeared on his show one or more times in the late 50s and early '60s. Black teen dancers were on *Bandstand* by the mid-'60s. By performing on *Bandstand*, black musicians gained national exposure and jumps in their records' sales they would not have had otherwise. Some of his other hit-making guest singers, who were not R&B artists in the late '50s and '60s included: Connie Francis, Buddy Holly, the Everly Brothers, Frankie Avalon, Brenda Lee, Paul Anka, the 4 Seasons, Johnny Tillotson, Bobby Rydell, Lesley Gore, The Lovin' Spoonful, Sonny and Cher, The Grassroots and The Righteous Brothers. A few of Clark's other R&B and soul artists in the early and mid-60s were Marvin Gaye, The Miracles, The Temptations, The Supremes, Sam and Dave, and Aretha Franklin.

Between his hundreds of guest recording artists, both new ones and already established stars and his rate-a-records, Clark's *Bandstand* was an important trendsetter for popular music in the late '50s and early '60s. *Bandstand* was on TV all five weekdays for an hour until it was changed to one-half hour, five days a week in 1963. Even when it was reduced to just one hour on Saturday beginning in September 1963, the teen dancing show was a key component of the popular music industry.

On *Ed Sullivan*, musicians usually sang a live version of one or two of their hit songs to a studio audience, while on *Bandstand* they often lip synced their songs to the show's own teen dancers. Ed Sullivan had a strong connection with Motown in the '60s and early '70s, featuring The Temptations, the Supremes, the Four Tops, Smokey Robinson and The Miracles, Gladys Knight and The Pips, Stevie Wonder, Marvin Gaye, and Jackson 5 (many of them appeared on more than one show.)

Ricky Nelson, real-life son of Ozzie and Harriett Nelson on *The Adventures of Ozzie and Harriet*, often played one of his songs with a few band mates at the end of the show to boost record sales of "A Teenager's Romance," "Be-Bop Baby," "Stood Up," "Poor Little Fool," "Travelin' Man" b/w "Hello Mary Lou," "It's Up To You," "For You," and "Fools Rush In." Nelson, like Presley, was handsome in his own right, but unlike Elvis he portrayed a more clean-cut image with his more subdued guitar playing style and lack of dancing and gyrating.

Record companies were keen to the concept that teen record buyers liked buying songs and watching hit makers who were teens or in their early 20s. Frankie of Frankie Lymon and The Teenagers was only 13, when he first sang "Why Do Fools Fall In Love (1956)," Little Peggy March (born Margaret Battivio) first sang "I Will Follow Him (1963)" when she was 15, and Brenda Lee (born Brenda Mae Tarpley) was only 15 singing her first two hits ("Sweet Nothin's" and "I'm Sorry") in 1960. Brian Hyland was only 16 when his "Itsy Bitsy Teenie Weenie Yellow Polkadot Bikini (1960)" became a number one hit on the Hot 100 and he also sang it on *Bandstand*. Anthony Gourdine of Little Anthony and the Imperials was 18, singing his first chart hit "Tears On My Pillow (1958)" and Marcie Blane was 18, when her hit single, "Bobby's Girl (1962)" first hit the charts. Leslie Gore was 17, when she first sang her hits "It's My Party," "It's Judy's Turn To Cry" and "You Don't Own Me" in 1963, and Diane Renay (born Renee Diane Kushner) was 18, when her "Navy Blue (1964)" was number 1 on the AC chart and number 6 on the BB Hot 100 chart. Stevie Wonder was only 15, when he first sang his second number one R&B hit, "Uptight (Everything's Alright)" in early 1966. He was Little Stevie Wonder (13 years old) when his live cover of "Fingertips—Pt. 2" from the Motortown Revue was number one on the BB Hot 100 and R&B charts in 1963. Stevie Winwood was still 18, when he first sang lead vocals for The Spencer Davis Group's "Gimme Some Lovin' (1966)" and "I'm A Man (1967)" before helping form the group, Traffic, late in 1967.

The *Buddy Deane Show* in Baltimore was a local favorite on WJZ-TV from late 1957 to early 1964 (it was the basis for John Waters' 1988 dance comedy movie *Hairspray*). Deane's show was much like *Bandstand* and some of its dancers became regulars who Baltimore teens enjoyed watching as much as the show's guest singers and bands. Baltimore's Michael Olesker wrote: "He [Deane] caused a generation of baby boomer adolescents to rush home from school every afternoon and turn on the television so they could learn how to be cool. "

Deane and the show's producers had great difficulty deciding whether to host shows with both black and white teens dancing together or keep separate shows for black teens and white teens. Deane's show featured black teen dancers one day a month and later one day per week, but the TV station's producers avoided integrated shows with black and white teen dancers together. We were listening to more and more music written and performed by black artists and many white kids didn't care if black kids were also on the show with them, but many white parents opposed integrated shows that would allow intimacy between black and white teens. In the end, the producers threw up their hands and ended the show altogether on January 4, 1964, just before the Civil Rights Act of 1964 was passed.

The Beatles and the British Invasion sparked two new weekly music/dancing TV shows in the U. S., *Shindig!* and *Hullaballoo*, a Beatles cartoon show and *The Monkees* from 1964-66. *Shindig!* (mostly black and white shows) began in Sept. '64 on ABC and lasted until January '66. One of its Fall '65 shows from London featured the Kinks, Rolling Stones, the Byrds and Everly Brothers. *Hullabaloo* (mostly color) started in January '65 on NBC and ended in the Fall of '66. Some of its guest performers included James Brown, Otis Redding, Diana Ross and the Supremes and the Beach Boys. *Shindig!* was created as a replacement for *Hootenanny*, a folk revival TV show that suffered poor ratings when the British Invasion's musicians first appeared in popular music in 1964. Producers of *Shindig!* decided right away that they needed to host a wider array of popular music genres if the show were to gain enough viewers on TV. *The Beatles* was an animated cartoon show on ABC-TV on Saturday mornings from September 1965, through a portion of 1967, followed by reruns into 1969. Thirty-nine different shows featured animated versions of John, Paul, George and Ringo singing a featured song for that episode, often running away from adoring fans, mostly girls, like in *A Hard Day's Night*. The Monkees, were a four-member group that NBC created for a new TV show in response to The Beatles. *The Monkees* sit-com TV show aired from September 1966, through March 1968. The Monkees (mop heads in their own right) with the aid of musicians from The Wrecking Crew issued over a dozen hit singles from 1966 through 1969, with six of those records becoming million sellers. "I'm A Believer (1966)," "Daydream Believer (1967)" and "Last Train To Clarksville (1966)" were their three top-selling songs. Many girls, especially pre-teens and young teens were as crazy about The Monkees' looks and songs as they were about the Beatles.

Two popular music/dance shows from the west coast that broadcast late in the afternoon on the east coast in the '60s were the *Lloyd Thaxton Show* and *Where the Action Is*. *Where the Action Is* aired from '65 to '67, was created by Dick Clark as a spinoff of *American Bandstand* and often featured Paul Revere and the Raiders as "its de facto house band." Freddie "Boom Boom" Cannon sang its theme song, "Action" with a similar sound to his hit "Palisades Park (1962)." The *Lloyd Thaxton Show* aired most of the '60s and featured at one time or another the Temptations, The Turtles, Four Tops, Sonny and Cher, The Byrds, Marvin Gaye, Roger Miller, the Kinks, the Bobby Fuller Four and others. I was shocked the time I was watching *Lloyd Thaxton* and Roger Miller forgot some of the words while singing his new song, "King Of The Road (1965)." I felt sorry for him! These TV shows gave teens in the '60s many more chances to see their favorite musicians than their older siblings had seeing their favorites in the '50s.

TV shows, alongside of many new songs and movies of the late '60s came a long way in pushing the envelope, testing the boundaries of what could be said and even talked about on broadcasts in the 'late '60s. *Laugh In* (from 1968-73) had "sketches with sexual innuendo" or political roots, *The Smothers Brothers Comedy Hour* (original release from 1967-69) opened political dialogue much to the chagrin of the show's producers and some of its sponsors, and *The Dating Game* and *The Newlywed Game* used new terms relating to sexual encounters, especially "making whoopee." They were in color, and colorful, and often surprised us with issues they covered and things that performers and contestants said. *The Smothers Brothers* often featured popular music artists who were shunned by sponsors of other TV shows because of the "political position or subject of some of their songs" including: Pete Seeger; Joan Baez; The Doors; Buffalo Springfield; Cream; Jefferson Airplane; Simon and Garfunkel; and Peter, Paul & Mary. The late '50s and early '60s shows like *Father Knows Best*, *The Donna Reed Show* (one episode featured Shelly Fabares singing her 1962 number one hit "Johnny Angel"), *Leave It To Beaver*, and *Ozzie and Harriett* felt so passe by comparison.

Country music began to receive its due with three TV shows in 1969—*Hee Haw* (CBS), *The Glen Campbell Goodtime Hour* (CBS) and *The Johnny Cash Show* (ABC). Now country music was coming into our living rooms. Country music fans were in their glory and equally important, these shows gave other popular music fans the chance to become more familiar with the genre. Campbell's show was a springboard for his country western tunes and crossover hits and his guest artists. *Hee Haw* featured a wide variety of country artists along with the show's co-hosts, Buck Owens and Roy Clark. Owens played his guitar and Clark picked his banjo in their duets. On their first show in mid-June '69, Buck Owens played his cover of "Johnny B. Goode" and Loretta Lynn sang her hit single, 'Your Squaw Is On The Warpath." Although the show's humor was labelled cornball by some critics, *Hee Haw* had a steady viewership. The skits were brief and spurred plenty of laughter on the show that poured into our homes—settings were in the cornfield, at the country store, the general store front steps and the like. One example, "Well you know how to catch a rabbit? Go in the woods and make a noise like a carrot."

Movies that had theme songs or other songs that were hit singles were abundant in the '60s. Some of the movies in the '60s that included popular songs on the BB Hot 100 were: *The Magnificent Seven* (1960); *The Westside Story* (1961); *The Pink Panther* (1963); *The Great Escape* (1963), *Goldfinger* (1964), *A Hard Day's Night* (1964), *Help!* (1965), *Thunderball* (1965), *The Good, The Bad, and The Ugly* (1966); *The Graduate* (1967); *Once Upon a Time in the West*; *2001: A Space Oydssey* (1968); *Romeo and Juliet* (1968); and *Midnight Cowboy* (1969).

James Bond movies in the mid-'60s hit the bullseye with their male viewers, starting with their movie's erotic intro theme song being sung by star popular vocalists. Shirley Bassey gave a stirring vocal of "Goldfinger" with a strong backing from John Barry's brassy orchestra during the intro for *Goldfinger* and Tom Jones belted out "Thunderball" during that movie's intro along with an erotic visual of nude silhouettes of women swimming, that left lasting impressions on men and boys in movie audiences. Whenever we heard those songs on the radio, their movies' intros flashed across our minds again. What guy didn't have at least a passing fantasy of being Bond, the consummate hero of the good guys vs. the villain and rescuing those ladies?

Movies often boost a song's popularity and they increased airplay time on AM radio and record sales for some songs in the '60s. "Born To Be Wild" by Steppenwolf was a hit single starting in July 1968, for 13 weeks and peaked at number two for three weeks. The song hooked more listeners starting in July 1969, when it was featured in *Easy Rider* and likely boosted Steppenwolf's LP sales. "Everybody's Talkin" by Harry Nilsson only reached number 113 of the Bubbling Under the Hot 100 singles in August 1968, but it became a top ten hit single in August 1969, when it played in the 1969 movie *Midnight Cowboy*. It's a certainty that Simon and Garfunkel's "Mrs. Robinson" released in April 1968, gained some of its popularity (number one for three weeks on the BB Hot 100) from an earlier version of the song that was featured in *The Graduate* beginning in December 1967. If we saw *The Graduate*, we can't hear the song without thinking of middle-aged Anne Bancroft's (Mrs. Robinson) sexual advances towards college graduate Benjamin Braddock (Dustin Hoffman).

Likewise, some Broadway musicals' songs reached higher record sales and more playing time on AM radio because of their popularity on Broadway, first. Barbra Streisand's "People" and "Funny Girl" became popular music hits on AM radio in 1964, a few months after she began singing them in the Broadway musical *Funny Girl*. The Cowsills' "Hair" was a number 2 hit single in the BB Hot 100 in 1969, as a spin-off of the hugely popular Broadway "tribal love rock" musical *Hair*. Oliver's (born William Oliver Swofford) "Good Morning Starshine" (a number 3 hit on the HT and AC charts) and Three Dog Night's "Easy To Be Hard" (a number 4 hit on the HT chart) in 1969, also had their origins in *Hair*.

7

45-records and record albums

ALONG WITH OUR RADIOS, we played our 45-records and record albums on our own phonograph/record player/turntable in the '60s. Brittle shellac record disks that were 78-rpm hit singles of 2 to 3 minutes were the record medium our parents used until Columbia Records developed a long-playing 33 and 1/3-rpm record album in 1948 and RCA Victor issued the first 45-rpm singles in 1949. In the '60s, we didn't always place much importance on owning a good quality stereo record player to listen to all our 45-records and LPs; we just needed to hear our music often and loud, whenever possible. Until the mid- '60s, records were recorded in monophonic, until stereophonic became the chief method in about 1968 after several years transition. In the '60s vinyl records were "king"—they were the only way we bought our music until 8-track tape players and tapes began to compete with records around 1968-69. Cassette tape players and tapes closely followed starting about 1970.

LPs and 45-records were priced low enough in the '60s (less than a dollar for a 45-record and less than four dollars for an LP) that many teens bought several of their favorite new songs each week. At the same time, portable record players became affordable which meant teens could play their music in their own bedrooms away from their parents' hi fidelity (HiFi) record players with wooden consoles in many families' living rooms. We learned early during our record collecting, that it helped preserve a better quality of sound on our vinyl records (less static and crackling) if we avoided putting multiple fingerprint/skin oil smudges on the records' microgrooves. We held the edges of our vinyl records with the middle section of our four fingers from each hand, then used a quick rolling action to flip the record over without ever touching the grooves with our fingertips or thumbs.

Most of the seven-inch diameter 45-records in the early '60s were songs that lasted two to three minutes. Then, in the mid-to-late '60s, some musicians started issuing singles that had longer playing times. Bob Dylan's "Like A Rolling Stone (1965)" was a trailblazer, increasing a song's limit on a 45-record at over six minutes and AM radio stations changed their format to play it. The Beatles' "Hey Jude (1968)" 45-record was over seven minutes. George Martin admitted to producer Jimmy Webb that "Hey Jude" was "only allowed to run over 7 minutes" on the 45-record because Richard Harris's "MacArthur Park (1968)" (produced by Webb) lasted 7 minutes and 20 seconds and received plenty of airtime on AM radio in the U. S.

In the mid to late '60s, recording artists often issued longer versions of some of their hit songs, anywhere from four to seven or eight minutes on record albums and two to three minutes of the same-titled song on 45's. In most cases, if we had the longer version of a song on an LP compared to its 45-record, we preferred to hear the longer version. We felt gypped when we heard the shorter 45-record version and knew where the song was ed-ited, often sounding clumsy or chopped. Examples were Vanilla Fudge's "You Keep Me Hanging On," Cream's "White Room," Iron Butterfly's "In-A-Gadda-Da-Vida," and The Chambers Brothers' "Time Has Come Today." Our 12-inch diameter LPs usually held a little over 20 minutes of music on each side of the record.

Sales of 45-records increased greatly in the mid to late '50s, especially with Elvis Presley's frequent hit singles on the BB Hot 100, starting with "Heartbreak Hotel (1956)." A 45-record cost the same whether it had a hit single on one side and filler on the other side or hit singles on both sides. The A-side of any artist's 45-record was the projected hit single and the flip B-side was often filler, but with Presley, his listeners were often treated to a double-sided hit. Some of Presley's biggest double-sided hits were "Don't Be Cruel" b/w "Hound Dog," "(Marie's the Name) His Latest Flame" b/w "Little Sister," and "Jailhouse Rock" b/w "Treat Me Nice."

In the '60s, the Beach Boys and the Rolling Stones had a few double-sided hits, but the Beatles were the clear-cut champions in this category, usually giving record buyers a two-for-the-price-of-one bargain. The Beatles' biggest double-sided 45's were: "I Want To Hold Your Hand" b/w "I Saw Her Standing There," "I Feel Fine" b/w "She's A Woman," "We Can Work It Out" b/w "Day Tripper," "Yellow Submarine" b/w "Eleanor Rigby," "Penny Lane" b/w "Strawberry Fields Forever," and "Come Together" b/w "Something. "

Musicians were wise not to take projected B-sides too lightly when pairing them with a projected A-side single, because sometimes DJs and their listeners much preferred a B-side compared to the A side. Them's "Gloria (1965)" was the projected B-side for "Baby, Please Don't Go" but "Gloria" became the bigger hit single and Them's original cover of "Gloria" was rated number 204 all-time by *Rolling Stone* in 2004. J. J. Jackson's "But It's Alright" was the projected B-side of "Boogaloo Baby" in 1966, but many DJs played "But It's Alright" deciding this was the better song of the two. "But It's Alright" fooled J. J. and his record company and became a boogaloo/shing-a-ling dance staple at teen centers, and listeners loved its basic lyrics by a shunned lover able to move on. "God Only Knows" was the projected B-side for "Wouldn't It Be Nice" in 1966, but years later *Rolling Stone* rated the B-side number 25, all-time, in 2004. "Wouldn't It Be Nice" might have been the chief reason for the high number of sales for the double-sided hit, but it was not rated in *Rolling Stone's* top 500 songs. Cliff Nobles' "The Horse" was the projected B-side and instrumental of "Love Is All Right" in 1968, but DJs played the instrumental so much that it gained the air time it needed and deserved. Listeners liked "The Horse" so much that it was a runaway hit and became its own dance, The Horse. If you listen to the iTunes sample of the vocal version ("Love Is All Right") today, it's obvious why "The Horse" carried the record's popularity. Rod Stewart's "Maggie May" was released as the projected B-side of "Reason To Believe" in 1971, but "Maggie May" became a number one hit thanks to DJs flipping the 45 to play the B-side and radio listeners requesting it. "Maggie May" became Stewart's early career anthem.

8

Taping with dad's reel-to-reel tape player

♪

I WAS LUCKY TO HAVE MY DAD'S REEL-TO-REEL TAPE PLAYER, so I could tape various songs directly off the radio. These reel-to-reel tapes held about 33 hit singles on each side, increasing my "ready access" playlist of songs many fold over the number of songs on my 45s and LPs. When a DJ gave the song's name before it began, it was easier for me to know I wanted it on tape and I recorded it from the beginning. Other times, I began recording a song at least a few notes after it began, because I recognized it after hearing the first few notes or words and knew I wanted to tape it. Having a song on a tape that was missing its first few notes was not a big deal, it was still better than not having those songs at all when I wanted to hear them. Dad's reel-to-reel tape player also had a better sound, a richer bass than my turntable.

My "career" as a recording engineer was brief. In search for loudness, I taped a few of my 45s or songs from my LPs on the reel-to-reel player, tried to synchronize a replay of the vinyl and reel-to-reel tape versions at the same time, but it was almost impossible to pull it off. Starting a 45-record or LP might give you a few seconds lead time before the actual song began, depending where the needle hit on the vinyl. Pushing the play button on the reel-to-reel player was easier to "time" with the vinyl medium if the reel-to-reel started to play the song as soon as you pressed the play button. Even if the start-up of the two happened to be close to the same note, the best I usually managed was one verse of a song where one medium playing it was slightly behind the other one, sounding like an echo effect. Then the recording of the song on the reel-to-reel tape often fell further behind the vinyl version.

Radio station DJs often told us the name of the record and its musicians before or after they played a song, but if you weren't paying attention you missed it. This was especially frustrating if it was a new song you had only heard a few times or had never heard it before—what's that song called and who sings it? Listeners often called a radio station to find out the name of the last song that the station played. Too, we often misunderstood what a DJ said on the radio and might or might not realize we misheard them. Proof of this lies in some of my typewritten lists of songs I taped in 1966 and 1967—some song titles are close, but not correct, and some artists I matched with some songs are wrong. I listed "Shake A Tail Feather" as being sung by "The Purify Bros." Little did I know that the song's artists always listed as "James and Bobby Purify" were cousins, James Purify and Bobby (Robert Lee Dickey). I labelled "Together" as being performed by The Manhattans; it was a hit single by The Intruders. I mislabeled J. J. Jackson's "Four Walls (Three Windows and Two Doors)" as "No One To Talk To." Otherwise, out of about 70 songs off the radio, I was on the money.

Today's technology labels songs for us in ways we could only dream about having in the '60s. Car radio screens on the dashboard "flash" the song's name and artist the whole time that a song is playing. Much to our delight, if you hear a song playing in a restaurant, bar or rest stop today, you can tap the smartphone apps, *Shazam* or *Soundhound,* and it starts recording the song currently playing. The App gives you the name of the song and its artist within a matter of five to ten seconds. We had none of these song identification luxuries in the '60s.

In '66 and '67, many of the songs I taped off the radio came from Baltimore's three black AM soul stations—WWIN, WSID and WEBB. Tom Douglass and his brother Bill turned me on to the music coming from those stations, otherwise I would never have heard many soul hits that peaked high on the R&B chart. Bill often played Motown and Stax songs on vinyl for Tom, his brother Matt and me. Many of the R&B chart hits did not make a good standing on the BB Top 100, especially the Top 40, if DJs on mainstream stations were not aware of them or just chose not to play them. Listening to some of these R&B records and following up by hearing them on black radio stations was the only way I heard Shorty Long's "Function At

The Junction," The Contours' "First I Look At The Purse," the Spinners' "Truly Yours" and Kim Weston's "Helpless. " Another bonus when I taped off the radio was when I occasionally recorded a DJ's theme song or narrative or the radio station's jingle that introduced songs that were oldies or flashbacks.

9

Listening to music with friends

♪

FOR BABY BOOMERS GROWING UP IN THE '60s, when was the last time you sat with a friend and played one whole side of a new (or old) record album? That requires 20 to 25 minutes and many people are not willing to spend that much time together, uninterrupted, listening to music. In the '60s, Tom and Bill Douglass introduced me to the Temptations' *Gettin' Ready* album during some of our "Kendi Road listening sessions." The back cover had solo photos of each of the group's five singers, dressed in suave three-piece suits with top hats and canes, making final adjustments while looking in large mirrors in a dressing room. The solo pics with each singer's name listed below them made it easy for us to know who each vocalist was when we saw them on TV. "Get Ready" and "Ain't Too Proud To Beg" were the album's 45-hit singles, but we usually played the whole album, both sides. Then, we'd switch to Otis Redding's *Otis Blue* album. We loved Otis's covers of "My Girl," "A Change Is Gonna Come," "Down In The Valley" and "I've Been Loving You Too Long." The clinchers were Redding's original version of "Respect" and cover of "Satisfaction." They were more exciting, more stirring than anything we ever heard from The Elvis look-alike guys. Only Elvis could give Otis a run for his money. I've stayed hooked on *Otis Blue* and *Gettin' Ready* ever since. Tom liked playing his 45-records

31

that were four of my favorites, "Kind Of A Drag" by the Buckinghams, "(I Know I'm) Losing You" by The Temptations, "Sunny" by Bobby Hebb and "Knock On Wood" by Eddie Floyd. Bill brought back his enthusiasm for the Rascals' (formerly the Young Rascals) and the Chambers Brothers music after seeing them play "live" in New York while he went to college at Steven's Institute of Technology in New Jersey. I was blown away by those bands' great sounds and impressed by Bill's enthusiasm, a different kind of peer group pressure. "Upstairs, in that room on Kendi Road there was magic happening on the stereo, and I know that now, listening to what is served up to most people on the radio or in their CD collections. Lord, nothing like that now," Tom wrote to me in July 2012.

Learning those songs with Tom and Bill, and sometimes strutting around their room while we watched Bill show us some of his dance moves was much better than doing it alone. It confirmed that soul was cool—it must be, if other guys liked it that much, too. It was a special camaraderie we had, playing, singing and dancing to soul music. We were in this special groove of music together and there was no turning back. When I went home and listened to soul music on AM radio or on my records alone, my love for it grew even stronger. Our "group sessions" were the seeds and my bedroom listening sessions were the fertilizer that made my love for soul music grow.

My cousin Ralph started me listening to *Rubber Soul* and *Revolver*, and even at 14 and 15 years old, I knew The Beatles were changing. No longer were they just writing and recording love songs; now they were delving into deeper themes like in "In My Life" and "I'm Only Sleeping. "One song, "Taxman" protested the high rate of taxation (especially for higher tax brackets) in Great Britain. Ralph learned many of those songs for his own guitar playing. He personified what many teens in the '60s felt who were playing in teen bands—he just wanted to play as often as possible and it was a special thrill for any musician to hear a new song they liked that they couldn't wait to learn to play with or without the sheet music. It was a thrill for them to learn to play such songs, maybe slowly at first and then sounding like the original version while playing in a teen band.

Debbie H. corralled me in June '67, insisting, "you need to come over my house and hear the Beatles' new album, *Sgt. Pepper's Lonely Hearts Club Band*!" We liked it, but we weren't sure what to make of it. *Sgt. Pepper's* had strange lyrics in Lennon's "Lucy In The Sky With Diamonds" and serious themes about life in McCartney's "She's Leaving Home" and "When I'm

Sixty-Four." It's no wonder we did not know how to label the album's music because the Beatles and their producer George Martin were experimenting with a wide variety of sounds—Western and Indian classical, circus, music hall, vaudeville, pop/rock and psychedelia. Songs like "Getting Better" and "With A Little Help From My Friends" sounded more like a few songs from *Rubber Soul* and *Revolver* that were closer to mainstream popular music. "She's Leaving Home" only used string instruments and McCartney's voice, making it sound and feel somber to go along with its lyrics much like "Eleanor Rigby." Still, listening to each side of the LP then and now, conveys mostly an upbeat feeling because of the circus, music hall, and vaudeville feel of many of its songs. The Beatles in their *Sgt. Peppers'* uniforms on the album cover with the many bright colors personified the Summer of Love in 1967. Not only was our real world in color, rather than black and white, but now our music and its accessories were converting to color (and many formerly black and white TV shows were being broadcast in color). Psychedelia had a new springboard with *Sgt. Peppers*. Being a national and international sensation, its impact was immensely widespread compared to the many regional hit makers for that new genre.

Jabber's house was where I first heard the self-titled albums, *Three Dog Night* (late in '68), *Chicago Transit Authority* (CTA) in May '69 and *Santana* in August '69. Vocals on *Three Dog Night's* hit singles "Try A Little Tenderness" and "One" were stirring. Blood, Sweat & Tears self-titled LP in December '68 was its first with lead singer David Clayton-Thomas and the band's producer James William Guercio gave us a preview of things to come with the group's music that was "a wedding of rock and jazz" according to its liner notes. Just when many of us were catching our breath getting use to *Blood, Sweat & Tears*, Columbia Records issued another Guercio production, *Chicago Transit Authority*, in late April '69. Jabber was spinning the LP on his turntable for me days after its release and I bought it just a few days later. He took me over to Luskin's to their large record department and I nabbed a copy when it was hard to keep it in stores. I was thrilled that I liked another new album of "jazz-rock fusion" as much as *Blood, Sweat & Tears*. Both LPs' songs are loaded with horns. It felt like we were immersed in music with a new level of sophistication. Mike, Tom and I sang "Beginnings" and "Does Anybody Know What Time It Is? " hearing Tommy's 8-track tape riding along Belair, Joppa and Ebenezer Roads in the summer of '69, and we liked the whole album. The forgotten gem from that album is its six and one-half minute orgy of horns in "Introduction," worthy of its own 45-record. Being the LP's intro song, it surely achieved its objective, preparing us for a joyful ride listening to the rest of the album. When Jabber played *Santana* in August 1969, it was the fourth time over eight months that I heard a new record album that remains one of my all-time favorites, 49 years later. *Santana* featured the 45-hit record "Evil Ways," the hard driving "Jingo" and equally raucous instrumental "Soul Sacrifice." Santana used lead guitar, bass, Hammond organ, piano, vocals and hard driving congas and drums that opened a new world of sound, Latin rock, to many teens and older listeners in the U. S.

I enjoyed *CTA, Santana*, and *Three Dog Night* so much that I bought all three, and wondered what could these bands do for an encore if they recorded second albums? They were hard LPs to follow up, but in all three cases, the bands met that challenge with second albums, *Chicago II*, Santana's *Abraxas* and Three Dog Night's *Suitable for Framing,* that were as good as their first LPs. We hoped we'd be hearing more from these bands; little did we know how much staying power they would have.

During our high school days, my friends kept bringing me more good music off their 8-track car tape players and phonographs. Glenn H. played Creedence Clearwater Revival's (CCR) *Bayou Country* 8-track tape as we zipped down Belair Road in his Thunderbird in the spring of '69. We were big fans of "Born On The Bayou" from the start, nodding our heads and doing quick arm pumps (three from the right, then three from the left, etc.) whenever it was playing (later I learned that "Born On The Bayou" became CCR's opening song for many of their shows, no doubt because of its kick start feeling as soon as it begins). Don L. played the *Are You Experienced* album by the Jimi Hendrix Experience and I introduced some of my friends to Hendrix, Cream and Blind Faith. Karen played *Donovan's Greatest Hits* for me every time I went to her house in the spring of '69. Until then, I was only aware of his hit songs "Sunshine Superman," "Mellow Yellow," "There Is a Mountain," and "Hurdy Gurdy Man." Debbie S. converted me into an avid Crosby Stills and Nash fan with their self-titled first album in '69, and CSN and Young's album, *Déjà Vu* in '70. Too, we played the *CTA* and *Chicago II* LPs every time I went to her house.

I began college in the Fall '69, at University of Maryland's College Park campus, where we had plenty of guys up and down the hall from each other in Ellicott Hall dormitory. It was one shared listening experience after another and our lifetime's all-time high for musical camaraderie. Hearing record albums for free before deciding to buy one was a national pastime for college students. Some of our dorm mates had deluxe stereo systems, especially Brad M. who regaled us with *Abbey Road* and Paul, whose dad, Henry O. Berman owned a small electronics store in Baltimore off Lombard Street. Paul was the first one in the dorm to blast *Grand Funk Live* in his room, loud.

While we ate meals together in the Ellicott Dining Hall, we listened to whole sides of record albums broadcast over the eatery's speakers from the campus radio station, WMUC. I regret now, that I didn't get a part time job there. I thought about walking over to its studio to see if they needed help, but I never did. I know I was leery the first semester I was in college full time about working part time, too, but I should have checked into it the following year. In the Fall '69 and spring '70, when we heard The Beatles' "Come Together" or "Here Comes The Sun" in our dining hall, we knew side one or two of *Abbey Road* was coming over the speakers. Despite hearing it almost daily while we ate together, many of us bought the album.

During its first full month in the U. S., *Abbey Road* played on the radio alongside strong rumors that Paul McCartney was dead, and we wondered, "what is that all about? "We saw and heard news reports much less frequently in 1969, than we do with today's 24/7 news coverage, so the "Paul McCartney is dead" rumor was much more difficult to dispel at first. Originators of the "Paul is dead hoax" and others who persisted with the conspiracy pointed to *Abbey Road*'s cover. They "labelled" the front cover photo of The Beatles walking on a crosswalk, a funeral procession, with John dressed in Angelic white, Ringo was in black signifying death, George wearing jeans as the gravedigger, and Paul was in bare feet, a symbol for the corpse. Long before the Paul is dead hoax, when "Strawberry Fields Forever" was released in 1967, some of us thought we heard John state "I buried Paul" near the end of the song (not "cranberry sauce" as John claimed during or after the hoax in 1969). In October 1969, a few of us sat in Joe F. 's car one weekend night eating our subs behind Perry Hall's Palms Subs and Pizza while listening to "Strawberry Fields Forever." We doubted the veracity of Paul being dead, but thought John was saying "I buried Paul" (some of the 1969 rumors suggested Paul died in 1966 and was replaced by a look-alike which we found even harder to believe). Hearing the song today, it still sounds clearly like, "I buried Paul" to me. Paul had been away from public view, mostly at his Scottish retreat with his wife, Linda, for several months around the time of the hoax and helped dispel the rumors of his death when *Life* Magazine published a new interview and photos of him in its November 7, 1969 issue.

Living on campus in the dorm was a privilege that our new college classmates who were commuters missed. The shared experiences we had in the dorm and for me later in the fraternity (cost $100 extra for social fees, while room and board were the same as the dorm per semester), were well worth the student loans I paid back after graduation. Now I consider it priceless or nearly so. It was an amazing life experience being on our own, starting at 18 years old, getting more education, not having to work fulltime yet, and our shared music experience was an important part of it. When we hear one of those songs now, they take us back to our rooms and hallways, the cinderblock versions in the dorms and the cozy ones with some woodwork in the fraternity.

Back in Perry Hall on winter break from college in December 1970, Tom D. played whole sides of George Harrison's *All Things Must Pass* for me at his house and I bought the triple album right away. In the dorm, Stuart started us listening to Traffic's *John Barleycorn Must Die* and Ed H. played Joe Cocker's *Mad Dogs and Englishmen* on Friday afternoons for Paul T. and me to start our weekends. Living on campus provided a very convenient way to see live bands in concert often, though I squandered many chances. I saw Al Kooper (Blood, Sweat and Tears' lead singer before David Clayton-Thomas) in the U of MD's Armory, Rare Earth at Ritchie Coliseum and Grand Funk Railroad at Cole Field House, but there were many concerts I missed from 1969-73. It was simply a matter of limited spending money every week. Should I buy another record album, go on a date, eat out once or twice, go to a mixer or the local bar, or go to a concert?

When I joined Theta Chi fraternity in the Fall of '71, record albums that my fraternity brothers played often included The Rolling Stones' *Let It Bleed*, *Beggar's Banquet*, and *Sticky Fingers*, the Allman Brothers' *Eat a Peach* and *Brothers and Sisters* and the Doobie Brothers' *Toulose Street* and *The Captain and Me*. By having many different guys living there, all of whom had their own favorites, we heard many different albums firsthand, and saw how much they were moved by the music (different than listening to music on the radio by yourself). Bart, Turk and Koby played The Stones and Allman Brothers, Kenny played the Doors frequently, Slow played Neil Young, Anton loved reciting "Alice's Restaurant Massacre," Shoe played The Doobie Brothers, and Doug played the Moody Blues. I played Rod Stewart's *Never A Dull Moment, Clapton At His Best,* The Beach Boys' *Surf's Up,* and Steely Dan's *Can't Buy A Thrill.*

At University of Maryland basketball games, beginning about January 1970, the school's pep band often played the chorus from "Amen" and Steam's "Na Na Hey Hey Kiss Him Goodbye." The most successful cover of "Amen" in the '60s had been the Impressions' R&B chart topper in 1964. Everyone in 1970 seemed to know the easy-to-remember lyrics of both songs. They became the primary go-to songs for the band to play late in games at Maryland's Cole Field House when the home team Terps appeared to be a shoo-in to win. Maryland's visiting teams hated to hear those songs and Maryland fans loved singing the lyrics while the pep band played the music. If we hear those songs today, we're brought right back into Cole Field House—all the red and gold colors everywhere; the capacity crowd; the shiny polished tan court; the cheerleaders; the players; coach Lefty Driesell; the public-address announcer's voice; and the banners hung high in the rafters, new ones for each game drawn with visiting teams' mascots' names (e. g., Dunk the Deacons, Trip the Tar Heels, etc.). It's all there in my mind's eye, front and center.

It was a warm stirring feeling of camaraderie to listen to music to-gether, whether it was listening to record albums or dancing once a month to live music when bands played at our fraternity house. It often started an adrenalin rush—it felt electric inside of us. Listening to LPs, we shared laughs and notes with each other about our favorites and why we liked certain songs. We were living our music with each other and loving it when we were in the same room talking about an LP or recording artist or song. We traded salvos back and forth with each other with our favorite tunes on record albums, hearing parts of an album from a next-door room through our walls. Those free listening sessions when we heard LPs we did not own, were a joyful expansion of our knowledge of popular music. They were also more chances for us to decide whether we liked an LP enough to buy it ourselves.

We had very little patience for radio listening; rather, we wanted instant gratification by playing our favorite music on LPs. When I hear The Doobie Brothers' early songs today it often takes me back to those frat dance/band parties when E. S. Grit was the live band playing our music. Like The Doobie Brothers, E. S. Grit had two drummers. Their sound was a revelation when they played The Doobie Brothers' "Listen To The Music," "Jesus Is Just Al-right," and "Long Train Runnin'." Many of the frat guys favored "Jesus Is Just Alright" because it had a fast dance tempo at the beginning and the end, but a slow dance tempo in the song's middle. It was happening again, first during junior high and high school years and now while living near campus at college. Once again, you don't usually share music this way with record albums and band/dance parties once you get married or live alone in the city, suburbs or country and work steadily for a living.

10

Sing-along songs

♪

W HEN WAS THE LAST TIME YOU DID A SING ALONG SONG other than
the occasional Christmas carol with friends and family if you're
a baby boomer? If it's been years, I recommend you do it soon,
with or without the aid of a little liquid courage. It's another gratifying way
to enjoy music at any age. During our high school years in the '60s, we gave
it our best shot doing sing-along songs all the time riding up and down the
road in our cars.

All of us saw teen girls singing along with songs while driving. On average, they had less inhibitions about singing than teen guys. How many
millions of teen girls sang along with the Angels' "My Boyfriend's Back;"
Leslie Gore's "It's My Party;" the Chiffons' "He's So Fine;" the Supremes'
"Stop In The Name Of Love;" or Martha and the Vandellas' "Jimmy Mack"
in their rooms or riding down the road in their cars?

The Beatles' "Hey Jude" became the late '60's premier sing-along song
for a couple years beginning in 1968. Even though I bought the 45-record
and played it hundreds of times, I never tired of it. The hit single first appeared on the BB Hot 100 in mid-September, and reached number one two
weeks later, remaining the top song for nine weeks. The video of "Hey Jude"
was first broadcast in the U. S. on the October 6, 1968 on *The Smothers Brothers Comedy Hour.* As usual, Ringo played drums, John and George on rhythm
and lead guitars, but Paul played piano backed by a 29-piece orchestra. If

you weren't already singing along with "Hey Jude" before you saw the TV broadcast, you were after seeing it. When Tom N., Mike A., Joe F. and I drove down Belair or Joppa Roads we could only sing-along with "Hey Jude" if it was on the radio. That song wasn't on an 8-track tape yet because it was not on an album when it was first released. When it came on the radio in our cars we gave it our best shot singing it, even imitating McCartney's screaming near the song's end.

Other popular sing-along songs included the upbeat, Manfred Mann's "Do Wah Diddy Diddy," the Lovin' Spoonful's "Daydream," the Rascals' "It's A Beautiful Morning" the Friends of Distinction's "Grazing In The Grass," Otis Redding's Fa-Fa-Fa-Fa-Fa (Sad Song) and Them's (Van Morrison's) "Gloria." It was fun to try, but it was a hopeless endeavor for most of us to sing along with the chorus near the end of the "Grazing in the Grass" that appeared twice with all the I can dig-its, we can dig-its, she can dig-its and they can dig-its in rapid succession. I dare you to play the song now and try to sing it at the same pace that Friends of Distinction does it. We sang along with Otis in the song, "Fa-Fa-Fa-Fa-Fa (Sad Song)." Otis sang: "Fa-Fa-Fa-Fa-Fa-Fa-Fa-Fa-Fa…" Then he told the Memphis horns it was their turn, and then everybody's turn (Otis, the horns and us). Many guys loved singing parts of Them's (Van Morrison's) or Shadows of the Knight's "Gloria," the parts about her coming around here and how she made him feel alright and then spelling Gloria's name and shouting it out loud. Girls I've known named Gloria knew the song's effect on guys. This song cast such a spell on wishful teen boys that I've never met a girl named Gloria who didn't like it.

The Beatles' "Yellow Submarine," "All You Need is Love," and "Let it Be," released from 1966 through 1970, also became popular sing-along songs and many of their other songs prompted sing-alongs, too. Lennon's "All You Need Is Love" became the staple song of 1967's "summer of love" theme on June 25, when it aired as a live sing-along performance as part of *Our World*, a multi-country live satellite broadcast (estimated viewers worldwide ranged from 350 to 700 million). Jagger and Richards, Clapton, Keith Moon from The Who, Marianne Faithfull, and Graham Nash were among friends of the Beatles who joined them to sing the chorus for the song's live broadcast.

"Yellow Submarine" stayed on the charts for a shorter time than "Hey Jude," but it was popular two different times. First, it was issued as a happy lighthearted antidote as the A-side on a single with "Eleanor Rigby" in August 1966, when it was also on the *Revolver* album. Then it was issued on the

Yellow Submarine album in January 1969. "Yellow Submarine" had a jollier sound than "Hey Jude" in part due to the laughter in the background, the circus-sound of some of the horns, and the background sound effects that imitated an ongoing party (drinking glasses clinking and laughter). When we were driving age in 1968 and 1969, you might occasionally hear our car-load riding down the road trying to sing "Yellow Submarine." It was easier to sing than "Hey Jude" because lead singer Ringo didn't have any very high or low notes.

Some of these songs we only sang along with by ourselves in our room out of earshot of others, and other songs we sang along with our friends only in a car. One song that was fun to try to sing, but I'd only do it if no one else was in our house was Billy Stewart's "Summertime" singing,— about his little darling spreading her wings and taking to the "sky-ly-ly-ly-ly" and telling her not to let a tear fall from her "ey-ey-ey-ey-eye. " Many artists have covered "Summertime" but no one else sang it in the '60s with the fervor and enthusiasm of Stewart, except Janis Joplin. I also tried my best to harmonize with the Beach Boys' "In My Room" while it played on my bedroom turntable (later it became a favorite for Melissa, Luke and me to sing together).

Sometimes we sang along with the chorus of a song and left the rest of the singing to the record or tape that was playing. One example was Lee Dorsey's "Working In The Coal Mine (1967)." Many of us sang the chorus: "Working in the coal mine, going down, down" and the next verse, but left the rest to Lee. Another was the Beatles' "Let It Be." For the most part we sang the chorus that contained several "Let it Be's" and the phrase, "whisper words of wisdom" and left the rest of the lyrics to Paul McCartney while the song played.

For sing-along songs, we didn't always know all the words to a song in the '60s, we just gave it our best shot. Musicians bought sheet music with the words, but the rest of us rarely, if ever, saw sheet music. Today, we have computer search engines like *Google* and websites like *Wikipedia* to see lyrics of songs within a few seconds. In the '60s, we didn't have any ready access to songs' lyrics at our fingertips. Even if we didn't know all the words, we still often enjoyed a song's tempo or the mood it created. Forty and 50 years later, it's strange when we hear a song for the umpteenth time, listen to it in the proper context and hear some of its words clearly for the first time and think, "that's what they were singing!"

Sometimes, we still wonder if the lyrics of a song, as listed on the internet, are correct. On "Just Right Radio" in Raleigh, NC, on August 19, 2017, Disc jockey Doug Austin said as "Louie, Louie" concluded on the air, "I admit I sing along to the song even though I don't know all the words. Who does know all the words?" Some of us back in the '60s, wondered if there was a conspiracy to keep the real words of "Louie, Louie" a secret because we suspected there were words in the song about sexual intercourse, but we thought the recording artists wouldn't admit it for fear of losing playing time on the radio. My neighborhood friend, Lloyd, brought his 45-record of the Kingsmen's "Louie Louie" over to my house in 1964, so we could play it over and over trying to decipher the lyrics while the U. S. Federal Bureau of Investigation was making its own inquiry. Lloyd and I decided that lead singer Jack Ely was singing, "At night in bed, I.... her again" instead of the song's listed lyric, "a fine little girl, she waits for me."

I tried singing popular music with my cousin Ralph when he brought his microphone and electric guitar over to Aunt Betty's house and we "covered" the Stones' "Get Off Of My Cloud" in the summer of '66. Ralph was a very good musician, guitar player, and singer, but I'm afraid I was just an average singer. Then I had a brief tryout singing "Ain't Too Proud To Beg" and "Kicks" with George W. and Don T. playing lead and bass guitar and Andy P. playing drums in the spring of '67, and I decided it wasn't for me.

The last time I remember doing any sing-along songs with friends was when "Live" bands played "Jumping Jack Flash" and "Honky Tonk Women" at our fraternity house from 1971-73. This was group dancing and singing fueled by many beers that reduced our inhibitions. We felt ten feet tall and bullet-proof, as the saying goes, a good feeling for having fun, but not always the best state of mind for making decisions.

Neil Diamond's "Sweet Caroline (Good Times Never Seemed So Good) (1969)" is another sing-along song that became instantly popular from its happy theme, lyrics and tempo. It is still played at many sporting events and has been adopted by many sports teams in the U. S. "Sweet Caroline" has been played at most Boston Red Sox home baseball games at Fenway Park in the middle of the 8th inning since 2002. In a 2017 *Hyundai* TV commercial, a man and lady are stopped at a traffic light momentarily, next to each other in their cars, windows down. He belts out the song's first few words, "Sweet Caroline...," then she grins with a smirk and joins in with him on the next part "ba, ba, ba, Good times never seemed ..." The song is so familiar to most of us that we're not surprised watching it that she knows the song's tempo and timing between the words with perfection and sings along with him without a hitch. The message of the commercial is, all you need to overcome the "driving in heavy traffic blues" is a *Hyundai* and some good sing-along music.

11

Music genres and our personality types

♪

"Genres" can be defined as categories of music grouped together according to stylistic, contextual, and historical similarities like rock, hip-hop, jazz, country, soul, classical, salsa and reggae. "Styles" are the sum totals of the ways musicians combine elements of music that create coherence and identity.

Music psychologists also divide types of music into several *categories* (groups of several genres in this case) that scientist and musician John Powell describes in his book, *Why You Love Music.* "Reflective and complex music" is a category that includes classical, jazz, folk and blues. "Intense and rebellious music" includes rock, alternative and heavy metal. "Upbeat and conventional music" includes pop, sound tracks, religious and country. "Energetic and rhythmic music" includes, rap, soul and electronic. Had these categories existed in the '60s, I think garage rock and psychedelic would have fit into intense and rebellious music, bubble gum and sunshine pop would have fit in "upbeat and conventional music," and psychedelic soul would have fit in "energetic and rhythmic music." Musical psychologists have found that pop music listeners who enjoy reflective and complex music are often "open, not good at playing sports, are good with words and politically liberal." Listeners of intense and rebellious music often "score high on openness and are skilled with words." They are often good at playing sports. Upbeat and conventional music listeners are usually "extroverted, agreeable, conscientious, good at sports and many of them are politically conservative." Fans of energetic and rhythmic music are usually extroverted, agreeable and politically liberal. Powell and music psychologists admit that these categories do not work all the time; there are [many] "exceptions to the rule" as to where people fall.

While our preferred music genres are usually formed when we are pre-teens and teenagers, if we can expand to other genres as we get older, it broadens our overall enjoyment listening to music. Finally, when I turned 64, I began enjoying Bob Dylan's vast array of songs, most of them written by him. I just wasn't ready to adopt him in the '60s and early '70s when the radio and a college friend, Steve D., first gave me the chance. I wasn't ready for reflective and complex music yet. Now I take it in as an overall listening experience of our greatest poet who was also a top songwriter and musician in the '60s. I'm much more interested now in what Dylan had to say then. The importance of his songs to the overall story of music in the '60s is mind boggling to me now. How did I ignore it so long? Now I've become more interested in jazz music thanks to Ken Burns' 2002 documentary *Jazz*. Ironically, back in 1969 when *Blood, Sweat & Tears* and *Chicago Transit Authority* were my favorite albums, I didn't realize how much their music stemmed from jazz.

12

Rock and roll before the Beatles— R&B and Elvis

♪

ROCK AND ROLL MUSIC IN THE LATE '50s AND '60s had its roots in '50s rhythm and blues (often called race music because it was written and performed by blacks), gospel music, folk music, country western music (later known as country music), and rockabilly music. These genres contributed to a new name and a varying blend of these genres in various songs called rock and roll.

Bill Haley, Chuck Berry, Little Richard (Richard Penniman), Ray Charles, Fats Domino (born Antoine Domino) and Elvis Presley accelerated R&B's crossover into rock and roll in the 1950s. Many musicians of the '60s had Berry and Presley's music in mind when they wrote many of their songs. Over in Great Britain in the early and mid '60s, many white artists were fascinated with the R&B sounds of Howlin' Wolf (Chester Arthur Burnett), Muddy Waters (McKinley Morganfield), Berry, and Little Richard when they wrote and performed their music. The Beatles and the Rolling Stones did covers of some of their favorite R&B songs in '63-'64, along with their earliest self-written songs. Thereafter, they mostly stuck with their own songs.

Ray Charles' "Mess Around (1953)" and Ruth Brown's "Wild, Wild Young Men (1953)" sound like forerunners of Big Joe Turner's "Shake, Rattle And Roll (1954)" and Bill Haley's "Rock Around The Clock (1955)." All of them had a pick-me-up beat for easier fast dancing, especially by

46

teenagers. Dick Clark asserted that Bill Haley was one of the originators of rockabilly music (black blues combined with country western), while Carl Perkins said Haley was "country" who also had a saxophone. Perkins called "Rock Around the Clock" a great trendsetter. These songs were among the most popular at sock/record hops throughout small- and medium-sized towns and large cities around the U. S. in the late '50s and early '60s.

Elvis Presley's breakout of hit records in 1956, stemmed from his heavy listening of country western, gospel, and R&B. Interviewed by The *Charlotte (NC) Observer* in June 1956, Presley said, "The colored folks been singing it and playing it just like I'm doin' it now, man, for more years than I know. They played it like that in the shanties and their juke joints." Presley honed his singing and live performance skills during many appearances on the *Louisiana Hayride* and other venues on the road in 1954 and 1955.

Presley's breakthrough on TV occurred in the midst of parents' heavy concerns about his effects on their teen children's morals. Juvenile delinquency and street gangs were rising concerns in the U. S. in the '50s as seen in the Broadway musical, *West Side Story* and the movie *Blackboard Jungle*. Musicians grappled with the issue in popular music songs like Frankie Lymon and the Teenagers' "I'm Not A Juvenile Delinquent (1957)" and Portuguese Joe's "Teenage Riot (1957)."

Elvis Presley's music prevailed in the long run, despite resistance from many local radio stations and by some towns' mayors and city councils across the U. S. DJs sometimes refused to play his songs and towns occasionally cancelled a Presley-scheduled concert, but Elvis was careful about maintaining a good image in part from the mentoring by his agent/manager "Colonel" Tom Parker, and it paid off. R&B singer Ruth Brown said: "When Elvis Presley came on the scene he did it right. He did it good. Where he was concerned, there was no color—eventually he made the music more permissible for white kids to listen to. "

When Presley first appeared on the *Ed Sullivan Show* in 1956, he was introduced by Charles Laughton standing in for Ed Sullivan who had been in a car accident. Seventy million TV viewers in the U. S. watched Elvis belt out "Don't Be Cruel" and slow the pace with "Love Me Tender" in his first set. In his second set, the cameras widened so the TV viewing audience could see Presley's gyrations while singing "Ready Teddy" and a portion of "Hound Dog." Flashing his sexy grin and sneer, he swung his guitar-picking right arm in windmills, swiveled his hips and did his own version of sensuous walks and slides. The girls in the audience screamed, cried his name, squeezed their faces, outstretched their arms towards him, and some of them fainted. Almost seven-years old, Bruce Springsteen recalled that after the show: "I sat there (on his living room floor) transfixed in front of the television set, my mind on fire. "

Elvis made singing and playing guitar look like fun, even thrilling to teens. Thousands of American teens, mostly boys, were inspired like Bruce. Presley's popularity throughout the late '50s and early '60s, spawned many look-a-like (and sometimes sound-alike) hit-making singers—Eddie Cochran, Frankie Avalon, Paul Anka, Brian Hyland, Bobby Vinton, Bobby Vee, Bobby Rydell, Fabian, Ricky Nelson, and Terry Stafford.

Just when Elvis's career was white hot in popularity, he was drafted by the U. S. Army and served in the military between March 1958 and March 1960. Tom Petty said years later, "An entertainer [Elvis Presley] is really a force to be reckoned with, right? So, let's put him in the Army and calm this boy down. [And] Chuck (Berry) was in jail. It's my own theory that that early period got too wild. Calm down! And it was taken over by business men, and Bobby Vee, Bobby Vinton, Neil Sedaka, Bobby Rydell and Fabian were thrust upon girls as an alternate boyfriend. "

Many of Elvis's fans were distraught about his entry into the Army and were afraid his singing career was finished. Elvis worried that by the time he was released from the Army, he'd be hard-pressed to revive the popularity of his music and his success in movies to pre-Army levels. He surprised everyone including himself while he was in the military by making seven top ten hit singles, and his movie career grew after he was discharged from the Army. By carefully spacing his hit single releases during his Army service, "Colonel" Parker made sure Elvis just whetted his fans' appetite for more.

Presley's rising popularity in 1956-58 coincided with Little Richard and Berry's best hit-making years and helped get them more playing time on white radio stations and limited TV appearances. Covers of some of their original hits by white artists often outsold them even though the covers were not as good as the black artists' originals (example—Pat Boone's larger selling cover compared to Little Richard's much better original of "Tutti-Frutti"). "White" radio stations usually didn't play black musicians' hit singles in the early '50s, and black stations had weaker transmitting signals, reaching smaller areas of listeners.

Sam Phillips, owner of Sun Records in Memphis in the early '50s had the good fortune to have Elvis Presley walk into his studio in the summer of 1953. It was a fortuitous moment for both men because Sam saw the raw talent, the possibilities that Elvis had as a popular music singer and Elvis sensed that day and the next few times he came there that Sam had Elvis's best interest at heart. Phillips loved blues and other black music and hoped to find white musicians who were willing and able to play it. In short order, he "discovered" Elvis, Johnny Cash, Carl Perkins, Roy Orbison and Jerry Lee Lewis. Orbison recorded nine Top Ten hits in the early '60s with "Only The Lonely (Know The Way I Feel) (1960)" and Crying (1961)" peaking at number two and "Running Scared (1961)" and his best song for dancing, "Oh, Pretty Woman (1964)" reaching number one.

Berry's impact on white musicians was widespread. He combined country and rhythm and blues to become one of rock and roll's biggest pioneers along with Presley. He developed a very up-tempo guitar riff, and a beat and stage show that drew large crowds because of his energy, enthusiasm and showmanship. While many of his songs sounded similar, the themes still varied enough to make many of his new hit singles as popular as the earlier ones. It was important, too, that Berry's songs were easy to dance to, making them popular requests at sock hops, on juke boxes everywhere, and songs frequently covered by other musicians. Berry's storylines –girls, cars, school bells, and dances, matched well with teens of the '50s and 60s, too. Berry's charisma and stage presence enabled him to gain many stage and TV appearances that were slower to come to most other black musicians in the late '50s and early '60s. Jackson Browne recalled: "Berry was a big influence. The first time I went to play one of his songs, I realized I knew the chords and all the words. "Carl Perkins recalled: "The first time I heard [Berry's] "Maybellene," I said, 'Look out,' here is a man who loves country music. "Eric Burdon of the Animals called Chuck Berry "the poet laureate of America. "Berry did his "patented" duck walk for concert and TV audiences while playing his guitar to "Maybellene," "Roll Over Beethoven," and "Johnny B. Goode."

13

"The Twist" breaks down the generation gap in music

♪

I N THE MID AND LATE '50s AND EARLY '60s, many parents worried about the effects of rock and roll on their sons and daughters, and many civic leaders tried to prevent white teenagers from embracing R&B and rock and roll as their own music. They thought it was too wild and inciteful, bringing out animal qualities and behavior in teenagers and more promiscuity that was harmful and degrading to teens.

Parents' fears were fueled by Elvis's early concerts and TV performances and those by Little Richard and Jerry Lee Lewis. Little Richard sang inspired versions of "Tutti-Frutti" and other songs while standing and playing his piano. He even sang one song and "danced" while he was on his back on the floor. Lewis put his crowds surrounding him nearby in a trance that looked like devil worship (like they were possessed) while he sang "Whole Lotta Shakin' Going On" and played the piano with his fingers, hands, elbows and feet, shaking his head and long hair on one side lustily.

In late summer of '60, this one-sided view of rock and roll and R&B by many parents softened when Chubby Checker's (born Ernest Evans) version of "The Twist" hit the radio and record stores. Hank Ballard wrote "The Twist" and released his original cover in July, but Checker's version in early August set the country in motion. "The Twist" was the most significant rock and roll record of all time. It was the first time that all generations could freely admit they liked rock and roll," said Dick Clark. Featured on Dick

50

Clark's *Bandstand* and white radio stations, Checker's version reached number one in 1960 (18 weeks on the Hot 100), and in 1962 (21 weeks on the Hot 100 from late '61 through early '62). Checker's smiling face and personality appealed to TV viewers. We even liked his nickname. He one-upped Ballard by doing "The Twist" while he sang it, and viewers were hooked. Some of Checker's moves looked a bit like Jackie Wilson's when he performed "Lonely Teardrops" on *Bandstand* just a year earlier.

When "The Twist" was playing somewhere, you did it; it was a national sensation. Teenagers and parents were doing it. Of all the dances in the '60s, "The Twist" was the most popular and is still played often at wedding receptions because its moves of the arms and legs are obvious—it's easy to follow. Some variations included doing swivels while on one foot. Many adults, including many celebrities, were seen doing the Twist in New York's Peppermint Lounge. My parents and their friends in their 30's played their 45s of "The Twist" that they danced to at neighborhood parties. "The Twist" was followed by Checker's "Let's Twist Again (1961)," Joey Dee and the Starliters' "Peppermint Twist (Part 1) (1961)," Sam Cooke's "Twistin' the Night Away (1962)," and Checker's (with Dee Dee Sharp) "Slow Twistin' (1962)," among many other "twist" songs. It was not a quick one and done fad. Joey Dee and The Starlighters and Sam Cooke's "Twist" songs were both number one songs for three weeks.

14

More rock and roll and soul in the early '60s

♪

IN THE EARLY '60s, the Shirelles spawned similar girl groups like The Chiffons, the Ronettes, and The Crystals, closely followed by the earliest Motown girl groups. The Shirelles' biggest hits were their number one songs, "Will You Love Me Tomorrow (1960)" and "Soldier Boy (1962)" and their other top five songs, "Dedicated To The One I Love (1961)" and "Foolish Little Girl (1963)." Motown's Marvelettes and Martha and the Vandellas sang songs that had a better rhythm and beat for dancing, thanks to Motown's musicians, the Funk Brothers and the songs' producers and arrangers. At the same time, female solo artists Connie Francis (from '58 through '69) and Brenda Lee (from '60 through '67) cranked out one big hit after the next on the Billboard (BB) Hot 100.

In '63 and '64, a flurry of car songs and surfing songs came from the West coast. California's Beach Boys and Jan and Dean issued top ten hit singles on the BB Hot 100. Ronny and the Daytonas ("G.T.O.") and the Rip Chords ("Hey Little Cobra"), recorded one-hit wonders that were favorites of car-loving teens. The Beach Boys issued "409," "Shut Down" and "Little Deuce Coupe" and Jan and Dean released the singles, "Drag City" and "Dead Man's Curve." The Beach Boys' "I Get Around" epitomized teens' favorite past time next to making out. It was "driving up and down the same old strip"—cruising in their own car or one of their best friends' cars. In the '60s, getting your driving license was often a bigger priority than it is with teens in 2018. It was the way you met more teens or found the ones you wanted to see or be with, or the way guys preferred to take a girl on a date. The Beach Boys issued most of the early '60s surfing songs that placed high on the BB Hot 100—"Surfin' Safari," "Surfin' U. S. A., " and "Surfer Girl" and Jan and Dean made the BB Hot 100 chart with "Surf City" and "Ride the Wild Surf. "While surfing had some limited popularity on the Mid-Atlantic and South Atlantic coasts of the U. S., it was much more popular off the coasts of California and Hawaii. It's no surprise that in 1964 and 1965, British invasion hit singles did not cover cars and surfing. Cars for teens were less common in the U. K. and there was no surfing there.

Popular music of the late '50s and early '60s abounded with the recurrent theme of love and the challenges of finding a lasting relationship. We had a rash of songs about teens that commiserated with their plight of falling in and out of love and trying to understand their own feelings and their boyfriend or girlfriend. What worked and what didn't and why or why not and did it vary with different ones? Some teens played hard to get and others "were too easy," some liked to flirt with other boys or girls while having a boyfriend or girlfriend and others did not. There were minefields everywhere as girls and guys plodded and experimented their way through relationships when they were preteens and teens. Some of the more popular "teen songs" were: Gale Storm's "Teen Age Prayer (1956)," Ricky Nelson's "A Teenager's Romance (1957)" and "Teen Age Idol (1962),"Tommy Sands' "Teen-Age Crush (1957)" and "Goin' Steady" in 1957 (a song that was an Elvis Presley sound-alike both in Sands' voice and his back-up singers), Dion and The Belmont's "Teenager In Love (1959)" and "Lonely Teenager (1960)," and Mark Dinning's "Teen Angel (1960)."

Doo-wop R&B of the '50s through the mid-'60s, was the forerunner of Motown and Memphis Soul. Doo-wop was all about vocal harmony and a slower tempo with more slow dance songs. "Doo wop music started because there were no instruments [available to many black teens]. So, the background singers had to do all the work. And that's why the bass singer would do the 'doo, doo, doo, ba, doo, doo, doo, doo ba, doo'," recalled Ben E. King. The Platters sang "The Great Pretender," "My Prayer," and "Smoke Gets In Your Eyes" in the '50s and charted with another doo-wop style song, "With This Ring" in 1967. The Miracles' singing in "Ooo Baby Baby (1965)" had a doo wop style of singing and only a few instruments in the song. The Dells sang their late '60s hits, "Stay In My Corner (1968)" and "Oh, What A Night (1969)" in doo-wop style, but their hit single, "There Is (1968)" had a dance beat that sounded more like early Four Tops or Temptations songs. Little Anthony (Anthony Gourdine) and the Imperials produced doo-wop style top 40 hits from 1958 through 1965: "Tears On My Pillow," "Shimmy, Shimmy Ko-Ko-Bop," "I'm On The Outside (Looking In)," "Goin' Out Of My Head," "Hurt So Bad," and "Take Me Back." The Drifters' doo wop harmony gave us "There Goes My Baby," "Saturday Night At The Movies," "Up On The Roof," and "Under The Boardwalk" from the '50s through 1964. Set in southern California in 1964, *American Graffitti's* soundtrack in 1973, featured many of the top doo-wop songs of the '50s and early '60s, including, The Orioles' "Crying In The Chapel," Frankie Lymon and The Teenagers' "Why Do Fools Fall In Love? ," The Diamonds' "Little Darlin'," The Skyliners' "Since I Don't Have You;" and The Flamingos' "I Only Have Eyes For You."

15

The Beatles in the U. S. in 1964

MOST POPULAR MUSIC WE LISTENED TO ON AM RADIO in 1963 had a sound that appealed to our parents as much or more than it did to preteens and teens. Elvis had only one song "(You're The) Devil In Disguise" that peaked as high as number 3 for two weeks, and by this time much of his music appealed to many young adults, anyway. We didn't realize it then, but the music was tame and often uninspiring compared to Beatlemania that was taking hold in Britain. The number one hits on the BB Hot 100 from June 15, 1963, through January 28, 1964, were good examples of the subdued sound we were listening to. Starting with June 15, the number one songs we heard were: "Sukiyaki" (three weeks), "Easier Said Than Done" (two weeks) "Surf City" (two weeks), "So Much In Love" (one week), "Fingertips—Pt. 2" (three weeks), "My Boyfriend's Back" (three weeks), "Blue Velvet" (three weeks), "Sugar Shack" (five weeks), "Deep Purple" (one week), "I'm Leaving It Up To You" (two weeks), "Dominique" (four weeks), and "There, I've Said It Again" (four weeks). Exceptions to the tame and subdued sound during this period were Martha and The Vandellas' "Heat Wave" and the number one songs listed above, "Fingertips—Pt. 2" and "My Boyfriend's Back." These were the kind of get up and go songs that teens needed to release some energy with some singing and dancing.

The Beatles from Liverpool, England were poised to make a lasting positive impression during their first visit to the U. S. in 1964, after refining their playing in West Germany and England in 1962-63. Carroll James, Jr., a DJ on Silver Spring, Maryland's WWDC-AM radio station scooped other U. S. DJs when he played "I Want To Hold Your Hand" on his show on December 17, 1963, at the urging of Silver Spring's 15-year old Marsha Albert. Marsha was so impressed with The Beatles when they appeared briefly in the *Walter Cronkite CBS News Report* on December 10, that she wrote Mr. James a day later. Then, James asked one of his stewardess friends to bring back a copy of the 45-record from England, and she did. Marsha gave the song's introduction on James' radio show on December 17, saying, "Ladies and gentlemen, for the first time in the U. S., here are The Beatles, singing, "I Want To Hold Your Hand." The adrenalin and thrill that Marsha felt while giving that introduction is hard to imagine. The only thing more thrilling for a teen, then, was to meet The Beatles. Interest in "I Want To Hold Your Hand" by other radio stations was immediate and widespread around the U. S. Many DJs obtained or made a tape of the song being played on WWDC.

Capitol Records ended up issuing the 45-record of "I Want To Hold Your Hand" six weeks earlier than planned, which would have been just days before The Beatles' first U. S. visit. Thus, a 15-year old teen and a DJ made a wiser decision promotion-wise for The Beatles than a major record company. Now there was no stopping The Beatles.

"I Want To Hold Your Hand" placed on the BB Hot 100 in the U. S. for the first time on January 18, 1964, and rose to number 1 on the chart on February 1, just days before the Beatles' first trip to the U. S. No British musicians had made much of an impact on U. S. popular music and its hit charts in the '50s and '60s, but the Beatles changed that in unimaginable ways beginning with their first appearance on *Ed Sullivan* on February 9, 1964.

Upon their arrival at New York's JFK Airport on February 7, U. S. reporters grilled the Beatles at their first press conference with questions designed to rattle and embarrass them, but it didn't work (one of the many signs at the airport held by Beatles fans said, "Beatles Unfair to Bald Men"). One reporter asked, "what do you think of the comment, 'you're nothing more than four British Elvis Presleys gyrating? "Ringo brushed it off, saying, "It's not true, it's not true (laughs)" while gyrating, and then John joined in with his gyrations. Making fun of their long hair another reporter asked, "when are you going to get a haircut? " and George replied, "I just got one yesterday," and both the Beatles and the press laughed again.

We were glued to *Ed Sullivan* on TV when Ed introduced "The Beatles!" to a screaming live audience on February 9. An estimated 73 million of the 170 million in the U. S. watched them that Sunday night. The Beatles sang "All My Loving," "'Till There Was You," "She Loves You," "I Saw Her Standing There," and "I Want To Hold Your Hand," in front of a delirious audience of mostly teenage girls. Some girls flashed looks of joy and others looked like they were in severe pain because it was so emotional for them. Every time the Beatles sang "Oooooh" and shook their long hair, the girls in the audience cried and screamed out to their new idols. When they sang "I Want To Hold Your Hand," it rattled most every girl in the audience. Holding her hand was so basic to any beginning of a guy and girl showing affection for each other; the first time you did it with someone, it sent an adrenalin rush through you. Here were The Beatles basically saying, "I want to hold *yours*." Ringo's rollicking initial drum roll in "She Loves You" sent a jolt through Beatles' fans, too. The song's call and response had Paul singing, "She Loves You" and the rest of the band responding with their chorus: "Yeah, yeah, yeah." The song's words about "you know I saw her just the other day and it's you she's thinking of" were the kind of assurance guys heard only rarely through the grapevine. Meanwhile, New York was in a frenzy about the Beatles. The Beatles' producer George Martin said, "During that first visit to the U. S., no matter where you turned your radio dial any time of the day, you would hear a Beatles song. It was complete saturation. Middle-aged men were walking down Fifth Avenue wearing Beatles wigs. "

The day after the Beatles' U. S. debut, Angela in our seventh-grade music class at Golden Ring Junior High School got permission from our teacher Mr. Valley to take a tally of everyone in class—who is your favorite? Elvis or The Beatles? Not surprisingly, the Beatles won easily among my 12 and 13-year old classmates. We were claiming the new hit sensation group; the older teens could have Elvis, we thought. It was the songs' innocence in their titles and lyrics and joyful upbeat sound (especially "She Loves You," "I Saw Her Standing There," and "I Want to Hold Your Hand") that kidnapped America's pre-teens and teens, lock, stock and barrel. Meanwhile, it's a sure bet that Elvis was losing sleep. What would The Beatles' impact be on his popularity and record sales?

The Beatlemania that took hold in Great Britain late in 1963, completely consumed America's teens, especially for the rest of 1964 and 1965. After their world tour in 1964, Beatlemania took hold in parts of Europe, Asia, Australia and Canada, too. They were an international teen culture sensation long before the internet. Bob Eubanks who was a disc jockey at KRLA (1110-AM) in Los Angeles in 1964 recalled, "After their first *Ed Sullivan* appearance, all the requests were for The Beatles. "

Young teenage girls in the U. S. were out of their minds, head over heels for the Beatles. Teen girls were by far the lion's share of fans at all Beatles concerts. Some teen boys decided if you can't beat them, join them, growing their hair like the Beatles if their parents let them and learning how to play guitar or drums. It seemed like every girl picked their favorite Beatle and many wore buttons to prove it saying, "I Love Paul," "George is my favorite," "I Love Ringo," or "My favorite is John" (this seldom happened with teen girl fans of other British groups). On their first *Ed Sullivan* appearance, at one point when the TV camera focused on John, words on the bottom of the screen said, "Sorry Girls, He's Married." Up until then, John and the press had conspired to keep it a secret that he was married, but it didn't matter, John seemed to have just as many girls who were head-over-heels for him as they were for the other Beatles (except maybe Paul).

Pre-teens and teenagers bought Beatles' 45-records and record albums at a startling record pace. Their first Capitol Records LP, *Meet The Beatles!* was issued January 20 in the U. S. and became the number one album on February 11, 1964. It stayed number one on the U. S. Billboard Top LPs chart for 11 weeks, until *The Beatles' Second Album* replaced it. *Meet the Beatles!* iconic album cover of the four portraits of them was a magnet for Beatles fans and the LP contained "I Want To Hold Your Hand," "I Saw Her Standing There" and "All My Loving." However, Vee-Jay Records issued *Introducing... The Beatles - England's No. 1 Vocal Group* on January 10, so it appeared in some U. S. record stores before *Meet The Beatles!* The Vee-Jay LP was arguably better because it contained "I Saw Her Standing There," "Love Me Do," "P. S. I Love You," "Twist and Shout," and "Do You Wanna Know A Secret." It was The Beatles vs. The Beatles, so The Beatles won either way. Beatles fans deciding between the two albums often picked *Meet The Beatles!* because they loved the album cover and it had "I Want To Hold Your Hand," which was number one for seven weeks. Some Beatles fans bought *Introducing... The Beatles* and the 45 record, "I Want To Hold Your Hand" to get the best combination of their early songs.

On April 4, 1964, the Beatles held the top five spots for hit singles and 12 spots overall on the BB Hot 100 (the only time a recording act has occupied the first five spots with different songs). The top five songs were: the number one "Can't Buy Me Love," "Twist And Shout," "She Loves You," "I Want To Hold Your Hand," and the number five "Please, Please, Me." One of the biggest questions the media posed just a few months after the onset of Beatlemania in the U. S. was "when will the bubble burst?" The media and Beatles fans had no way of knowing that The Beatles would remain at the top of the heap for the rest of the 1960s despite an unprecedented on-slaught of competition from other talented musicians. In 1964, The Beatles had six number 1 hits on the BB Hot 100, and there were more to come (twenty total) through 1970.

Current and future musicians watched Beatlemania unfold, too. Bruce Springsteen was 14 years old that spring and recalled, "Every Wednesday night I sat up in my room charting the Top Twenty and if The Beatles were not firmly ensconced each week as lords of the radio, it would drive me nuts. When 'Hello Dolly' grabbed the top spot on the charts week after week, I was beside myself [actually 'Hello Dolly' was only number one for one week on the BB Hot 100, on May 9]. Jackson Browne recalled later: "These girls were losing their minds (over the Beatles). I mean, this appealed to me in a very fundamental way (smiling). I think I was 13 or 14. These girls were going nuts." Right then and there, Browne knew what he wanted to be when he grew up. Ben E. King said, "[When the Beatles arrived] it was all over but the shoutin'. We had never seen an airport that you couldn't get in and out of because so many kids were there. We knew it was a problem [from a competition point of view] and it just landed." Jerry Lee Lewis said, "I knew that they were different, and their voices blended together, and I knew they had great talent. And I knew they were gonna be big and I hated them for that (laughs)." Tom Petty praised the luck he had to experience the Bea-tles from their start in the U. S. : "The Beatles were like a gift from God. I was just the perfect age for that—14. They gave us all an identity. It was such a bonus that the music was the best, ever (laughs). The Beach Boys' Brian Wilson recalled his initial shock and panic: "We had a meeting and we said, 'What are we going to do here? We're getting eclipsed by a group called The Beatles from London (winces). We were completely jealous as hell. "

When The Beatles performed at Baltimore's Civic Center for one evening on September 13, 1964, it was pure bedlam in the audience, just like everywhere else in the U. S. where they appeared that year. Fans in the first few rows recalled they "really couldn't hear the music because the fans' screaming was so loud." Photos in Baltimore newspapers the next day showed the range of emotions that occurred everywhere The Beatles played—kids holding their heads, mouths wide open, stunned looks on some faces, smiles scattered everywhere along with faces in tears. More than 50 years later, Beatles fans who were there that evening still recalled it with pure joy—an experience of a lifetime for pop music listeners. They also recalled the detractors of The Beatles among the media and many parents and proudly asserted that "we knew what we were listening to and enjoying at our young ages—we recognized real talent."

16

The British invasion of pop music

♪

THE BEATLES' IMMEDIATE SUCCESS IN THE U. S. IN EARLY 1964, spurred the British invasion, an avalanche of hit songs by other British groups on U. S. airwaves. British groups that rode the crest of the Beatles' popularity in the U. S. and had some staying power included: The Rolling Stones (still performing 50 plus years later), The Moody Blues, The Who, Herman's Hermits, The Dave Clark Five (DC5), The Animals, The Kinks, The Hollies, Manfred Mann and Donovan. Short-lived groups included Peter and Gordon, Gerry and the Pacemakers, The Searchers, Chad and Jeremy, The Zombies, Freddy and the Dreamers, The Yardbirds, the Spencer Davis Group, and Billy J. Kramer and the Dakotas. Who could forget the simple-minded "Freddie dance" that Freddie and The Dreamers did when they performed their number one hit, "I'm Telling You Now" and "Do The Freddie" live? They alternately swung both arms up at about a 45 degree angle while lifting their right leg at the same time, then their left leg, then their right leg and so on, until the end of those songs. Many of these groups made guest appearances on *Ed Sullivan*, *Shindig!* or *Hullabaloo*.

We heard British accents singing on our local AM radio stations often from 1964-66. The Beatles and other British bands and vocalists along with British actor Sean Connery in *James Bond* movies appealed to many girls and women in the U. S. in the '60s because of their British accent. We

thought the British accents sounded refined, clever, more polished, intellec-
tual or sexy or sometimes two or more of these traits.

Songs' lyrics from 1964 and 1965 were easy to listen to and remember,
but the thing that sticks with many baby boomers so many years later is we
can *hear* Gerry and The Pacemakers singing "Ferry Across the Mersey," and
Peter Noone and Herman's Hermits singing "Mrs. Brown You've Got A
Lovely Daughter" in our minds. We can *hear* the Rolling Stones singing
"Time Is On My Side," Dave Clark singing "Glad All Over," The Hollies
singing "Carousel," Eric Burdon singing "House of The Rising Sun" and
The Beatles singing "And I Love Her." We can hear those *different* British
accents when we replay those different songs in our mind without the actual
song playing in the background. We can just think about several verses in
succession or we can sing them out loud trying to imitate those different
British accents (especially if no one else is around). In other words, by hearing those songs often we became good at imitating the different British accents in them. If someone tries to play a different artist, even a similar
sounding artist performing one of those songs, we'd identify in seconds that
the song was an imposter. Our minds are remarkably good at remembering
songs and the way various artists sounded when they sang them, whether
they were from Great Britain or not, and those British artists' different accents are clearly etched in our memories.

The DC5 and Herman's Hermits were not nearly as talented as the
Beatles, but their timing was perfect. The DC5 appeared twice on *Ed Sullivan*
in March 1964, starting with their hit "Glad All Over." They charted eight
different hit singles that became gold records from 1964-65, and 25 hit singles in the BB Hot 100 from 1964-67. They had a consistent rock 'em, sock
'em beat with an organ, but they sounded a bit repetitious, except for their
two ballads, "Because" and "Come Home." Clark wrote most of their songs
and he had a good voice, but they never experimented with more thoughtful
lyrics and the use of different instruments and sounds the way the Beatles
did beginning with *Rubber Soul* in 1965. Herman's Hermits had 13 hit singles
that peaked at number 13 or better on the BB Hot 100 between October
1964 and February 1967. Their lead singer Peter Noone known as "Herman" for the group's band name's purposes turned just 17 years old a few
weeks after their first hit single, "I'm Into Something Good" entered the BB
Hot 100 chart. Like the DC5, Herman's Hermits did not experiment much

with different instruments or sounds or more thoughtful song themes to expand their repertoire. The Moody Blues started slow compared to many other 1964-65 British groups, but they finished strong in the '70s and '80s, long after most of the British '64- '65 groups disbanded. The Moody Blues released "Go Now!" in 1965, which stayed in the BB Hot 100 for 14 weeks and "Tuesday Afternoon" which remained in the BB Hot 100 eleven weeks in 1968. "Nights In White Satin" fizzled when it debuted as a single in '68, but it reached number 2 when it was re-released in 1972. Once Justin Hayward and John Lodge joined the group in 1966, the group gained their new more distinct dreamy orchestral sound.

The Rolling Stones quickly became the Beatles' chief competition from England. Starting in 1965, Mick Jagger and Keith Richards teamed up to write many of their own songs. Just as important, the group's "bad boy image" compared to the more wholesome Beatles, gained a very strong following. They even appealed to many Beatles fans as an alternative, and they still do (some music fans liked the fact that the two groups were much different). Jagger recalled, "The first tour [of America] was tough. We were popular in New York and L.A., but the rest [of the stops], forget it. We played in mostly empty stadiums. It was tough. America was very conservative in attitudes." The Who's Peter Townshend said that image and behavior were very important. "Music was kind of important. What was more important was where the music you played originated," said Townshend. "And for the Stones, they played the Blues. They took their name from Muddy Waters [presumably his recording, "Rollin' Stone"] and barreling style from Chuck Berry," he added.

The Stones were big hitmakers in the '60s, 70s and '80s. Jagger, Richards and drummer Charlie Watts continued to perform together often 40 and even 50 years after their first top ten hit in 1964, giving many music fans reason to crown them rock's or rock and roll's all-time greatest band for productivity combined with longevity. In the '60s, they followed "Time Is On My Side (1964)," with "The Last Time (1965)," "(I Can't Get No) Satisfaction (1965)," "Get Off Of My Cloud (1965)," "As Tears Go By (1966)," "19th Nervous Breakdown (1966)," "Paint It, Black (1966)," and "Ruby Tuesday (1967)." They had the three hit singles that were widespread dancing favorites– "Jumpin' Jack Flash (1968)," "Honky Tonk Women (1969)" and "Brown Sugar (1971)," and a string of album cuts that were longer and among their fans' favorites: especially "Sympathy For The Devil (1968)," "Gimme Shelter (1969)," "Midnight Rambler (1969)," and "You Can't Always Get What You Want (1969)."

The Kinks and the Animals had short, but very productive runs in the BB Top 40. Graham Nash recalled, "The Kinks were completely crazy. They would cut wires while you were playing. They were completely nuts. But once you heard them sing, 'You Really Got Me', you knew they were destined for fame and glory. "The Animals' Eric Burdon said, "We were on tour with Chuck Berry. I realized if you try to out rock Chuck Berry, you're wasting your time, so I was looking for a song to have a different feel to it that would be erotic, so we did 'House Of The Rising Sun'." Burdon gave a stirring vocal on "House Of The Rising Sun" which became a number one hit in the U. S. starting September 5, 1964, for three weeks. The Animals' early music (1965) was often more assertive and rebellious than many other British groups with songs like, "'Don't Let Me Be Misunderstood," "We Gotta Get Out Of This Place," and "It's My Life." Burdon recalled, "There was a great sense of brotherhood [among the British groups]. Hey, we're all in this together. Let's go over to America and kick ass, you know," he added.

British-born vocalists Tom Jones and Petula Clark also rode the momentum of The British Invasion and fit in another niche in popular music in the mid-'60s. They placed a large set of hit singles on the BB Hot 100 *and* AC charts. I would have never guessed in the mid-'60s that Tom Jones was the same age as John Lennon and only two years older than Paul McCartney. Because Tom's songs and performing style appealed to adult women more than teens, his hit singles usually placed higher on the AC chart than the Hot 100. His first two hit singles in 1965 ("It's Not Unusual" and "What's New Pussycat? ") clinched his popularity with many adult women listeners of popular music. His sexy edge, British (Welsh in this case) accent and raucous live performance style like Elvis, appealed to many women in their 20s and 30s. Petula was 33 in 1965, eight years older than Jones and Lennon, but her first three top ten hits in the U. S. —"Downtown (1964)," "I Know A Place (1965)," and My Love (1965)," placed higher on the BB Hot 100 chart, than the AC chart. Thereafter, her hit singles usually placed much higher on the AC Chart than the Hot 100 ("A Sign Of The Times (1966)," "I Couldn't Live Without Your Love (1966)" and "Don't Sleep In The Subway (1967)").

Once the large number of British groups became popular in the U. S.

in 1964 and 1965, solo singers were less prominent as big hit makers on the BB Hot 100. At the same time, most music fans only knew each group member's name if he was in the Beatles—John, Paul, George, and Ringo; the Rolling Stones—Mick, Keith, Bill, Charlie and Brian; and the Beach Boys—Brian, Mike, Carl, Alan and Dennis, and some of us knew all the names of The Temptations. Many girl music fans knew the names of all three of the Supremes, but not many knew all the names of the Marvelettes, Martha and the Vandellas and other "girl groups. "Most of us only knew the lead singers' names in many groups—Frankie Valli of the 4 Seasons (with that high falsetto voice), Peter Noone of Herman's Hermits and Dave Clark of the DC5.

17

U. S. musicians respond in 1964-65

♪

EVEN AS THE BEATLES AND OTHER BRITISH GROUPS were racking up one
hit single after another, some American singers and musicians were
also in some of their peak years. The Beach Boys, the 4 Seasons, Jan
and Dean, and Lesley Gore released many of their biggest hit singles in 1964-
65. The 4 Seasons followed their three number one hits, "Sherry (1962),"
"Big Girls Don't Cry (1962)" and "Walk Like A Man (1963)" with eleven
Top 40 hits from 1964-65. "Rag Doll (1964)" peaked at number one, and
"Dawn (1964)" and "Let's Hang On! (1965)" reached number three on the
BB Hot 100. Gore was at her high point when she was 18 years old in 1964,
and she sang all her biggest hits on the Teenage Awards Music International
Show (called the TAMI Show) at Santa Monica, California. The show's producers picked Mick Jagger and the Stones to be the last act, but that strategy
backfired. The more seasoned James Brown resented playing just before the
relative newcomers, the Stones, and stole the show with his dancing, theatrics
and scintillating live performance. Brown's performance inspired Jagger who
became one of his biggest fans and was executive producer for music in the
2015 biopic about James, *Get On Up.*

James Brown's peak years (1965-1968) for top ten hits on the BB Hot
100 and R&B charts coincided with the U. S. musicians' rebuttal of Britain's
hit makers. Often called "the hardest working man in show business," he
belted out shrill screams of joy and pain and danced on the balls of his feet,

slipping and sliding side to side in a rapid manner that thrilled concert goers. Emcees and other bandmates typically introduced him at concerts as "The Godfather of Soul," "Soul Brother Number One" and "Mr. Dynamite." For James, it was all about the beat—many of his songs had a prominent bass along with the drums (and often the piano, too) and he always made sure he had top notch horns in his songs. His live shows were often where he experimented—its where his dance moves played off his band's music and his vocals, and his music played off his vocals and dancing. Jerry W, Mike A. and I hoped to go to Brown's concert scheduled at Baltimore's Civic Center in early April 1968, but it was cancelled in the wake of Martin Luther King's assassination and the ensuing riots there. Brown's three hit singles, "Papa's Got A Brand New Bag (Part 1) (1965)," "I Got You (I Feel Good) (1965)," and "Cold Sweat - Part 1 (1967)," won a legion of fans who loved dancing. No imitator of James' style or covers of his songs came out of the U. K., or the U. S. for that matter, as the decade unfolded.

The Byrds played music that was sometimes classified as folk-rock, a new genre coming out of Southern California and New York City. Their biggest hit single was their cover of Bob Dylan's "Mr. Tambourine Man" issued in mid-1965. It reached number one for one week and was on the BB Hot 100 for 13 weeks. It still sounds as fresh and new today as when it first came on AM radio. The Byrds' cover of "Mr. Tambourine Man" has guitar playing (especially the electric lead guitar riff) and singing harmony that trumps Dylan's original version easily. This was one of the key songs of the mid-'60s that convinced many guys to go buy a guitar and learn how to play it. We heard this song's lyrics crystal clear, making it easy to sing along with it. We listeners had no idea at the time that the extra richness in layers of instrumentation on "Mr. Tambourine Man" came from several of the talented musicians from the "Wrecking Crew" in Los Angeles' Gold Star Studios (no credit was given to them on the album liner notes), rather than most of The Byrds.

The British invasion was more expansive than just the music. It extended to mop head hairstyles and fashion. "All the sudden, kids in the U. S. had to have long hair like they did in England," recalled Dick Clark. "We began talking like Englishmen. We wore the same clothing," he added.

American pop groups and vocalists followed suit of the British mop heads in music, hairstyle and fashion from 1964-66, including The Byrds, The Grassroots, Paul Revere and the Raiders, Sonny Bono, the Monkees, the Turtles, and The Beau Brummels. Some groups in '67-'68 still had the mop top hair style like Gary Puckett and the Union Gap. By 1966, clothing fads were influenced by The Byrds (granny or Ben Franklin glasses), The Rolling Stones (plaid and checkered pants), Sonny and Cher (hip-hugger belts), Paul Revere and the Raiders (paisley shirts and leather vests), and Herman's Hermits (round-toed boots).

One New Jersey based group, The Knickerbockers, cashed in on their Beatles-sound-alike song, "Lies" that debuted late in 1965, reached number 20 in early 1966, and stayed on the BB Hot 100 for 13 weeks. It was uncanny how much they sounded like The Beatles, even the scream for 3 or 4 seconds in the song's middle that was reminiscent of McCartney on some of The Beatles' songs. Some of us wondered, are they from England? If we read teen magazines, or heard them introduced on TV, we found out they were from New Jersey.

The British Invasion was also "re-introducing" American black R&B music back to "mainstream America" and American musicians covered some of the new British groups' songs. The Beatles recorded Smokey Robinson's "You Really Got A Hold On Me" and Smokey recorded "Yesterday." The Beatles covered Little Richard's "Long Tall Sally," The Spencer Davis Group recorded the R&B hits, "Gimme Some Lovin' (1966)" and "I'm A Man (1967)," and The Stones covered, "Little Red Rooster." By 1966, Otis Redding covered The Stones' "Satisfaction" and The Beatles' "Day Tripper."

18

Less album filler

♪

IN THE EARLY '60s, record albums often contained one to three hits and the rest of the songs were filler that didn't appeal to most listeners. When we played those record albums that didn't have whole sides of songs we liked, we lifted the record player's toning arm (that also held the needle at one end) and tried to place it gently down on the interval of the disc just before the song we wanted to hear. We became adept at doing it with all the practice we had, but sometimes we slipped and created a skip in the record (a disaster if it was our favorite song on the LP). Whenever we tried to play that side of the LP after that mishap, the skip in the record over some microgrooves brought us to a new place in a song and the skip thereafter, always brought the record player's needle to the same point in the record. A new saying was born from this mishap—if someone repeated themselves often and we tired of hearing it, we said "you sound like a broken record."

Many of us bought a combination of record albums and 45-records to make up our direct go-to play list. It was our limited number of songs we could play in our room on a record player without waiting to hear one of those songs on our radio. Buying some 45s and some LPs allowed us to pick the occasional album we knew had several good songs on it, while still buying a 45-record that we considered a standout, a possible one-hit wonder, or one that appeared on an album that did not have other songs we liked, or we were not willing to risk buying the LP before hearing it first.

The Beatles' first few albums released in the U. S. were collections of current and recent hits that tried to catch up with the large number of hit singles they released in 1964-65, and two LPs, *A Hard Day's Night* and *Help!* that were based largely on those movies. Starting with *Beatles '65* and *Rubber Soul*, The Beatles usually issued albums that had all new songs that we played uninterrupted, side one, then side two. *Rubber Soul* set the bar for future LPs. It had no filler and had more songs with thoughtful lyrics. The Beatles continued to build a reputation for LPs that *usually* had little or no filler when they issued *Revolver* (1966), *Sgt. Pepper's* (1967), *Magical Mystery Tour* (1967), and *Abbey Road* (1969). While the listenership of The Beatles was more widespread than for Bob Dylan, his fans felt the same way about his LPs, starting with *The Freewheelin' Bob Dylan* (1963).

Brian Wilson and The Beach Boys set out to compile such an album with all new songs in *Pet Sounds* in 1966, and many music fans and critics hailed the LP for reaching its goal. *Pet Sounds* had several hit singles, "Sloop John B," "Wouldn't It Be Nice," and "God Only Knows." Still, the Beach Boys' "Good Vibrations" was their biggest hit song recorded during those sessions, but it was not included in the LP. The Doors, Simon and Garfunkel and the Rolling Stones quickly followed The Beatles example, issuing albums that had enough good songs versus "filler" to make it easier to buy one of their LPs, instead of a 45-record.

We always wanted more records than we could afford, but we could choose between 45-records, new LPs by a recording artist or Greatest Hits (often I bought a 45 and an LP at the same time). The Greatest Hits LPs were a sure bet if we liked a recording artist and had few, if any of their records, but a new LP offered the chance to hear new songs other than an LP's featured hits, a risky decision if we had not heard the album yet. By listening to LPs that were not greatest hits records, we found little known songs that we liked that many of our friends didn't know about.

The downside of less album filler, was that many quality songs were never issued as singles, especially in the case of the Beatles. This was problematic for youngsters, especially preteens or teens who could afford to buy 45s once-in-a-while, but not many LPs. George Martin recalled that he and Brian Epstein (The Beatles' manager) discussed the goal in late '64 or so, to release a new single, every three months and a new album, every six months.

Maybe they were concerned that more frequent releases of new 45-records would supersaturate the airwaves with The Beatles and fans would grow tired of them. Still, examples of Beatles songs that would likely have been hit records if they had been issued as singles are: "No Reply (1964)," "In My Life (1965)," "Norwegian Wood (This Bird Has Flown)(1965)," "Girl (1965)," "Drive My Car (1965)," "Think For Yourself (1965)," "Here, There, And Everywhere (1966)," "Michelle (1966)," "Got To Get You Into My Life (1966)," "Back In The U. S. S. R. (1968)," "Ob-La-Di, Ob-La-Da (1968)," "Hey Bulldog (1969)," and "Here Comes The Sun (1969)."

Some of the better recording artists in the late '60s issued "double albums," two LPs issued together at the same time in one package, instead of one each, released in succession, months apart. Bob Dylan's highly acclaimed *Blonde On Blonde* became rock's "first great double album" in 1966, and contained the hit songs "I Want You," "Just Like A Woman," and "Rainy Day Women 12 And 35." Did the lyrical phrase "everybody must get stoned" refer to smoking pot or occasionally being hit hard by your critics (in his case the folk purists who didn't like when he "went electric'), or both? The double album, *The Beatles* (often called the *White Album)* was a big departure from The Beatles' *Sgt. Pepper's* and *The Magical Mystery Tour* LPs. This time the Beatles used no cover art on the album at all, a stark contrast to the colorful, almost eye-popping covers of the two previous LPs. More important, the *White Album's* songs didn't rely as much on studio technology. Lennon and McCartney (and Harrison) wrote most of the songs while taking a Transcendental Meditation course with Maharishi Mahesh Yogi in Rishikesh, India early in 1968. No 45-records were released from the LP. "Hey Jude" b/w "Revolution" were not included on the *White Album*, but they were recorded during the *White Album* sessions and were issued as a top-selling 45-record ("Revolution 1" in the LP was a bluesy version of that song whereas the 45 cut of "Revolution" was hard charging rock with Lennon's primeval scream). Many of the LPs' other songs had a blues edge to them and a couple reverted to the music hall sound.

Many Beatles fans couldn't get enough of "Birthday," Ob-La-Di, Ob-La-Da," "Back In The U. S. S. R.," "Rocky Raccoon" and "While My Guitar Gently Weeps" from the *White Album*, but I felt some of the double album, especially many of the Disc 2 songs were extraneous and could have been left out. I was surprised years later to learn that the Beatles' producer George Martin said in the book, *The Beatles' Anthology*: "I thought we should probably have made a very, very good single album rather than a double. But they insisted. I think it could have been made fantastically good if it had been compressed a bit and condensed." Martin did not specify which songs he would have left out of the double album to make it a "better" single LP. Meanwhile, Cream crammed two LPs of music into *Wheels Of Fire* (1968), in part because some of the live songs "Spoonful" and "Toad," were over 16 minutes long, each. Chicago churned out excellent double albums for its first three releases, *Chicago Transit Authority* (1969), *Chicago II* (1970) and *Chicago III* (1971) and Crosby, Stills Nash and Young issued their live double album, *4 Way Street* in 1971.

19

Soul (R&B) music

♪

"RHYTHM AND BLUES" HAS AN AFRICAN AMERICAN ORIGIN arising from blues and the addition of driving rhythms taken from jazz. "Blues" originated in the Deep South around the end of the 19th century" with its roots coming from African American work songs and spirituals, and its early songs used field hollers, chants, and shouts. "Soul music" developed in the late '50s and early '60s, combining African-American gospel music, rhythm and blues, and jazz. Its trademark is often a catchy rhythm, hand claps and a call and response between the lead vocalist and chorus.

In the '50s black stations became more abundant and gave R&B and gospel music more playing time on the radio. Many of R&B's best vocalists in the '60s got their start singing in church choirs as youngsters in the '40s or '50s, including Sam Cooke, Jerry Butler, Otis Redding, Marvin Gaye, Aretha Franklin, and Dionne Warwick.

By the early '60s, R&B hit singles were more in demand by white listeners. DJs on stations that featured the BB Hot 100 or the BB Top 40 were able to pick and choose songs from the BB and Cash Box R&B charts to play on their stations. When *Billboard* discontinued its separate Hot R&B Singles Chart of 30 songs beginning November 30, 1963, only *Cash Box* had a separate R&B chart. This made it more difficult for a wide variety of black R&B artists to get the attention of white disc jockeys for airtime on

BB Hot 100 stations. By late November 1963, Motown, Stax/Atlantic, Brunswick, and Chess Records had their feet in the door for some playing time on "white" stations in 1964, but it was still a big boost to R&B record sales when *Billboard* re-started a separate Hot R&B Top Singles chart of 40 songs on January 30, 1965. Now, both black and white DJs had more R&B songs to choose from with two national R&B charts again, along with visits from record promoters.

Right on the heels of the Beatles' first U. S. visit, Berry Gordy's Motown Records and its subsidiary labels, Tamla, Gordy, and Soul found their groove in 1964. Martha and the Vandellas' "Heat Wave" and the Miracles' "Mickey's Monkey" in 1963, paved the way for the hit singles, "My Guy," "Dancing In The Street," "Where Did Our Love Go," "Baby Love," "Come See About Me," and "My Girl" in 1964, each reaching number 1 or 2 on the BB Hot 100. It was a strong rebuttal to the British invasion pop hit single success. Motown's greatest rate of hit singles played on AM radio from 1964 through 1968 (averaging about 37 new hit singles per year). By the mid-'60s, Motown, called itself *Hitsville, U. S. A.* and *the Sound of Young America* and it fit.

Motown's songs resonated with our feelings about love and infused us with energy for dancing. It's no wonder that many of us who were teens have so many memories about teen love. It's the time of first dates, first boyfriend or girlfriend, first dances or any dances we went to and Motown was everywhere, all the time, on our airwaves and at teen dances in the '60s. "Motown brought my world into an abundance of color and soulfulness because of those melodic lines and those fantastic chord changes and beats," singer Annie Lenox recalled. "Dancing In The Street—they would always kick off the night in any club with that one. One of the great Motown hits," recalled guitarist Jeff Beck.

In the '60s, it was a rarity to hear any white artists' songs on Baltimore soul stations because their airwaves were the primary medium for a wider variety of R&B and gospel songs. Exceptions in Baltimore were when its soul stations played the Righteous Brothers' hit singles starting with "You've Lost That Lovin' Feelin' (1964)," some of the Rascals' songs (e. g., "Groovin' (1967)" and "People Got To Be Free (1968)"), and other occasional crossover hits like the Soul Survivors' "Expressway To Your Heart (1967)" and The O'Kaysions' "Girl Watcher (1968). "

Atlantic Records' The Young Rascals (and later The Rascals) were a white group from New York who had 15 hit records on the BB Hot 100 in the '60s. Tom Petty recalled, "I never saw a Hammond organ in my life until I saw The Rascals. We went out and scrounged up somebody's old Hammond organ and here's a whole 'nother texture of sound." John Sebastian recalled, "People don't realize the contribution The Rascals made." "Their attitude was 'we're the uptown band. 'They had this vicious rhythm section. I mean it was poppin' between Felix's left hand (on organ) and Dino Danelli (on drums)."

In the mid-'60s, we most often identified soul music with Motown and the Memphis sound of Stax Records, Atlantic Records, Chess Records in Chicago and some Philadelphia record labels, too. The Stax/Atlantic Records soul sound featured Aretha Franklin, Otis Redding, Sam and Dave, Booker T. and the MGs, and Ray Charles, while the Motown sound was led by Smokey Robinson and the Miracles, the Temptations, Diana Ross and the Supremes, the Four Tops, Stevie Wonder, and Marvin Gaye.

The *styles* of Motown and Memphis soul had differences and similarities. Motown had as many Top 40 and number one hits coming from its vocal groups as solo singers. Stax and Atlantic had most of their hits coming from solo artists. Berry Gordy often used orchestral strings in Motown's songs. Motown's lyrics were all about love—falling into love, out of love, and losing your love partner. While love was usually the theme for Stax and Atlantic, too, their lyrics and delivery of their songs often had a harder edge than Motown. Examples of that harder edge to R&B are Ray Charles' "What'd I Say (1959);" Carla Thomas's "B-A-B-Y (1967);" Redding's "Respect (1965)" and "Try A Little Tenderness (1966);" Aretha's "Respect (1967)" and "I Never Loved A Man (The Way I Love You) (1967);" and "The Wicked" Wilson Pickett's "In The Midnight Hour (1965)." Pickett's voice was gritty and every bit as serious and soulful as Otis. I bought his *The Exciting Wilson Pickett* LP within the first few weeks it was issued. The pink background on the LP cover was an eye catcher and it did just that during one of my trips into Michael's. I grabbed it, made a quick look at the song list and knew I had to buy it for home consumption—"Land Of 1000 Dances;" "In The Midnight Hour;" "Mercy, Mercy;" 634-5789;" "Barefootin';" and the clincher for me—"Ninety-Nine And A Half (Won't Do)."

Motown and Stax issued plenty of songs in the mid-60s and later, that teens loved dancing to. Motown's list of teen favorite dance songs included "Ain't To Proud To Beg" and "Get Ready," The Four Tops "I Can't Help

Myself," and "Reach Out I'll Be There," Stevie Wonder's "Uptight (Everything's Alright)" and Edwin Starr's "Twenty-Five Miles." Some of Stax's (and Atlantic Records') hard driving songs that were fast dance favorites included: Otis Redding's "Respect" and "I Can't Turn You Loose," Aretha's "Respect," Sam and Dave's "Soul Man" and Arthur Conley's "Sweet Soul Music."

At Teen Center, when "Soul Man" started with those opening guitar notes, drum beats and horns you'd get goose bumps sometimes—out to the dance floor we'd go. Then the singer started, "Comin' to you on a dirt road... " Our arms and body swayed twice to the right, twice to the left and so on, with our heads bobbing up and down and to the right and left. It was a groove in the true sense of the word as we fell in line with the beat and the loudness as the song played. If "Sweet Soul Music" played next the beat quickened and we were dancing on our toes just like Arthur Conley did in his live performances on TV. Side to side swaying, head bobbing. We kept our rear ends and knees loose and moving. Grinning like Cheshire cats as we danced and strutted on the dance floor. How could you not do it? The clever thing about songs like these was their length of three minutes or less meant you wished they weren't ending. You wanted to hear them again, soon.

There was a healthy competition going on between The Miracles, The Four Tops, The Temptations and The Supremes in the mid—'60s. Plenty of listeners had their favorite of the four groups and mine became The Temptations when they rolled out four straight number one R&B hit singles in '66. In March, May, August and November they issued "Get Ready," "Ain't Too Proud To Beg," "Beauty Is Only Skin Deep," and "(I Know) I'm Losing You" fulfilling the new-hit-single-every-three-months goal that many musicians strived for. Part of the reason those songs connected with me so strongly was that I was 15 years old and just starting the dance scene, so the adrenalin felt like it was running sky high.

Berry Gordy hired choreographer Cholly Atkins to sharpen the "group" dancing skills of the Temptations, Four Tops, the Miracles and the Supremes for their live shows and it paid off. The dance moves and routines were Motown's signature feature for its vocal groups. Watching *You Tube* videos of The Temptations and the other Motown groups today transports baby boomers all the way back to the '60s. Motown groups' dance moves aided local teen bands' vocal groups with their dance routines. Local vocal groups did not have equipment for video recording, so they watched closely when any Motown group appeared on TV or made a live appearance in town. Black male vocalists in teen groups across the U. S. often imitated dance routines they saw on TV when The Temptations' performed "Ain't Too Proud To Beg" and "Get Ready;" the Four Tops sang "I Can't Help Myself" and female vocalists sometimes copied some of the Supremes' dance routines.

There were group name changes at Motown during the '60s to deal with egos or the insistence by Gordy that one singer have top billing in a group. It had been Martha and The Vandellas since their first hit single, "Come And Get These Memories" in 1963, but their name was changed to Martha Reeves and The Vandellas starting with "Honey Chile" in 1967. Beginning with "The "Love I Saw In You Was Just A Mirage" in March 1967, the Miracles name was changed to Smokey Robinson and The Miracles. Smokey began his solo career in 1972 and was replaced by Billy Griffin. The Supremes' group name was changed to Diana Ross and the Supremes beginning with their hit single "Reflections" in 1967 and ending with "Someday We'll Be Together" in late 1969. Jean Terrell replaced Ross late in 1969, joining Mary Wilson and Cindy Birdsong for their new hits "Up The Ladder To The Roof" and "Stoned Love." The Four Tops' and The Temptations' group names never changed during their time with Motown, but David Ruffin attempted to have the Temptations' name changed to David Ruffin and The Temptations late in 1967. Other members of The Temptations strongly nixed that idea and Ruffin was removed from the group in 1968, due to David's problems with drugs and missing practices and performances. Starting with "Cloud Nine" Ruffin was replaced with Dennis Edwards.

By the mid and late '60s, DJs, musicians and music listeners everywhere usually called R&B music "soul." Song titles seldom if ever had "R&B" in their titles, but the word "soul" appeared in some major hit singles from Stax/Atlantic Records: "634-5789 (Soulsville, U. S. A.)," "Soul Twist," "Soul Man" "Sweet Soul Music," "Memphis Soul Stew," and "Soul Dance Number Three." More examples included the 5th Dimension's "Stoned Soul Picnic" and "California Soul" and Dyke and the Blazers' "We Got More Soul. "

R&B LP titles started using the word "soul" more often in the mid and late '60s, especially on Stax Records—*Otis Blue/Otis Redding Sings Soul* (1965), *The Great Otis Redding Sings Soul Ballads* (1965), *The Otis Redding Dictionary of Soul: Complete and Unbelievable* (1966), Redding's *The Soul Album,* The Temptations' *With a Lot O' Soul* (1967), *Soul Men by Sam and*

Dave (1967), and William Bell's *The Soul of a Bell* (1967). Motown issued hit singles and LPs by Jr. Walker and the All-Stars, Gladys Knight and The Pips, Jimmy Ruffin, and Shorty Long on its subsidiary label, Soul Records, and Johnny Rivers issued many of the 5th Dimension's hit singles on Soul City Records.

Michael McDonald, Rod Stewart and Phil Collins are among the many hit-making musicians from the '70s and beyond, who grew up listening to '60s music and developed a deep attachment and respect for soul music of that era. Stewart covered "(I Know) I'm Losing You" in his 1971 album *Every Picture Tells a Story*. The Doobie Brothers covered Kim Weston's "Take Me In Your Arms (Rock Me A Little While)" in 1975, Peter Frampton recorded a rousing version of "Signed, Sealed, Delivered (I'm Yours) (1977)," and Phil Collins covered "You Can't Hurry Love" in 1982. Stewart and Ronald Isley (earlier with the Isley Brothers) issued their cover of "This Old Heart Of Mine" in 1990. Huey Lewis and The News released a sound-alike cover of J. J. Jackson's "But It's Alright" in 1993. Later, Stewart, McDonald and Collins each recorded whole albums of their own covers of '60s soul songs. Collins even brought back two members of the Funk Brothers to add more authenticity to his covers of Motown songs.

Several artists paid tributes to Smokey Robinson. George Harrison recorded "Pure Smokey" in 1976, named after Smokey's 1974 album *Pure Smokey* and gave thanks for Smokey's gifts of music to listeners. ABC recorded "When Smokey Sings," a rousing, heartfelt up-tempo tribute to Smokey Robinson sung by lead singer Martin Fry (a great singer in his own right) that reached number 5 in 1983. Stewart and the Temptations' "The Motown Song (1991)" pleaded for listeners to "bring over some of your old Motown Records" play those tunes through speakers in the window, and let's listen to the Miracles as the songs "echo in the alley down below."

20

At the dance with the teen center beat

♪

A T 15, I STARTED GOING TO WEEKLY DANCES AT TEEN CENTER in Perry Hall Elementary School on Saturday nights in the fall of 1966, and kept going until I graduated from high school. Talk about a bargain, for about $1. 25 every Saturday night, year-round, we listened and danced to *live bands on stage* for three hours.

Teen Center was a weekly party, a celebration. It was where 150 to 200 teens showed up every week with some bands like the Jetsons (later The Jetsons with The Tangiers) pulling in the biggest crowds, making our chaperones turn some people away at the front door. Most weeks it seemed like the only chaperones were Mr. and Mrs. Weiner (I still remember their faces) and they had very little trouble with fighting among teens. "Teen Center was our life line," one of my girl classmates told me in 2017. It was the place we enjoyed music the most because it was where real life played out for us— listening and dancing to our favorite music while often intertwined with the love scene. Sometimes, just before we left home when we had a date or went to Teen Center, we played a few of our favorite songs on our record player to spike our anticipation of that evening even more. It was like taking a shot of liquid courage. As if once a week wasn't enough, we had a monthly bonus during the school year at Perry Hall High School with live band dances on some Friday nights.

Teen center and high school dances were where the cool cats gathered, the place to learn a new dance and hear the area's bands with a few jitters belt out their new cover of a hit song currently on Top 40 charts. In many ways, some of the lyrics from Shorty Long's "Function At The Junction (1966)" reflected what Teen Center and high school dances were like for us. It was the place girls and guys "dressed in the latest styles." We felt "everybody's gonna be there" and there were plenty of "breathtaking hip-shaking cuties" there (and teens going to teen dances around the U. S. felt the same way).

We liked hearing in some of our songs' lyrics that teens and others elsewhere in the U. S. were also listening and dancing to many of the same songs, and we naturally identified with a song if it included our city's name in the lyrics. Songs like Chuck Berry's "Back In The U. S. A. " and "Sweet Little Sixteen," Martha and the Vandellas' "Dancing In The Street" and James Brown's "Night Train" reeled off cities' names to remind us that everybody was listening and dancing to our '60s music nationwide, not just us. "Dancing In The Street" and "Night Train" mentioned Baltimore, so it sent an extra jolt through us in Perry Hall and elsewhere in the Baltimore area when we heard them played by a live band. Likewise, when we watched the James Bond movie *Goldfinger* in Overlea's Paramount Theater (near Baltimore) in 1964, the audience applauded and roared its approval when the airline pilot in the movie announced to the few passengers on the small plane: "we are now approaching *Baltimore's* Friendship Airport."

Teen center and high school dances felt personal deep down because we knew many of the people there and knew who most of the dancers were. There was competition for boyfriends and girlfriends, too, adding to the excitement and butterflies we felt. For teens like me and my neighborhood friends who lived within a ten-minute walk of those dances, it was liberating at 15 or 16 years old to be able to walk there and back home instead of catching a ride with our parents (and even more liberating for teens who could drive and park there).

The weekly interval of teen center aligned well with the frequent changes in the Top 40 records rankings on the BB Hot 100 and it gave us many chances to hear many different local bands. If one night was uneventful in not meeting anyone new, or being with your boyfriend or girlfriend, or hearing one of your favorite bands, there was always next week. That frequent, re-occurring interval made us optimistic that more good times were on the way, soon.

Our first adrenaline rush came when we walked through the front door to get in line at the payment table and the band was already playing. Butterflies in our stomach. We glanced to the left into the "multi-purpose room" to see who was already there, dancing. It was all about the beat of the music, seeing teens dancing to it, some of them your best friends, and often the band was belting out one of your favorite songs. About half the dancers were girl-guy couples and the rest were groups of two to four girls dancing together (many guys lined up along the walls or standing in groups). I had already learned many fast dance steps from Bill and Tom D., and while slow dancing is easy, I was glad I had a couple quick slow dance lessons from Bo in her basement across the street from my house. They played the Beatles' slow dance number, "This Boy" and I was on my way. This was also the time when many guys starting using cologne (English Leather, British Sterling, Jade East or Hai Karate). The guys figured, "I can use all the help I can get." Many of the girls had already been using perfume for a couple years.

Hearing songs 40 and 50 years later by the original artists still reminds us of teen bands who played them. If I close my eyes and hear "Ain't Too Proud To Beg" and "If You Can Want" today, I still see the Jetsons with the Tangiers playing it at Teen Center. Hearing Parliament's "(I Wanna) Testify," the Platters' "With This Ring" or Robert Knight's "Everlasting Love" today, conjures up memories of Nate Simms and the Chevelles singing them at our high school ring dance and Teen Center. Wilson Pickett's "Ninety-Nine and A Half (Won't Do)" and "In the Midnight Hour" stir memories of Denny Picasso from Denny and the Hitch-hikers singing them, and hearing the early Blood, Sweat & Tears' song "I Love You More Than You'll Ever Know" brings back the Capris playing it at a Perry Hall High School dance. All those great horns in the Capris band. The Four Tops' "Reach Out I'll Be There," Spencer Davis Group's "Gimme Some Lovin'," the Lovin' Spoonful's "Summer In The City," and the Grassroots' "Midnight Confessions" stir memories of Teen Center, but I no longer remember which teen bands played them. Other popular Perry Hall Teen Center bands included the Admirals and Mike and the Majestics.

By the mid-'60s, teen center bands seldom played songs from the '50s. There were plenty of new songs for teen bands to play and teens wanted to hear the current and recent songs being played on the radio, not the ones their older brothers and sisters played at home just a few years earlier. Some of the fast dance songs we danced to most often at teen center and our high school dances were: "Sweet Soul Music," "Land Of 1000 Dances," "Going To A Go-Go," "Mickey's Monkey," "Soul Man," "Hold On! I'm Comin'," "Midnight Confessions," "But It's Alright," "Mony Mony," "Wooly Bully," "Gimme Some Lovin'," and "I Can't Help Myself." Their stirring dance beats made them top sellers and our most requested dance floor songs.

Our arms, shoulders, hips, legs and feet swung and spun in assorted ways and we often had our own version of various dances. For the twist, some twisted on two feet, others swiveled on one. The frug, mashed potato, the swim, the twist, the limbo, and the cha cha cha were mostly in the early '60s. The jerk, the skate, boogaloo, shing-a-ling, and the Horse took over as our dance floor favorites in the mid and late '60s. We learned or modified our dance moves from watching other teens, another example of the phenomena that we were all in this thing together, even among people we barely knew in high school, but usually knew their name and not much more. We watched teen dancers on *Bandstand* and the *Buddy Deane* Show or *The Kerby Scott Show* in Baltimore for more dance move ideas. *The Kerby Scott Show* was "a rock and roll music dance show" on Baltimore's WBAL -TV in 1967. It began as a one-hour show early on Friday evenings that was broadcast for one and ½ hours at 4:30 beginning in mid-September. Like the *Buddy Deane Show* a couple years earlier, teens flocked home to see the live dancing, lip syncing by live local bands (who recorded their song for playing in the studio earlier) and national bands on *Kerby Scott*. On September 15, *Kerby Scott* featured the local bands, Denny and The Hitch-hikers and Billy Storm and The Tempests, and Motown's Four Tops singing their new single "You Keep Running Away" and their recent number one hit, "Reach Out I'll Be There."

We learned dancing from some of our favorite singers on TV. Elvis Presley, Jackie Wilson, and James Brown were some of our premier fast dancers during their live performances. Even Chubby Checker's performance of The Twist on *Bandstand* had an extra flourish to it. Mick Jagger would strut around during Rolling Stones songs like a king rooster and the Temptations had the most variety in their dance routines out of all the Motown groups.

Some songs were about one dance craze or listed our current favorites. Before the Twist; the mid-tempo cha, cha, cha became popular in the late '50s and early '60s. It was several steps forward —one, two; cha cha cha, then backward—three, four, cha, cha, cha; then forward again and backward again until the song ended. My parents and their friends played 45-records of Sam

Cooke's "Everybody Loves to Cha Cha Cha (1959)" and Elvis Presley's "It's Now or Never (1960)," practicing the cha, cha, cha. Bobby Rydell's "The Cha, Cha, Cha" was on the BB Hot 100 for 12 weeks in 1962, and girls at our Teen Center danced the Cha, Cha, Cha to the Four Tops' "Ask The Lonely (1964)" and Jr. Walker's "Hot Cha (1965)" when bands played it. Presley's "It's Now Or Never" is his all-time best-selling hit single with over 25 million copies sold worldwide, and part of its popularity stemmed from the ease of doing the cha, cha, cha to it. Even the last three solo drum beats of "It's Now Or Never" were played to the familiar "cha, cha, cha" beat. Major Lance's "Monkey Time" and The Miracles faster tempo "Mickey's Monkey" sang about The Monkey in 1963, telling us to twist our hips, let our backbone slip and move our feet. When a band at Teen Center began with the intro, "Alright, is everybody ready? " we knew they were starting "Mickey's Monkey. " The Miracles ("Come On Do The Jerk"), The Contours ("Can You Jerk Like Me"), and The Larks ("The Jerk") sang about The Jerk in 1964. Wilson Pickett's cover of "Land Of 1000 Dances (1966)" reeled off a few dances—the Pony, Mashed Potato, Alligator, Watusi, and the Jerk. Some teen bands added The Young Rascals' verse to "Land Of 1000 Dances": "Clap your hands! Stomp your feet! I said, Na, Na, Na, Na…" Pickett's "Soul Dance Number Three (1967)" sang about the boogaloo, the skate and the shing-a-ling, "a brand *new* dance." The Esquires sang in "Get On Up" that we're gonna do the Boogaloo, the Monkey, the Philly Dog, The Jerk, and the shing-a-ling.

New fast dance crazes came our way in rapid-fire succession in the '60s. Live bands played mostly fast dance songs that never let us rest easy for long at teen dances and that's the way we wanted it. Most girls loved fast dancing and the guys seemed to fall into an even split—about half loved fast dancing and the other half were dubious about dancing or did not like it (some guys only opted to dance to slow dance songs). Girls were usually better dancers than guys. They were often more extroverted, liked to let loose on the dance floor, and practiced dancing more with each other at home and at Teen Centers.

I liked fast-dancing from ages 15-22—it was in my genes. My mother and father couldn't get enough of it and neither could dad's sister Norma and their mother Camilla. Camilla danced on their dining room table more than one time when she was in her thirties and Norma was a teenager (In 2018 the table still resided in Aunt Norma's apartment). They were all crazy about dancing. Norma brought her portable wind up Victrola phonograph with records outside and taught the boys on Sargeant Street in Baltimore how to fast dance during WWII.

The importance of feeling confident about your dancing can't be overstated, maybe more from the guys' point of view because most of them didn't practice at home the way many girls did with their friends. The Contours nailed it in "Do You Love Me (1962)" when they sang about a guy who was turned down by a girl because he couldn't dance, so he learned how to be a good dancer and now he was back to show her and anybody else his dance moves.

Many teens were less inhibited about dancing at that age than we were years later. It paid to loosen up, be light on your feet and let yourself go. It was all about the frequency—the more you did it, the less inhibited you were. Having the opportunity to dance every week meant that many guys broke the barrier of intimidation about fast dancing and stayed that way once they conquered it. Much later, many of us being older adults are more inhibited about dancing because we do it so rarely—it's tougher to get up and start grooving to music at wedding receptions and at high school reunions among friends and classmates than when we were doing it more often.

When we heard the first five to ten notes of many songs by a band at teen dances, we felt butterflies in our stomach along with the urge to look for a dance partner. Most of the time, guys asked girls to dance (fast and slow dance songs) in the '60s, not the other way around. Guys felt plenty of excitement and high anxiety when we went up to a girl to ask her to dance. You dropped that line, "Hey do you wanna dance? " and waited for the look she gave you and her answer. If she said "yes," your spirit soared, and if she said, "No," you felt like crawling in a hole.

Teen band singers often urged dancers to keep moving and sped up the tempo during extended or improvised versions of a song, in much the same way popular recording artists exhort their crowds at live concerts. Bands often played a medley of several good dancing songs in a row, without ending one song before beginning the next one, or several songs by the same recording artist, strung together without stopping. Keeping dancers on the floor for several songs in a row, nonstop, meant sometimes when a guy asked a girl to fast dance and she said, "Yes," he got more than he bargained for. Sometimes you could see a dancer (most often a guy) sigh as the second, or even the third song started.

Teen Center and high school dance bands played several slow songs during a three-hour dance and always saved one of the best slow dance tunes for the night's last song. This is when boys smelled a strong whiff of Chanel or Tabu perfume from the girls, or the girls caught an overdose of Brut, Jade East or Hai Karate cologne from the guys. Our most popular slow dance songs in the mid-60s at teen center and high school dances were "When A Man Loves a Woman," "Tell It Like It Is," "The Tracks Of My Tears" and "Try A Little Tenderness. "In '69 and '70, Chicago's "Colour My World" joined the short list of popular slow dance songs played at teen dances. "Try A Little Tenderness" went beyond the serious and sentimental feelings of these other classic slow dance songs. It exuded sex in its lyrics and the buildup in tempo during the song. "Try A Little Tenderness" went through you like electric pulses and felt more urgent near the song's end.

Asking a girl to slow dance was a bigger deal than asking her to fast dance. If you think about the intimacy, the trust someone places in you, the thrill and privilege of holding someone close if you are attracted to them, this was and still is a big deal to teens. Usually in everyday life in the '60s, people only hugged each other if they were boyfriend-girlfriend or were close friends or maybe had known each other for a long time. Sometimes you figured the answer would be, "yes" for a slow song if you heard good things "through the grapevine," but your heart still pounded. The Beatles' "I Saw Her Standing There" hit the bullseye about these moments when they sang, "Well my heart went boom, when I crossed that room and I held her hand in mine. "

A girl's heart pounded when a guy she liked or had a crush on, went up to her when a song was starting, and asked her to dance. On the other hand, she dreaded the dance question from someone she did not want to dance with. To make matters worse for the guy, girls usually stood with another girl or in a girl group, so other girls knew at once when a guy was turned down. Still, guys often knew from various signals that girls gave them whether asking for a slow dance was a good move or not. Since girls did not often walk up to a guy and ask him to dance, they smiled or stared at a guy or kept glancing at him repeatedly if they liked him (or let it be known "through the grapevine" that they liked him).

Teen girls identified with Lesley Gore's "You Don't Own Me" in 1963, and from the mid-'60s through the end of the decade, Aretha Franklin was their idol. It was obvious at teen center the way they acted, danced and sang-along when a band played Aretha's songs. She was their chief spokeswoman, much the way Carole King was in the early '70s. Aretha's cover of "Respect" drove home the point further by spelling it out. Teen girls loved singing along with Aretha's version of "Respect": spelling it out and singing the "sock it to me, sock it to me, sock it to me, sock it to me" part. Girls also identified strongly with the lyrics of Aretha's "(You Make Me Feel Like) A Natural Woman," "Chain Of Fools," "(Sweet Sweet Baby) Since You've Been Gone" and others.

Many soul songs had verses that sang about the joy of dancing. Junior Walker's (born Autrey DeWalt Mixom) "Shake And Fingerpop" called out to his woman to put on her wig because they were going out to "shake and fingerpop." It was time to get out on the dance floor. The Esquires asked a girl in "Get On Up" how could she sit down and rest when she knows he's trying to dance with her. Archie Bell and the Drells sang in "I Just Can't Stop Dancing" that upon hearing a good dance song and the drummer's funky beat it was time to put his hamburger down and dance. Sly and the Family Stone's "Dance to the Music" always spurred teen dance goers to get up off their seats and start dancing to the song's beat. In Archie Bell and the Drells' "There's Gonna Be A Showdown" they sang about a self-proclaimed hometown dance king challenging a newcomer to a dancing contest.

The large cluster of R&B/soul and other pop songs from 1964-1968 brought great joy to millions of black and white teen dancers in the U. S. and elsewhere (especially in Great Britain). By the end of 1965, the new soul song list that bands could choose from and learn to put on their playlists included: "Dancing in the Street," "Shotgun," "I'll Be Doggone," "I Can't Help Myself," "In The Midnight Hour," "The Tracks Of My Tears," "Papa's Got A Brand New Bag," "Shake And Fingerpop," "Respect" (Otis Redding version), and "Rescue Me." By the end of September 1966, the new soul songs that teen bands often added to their playlist for another school year of dancing included: "I Can't Turn You Loose," "Going To A-Go-Go," "Uptight (Everything's Alright)," "This Old Heart Of Mine," "Get Ready," "Hold On! I'm Coming," "When A Man Loves A Woman," "Ain't Too Proud To Beg," "Land Of 1000 Dances," "You Can't Hurry Love," and "Reach Out I'll Be There." The new soul songs that were good for dancing kept coming. By the end of September 1967, many teen bands were learning: "But It's Alright," "You Keep Me Hanging On," "Try A Little Tenderness," "Together," "Sweet Soul Music," "Respect (Aretha Franklin's version)," "Funky Broadway," "Expressway To Your Heart," and "Soul Man." From October 1967 through September 1968, teen bands often learned another new set of good dancing songs including; "Dance To The Music," "Tighten Up," "The Horse," "Jumpin' Jack Flash," "Mony Mony," "I Can't Stop Dancing," and "Midnight Confessions." We loved this sustained barrage of great dancing music (mostly soul) that kept coming our way. It made us feel high on life.

Bands liked playing good dance songs like "Memphis Soul Stew," "Tighten Up" and "Dance to The Music" that introduced different musicians and their instruments for a few chords early in the song, giving each musician a short stint in the spotlight. Teens loved listening to King Curtis in "Memphis Soul Stew" introduce his band members' instruments (with a bass guitar playing in the background) including: a half teacup of bass, a pound of fatback drums, four tablespoons of boiling Memphis guitars, a pinch of organ and a half pint of horns, with each instrument following his vocal intro with a short riff. Archie Bell gave each band member of Archie Bell and the Drells, a chance to show their stuff at the beginning of "Tighten Up," with his intros of the drums, then the bass, followed by "guitar falling in," the organ and then the horns (that made it mellow). Sly and the Family Stone gave various instruments a brief time in the spotlight in "Dance To The Music. "They started with vocals and interspersed them throughout, first highlighting the drums, then the lead guitar, followed by bottom (the bass), then the organ and then horns (trumpets).

Like Perry Hall, other Baltimore suburbs and Baltimore city had plenty of teen centers and live bands and it was that way nationwide in the U. S. in the '60s. These bands were composed mostly of teens, oftentimes some of our classmates and occasionally someone in their early 20s. The nationwide sensation of teen band formation was a spinoff of teen boys seeing that guys playing in bands often attracted teen girls. It was a status symbol. Some teen girls were inspired enough by Aretha Franklin or Diana Ross and the Supremes or Martha and the Vandellas to become singers for a teen band. The tidal wave of boys forming teen bands took flight and grew after the Beatles played on *Ed Sullivan* the first time, and new TV shows following the Beatles first U. S. appearance, that featured British and American pop groups.

Watching teen girls' reactions in the audience to pop music performers hooked young boys who hoped the same adoration would come their way. The Byrds sang about it in their hit single "So You Want to Be A Rock 'N'

Roll Star (1967)" telling listeners to get a guitar, learn how to play, and over-simplified the ease of the next three steps—then go to the agent man, make a record that hits the charts, and watch out for the adoring girls. We heard screaming fans in the song's background that conjured up images of The Beatles' fans chasing them down the street in *A Hard Day's Night.*

In Baltimore and its suburbs and elsewhere, white teens often formed the core of the musicians in a teen band/group and sometimes the vocalists, but if a band played mostly soul music then the vocals were often performed by one or more black teens. Many local bands specialized in British (i. e., Liverpool) and U. S. rock and roll (including garage rock), or Motown and Memphis soul. Some bands made the switch from British music to soul around 1966, partly because most soul music was better for fast dancing. One article in the Baltimore *Sunday Sun Magazine* in August 1966, estimated that between 75 to 150 teen bands were working in the Baltimore area. Usually, they operated with a couple Fender guitars, an electric piano/organ and drums, and many bands featured horns. An electric guitar with a necessary speaker and pre-amp unit ranged from $400 to $1,800. Band members made $15 to $20/night playing at teen centers, discotheques, proms and pool parties. Some bands were on the cutting edge for making new sounds with reverb and fuzz-tone units shortly after the Beatles used an echo unit in "Paperback Writer" and the Stones used a fuzz-tone distortion device in "Satisfaction. "

The Beatles recalled that in their early days: "We just wanted to play. Playing was the most important thing." It was the same way with many teen bands when they found the right mix of members. Most of us who did not play in bands were clueless about all the hours of practice that went into learning a new song, learning how to play it together, the experimentation with sound and volume and equipment hookups. We also didn't realize the fun that teen bands and regional or nationally popular bands had jamming and just spending time together. We just heard and saw the finished product at a teen dance or on TV or heard it on our 45s and LPs. Sometimes, a few of us were able to sit in on some practice sessions.

"Battle of the Bands" was a frequent event in the mid and late '60s in the Baltimore area and scattered everywhere in the U. S. It was a chance for three or four bands to play a few samples of their best sounding covers of current or recent BB Hot 100 songs and compete for a prize. For example, in Perry Hall High School, the winning band, The Expressions, convinced a student panel they were the best of the competing bands in 1967 and 1968, winning a trophy and a contract to play at one school dance.

Coveted gigs for local bands in the '60s were backing up or opening for a national recording group performing in town. One example in the Baltimore area was the Club Venus at Joppa Road and Perring Parkway, beginning in 1966. Club Venus was an affordable dinner/music show venue that hosted Smokey Robinson and The Miracles, the 4 Seasons, The Temptations and other national sensations so that local bands who were tabbed to open for these groups or play music for their performances felt a step closer to reaching stardom.

Teen bands throughout the U. S. paid for time in a recording studio to make an acetate of a 45-record in the hope of rising popularity and fame. They aimed for playing time on local pop or R&B/soul stations, then regional or national stations, and a listing on the BB Hot 100, or the BB Bubbling Under (BU) the Hot 100. The BU chart listed as many as 35 songs each week believed to be in the running for a spot on the following week's BB Hot 100. The BU number 101 was number one on that chart. Examples of a few songs pressed by local Baltimore bands included Tommy Van and the Echoes' "Too Young (1966)" on Academy Records, The Tangiers with the Jetsons Band's "Baby It's Cold Outside (1967)" on Date Records and Bob Brady and the Con Chords' "More, More, More Of Your Love (1967)" on Chariot Records. All three were played on Baltimore's local popular music stations. Tommy Van's "Too Young" was on the BU chart for 5 weeks and peaked at number 103. Bob Brady's hit single was on that chart for 4 weeks and peaked at BU number 104. Baltimore's The Royalettes was a four-girl R&B group that placed "It's Gonna Take A Miracle (1965)" on the BB Hot 100 for 11 weeks peaking at number 41. Oddly, it was only on the R&B chart for 6 weeks, but we heard it often on Baltimore radio stations due to their strong local group of fans.

When teen dances ended at 11pm in Perry Hall, we made beelines straight to Palm Subs and Pizza or Persing's Meat Market for a steak and cheese sub or pizza or skipped Palm's and Persing's and went straight to Ginos Hamburgers and Berg's or Ameche's in Towson or other hangouts in Essex. Berg's Farm Dairy was often our nightcap stop for burgers, shakes and ice cream and one more fix of jukebox music. Unless we lived nearby and walked, we drove or caught a ride home and listened to a few more songs on the car radio or 8-track tape players. It was the same way at burger and shake shops with jukeboxes all over the U. S. We teens drowned happily in our music together, especially on weekends.

When I started attending University of Maryland College Park in the Fall of 1969, I lost that magic feeling of close camaraderie at live band dances for a while and figured it was gone forever. At large dances at dorm dining halls, other campus halls, or fire houses, a few of my dorm mates and I knew no one except the few people we came with. It was not easy meeting people in those settings.

Two years later, when I joined Theta Chi fraternity near campus and lived at the fraternity house, I regained that camaraderie we had at Teen Center and high school live band dances tenfold. We had a monthly live band dance on a Saturday night *in the house* where about 25 out of 40 fraternity brothers lived. When we danced to those live bands we knew almost everyone including the guys' dates. Those bands played a combination of rock and soul music left over from the '60s, along with Rolling Stones (old and new tunes), Doobie Brothers and Rod Stewart and other music from the early '70s. The magic that comes along with dancing with a group of people we know, was back.

21

Folk music

♪

FOLK MUSIC IN THE LATE '50s AND '60s was a direct outgrowth of an "American folk music revival" started in the '40s. The Carter Family and the Almanac Singers (founded by Millard Lampell, Pete Seeger, Lee Hays and Woody Guthrie and active between 1940 and 1943) were among the artists who paved the way for folk music of the early '60s. The Almanac Singers sang songs about peace and isolationism during the early stages of World War II, until the Soviet Union was invaded by Germany. Guthrie wrote "This Land Is Your Land" (originally called "This Land") and protested in its middle two verses about inequalities of treatment of the poor compared to the wealthy in America, but the version we sang in schools in the late '50s and the '60s, only had the more positive verses about the U. S. We weren't aware of the middle verses.

Folk music was traditional music handed down, often without the song's authorship known, but in the '60s, new folk music had known song-writers/singers. The late '50s and early '60s folk music was often played by singing groups harmonizing, while the mid '60s tunes were often performed by individual singers. It was often played in coffee houses and at hootenannies and accompanied by acoustic guitar, sometimes bass fiddles and occasionally bongos or harmonicas. Folk music contributed to country western, jazz, and rock and roll. It was decidedly "lighter" and not usually as high charging and rambunctious as rock and roll and soul.

Jim (Roger) McGuinn (who was in the Chad Mitchell Trio before he helped form The Byrds in 1965) said, "there was this folk scene going on in New York—the bohemians and poets, and comedians. "In Greenwich Village, there was a fertile mixing ground of musical talent learning from each other. John Sebastian (who played jug band music before he helped form the Lovin' Spoonful in 1965) explained: "those clubs provided a nucleus for an instrumental and musical style. [There were] young modern songwriters with bluegrass players, old timey music people and 60- to 70-year old blues men." Judy Collins nailed the essence of the new creativity: "What happened was rules were being broken. No longer did you have 'Earth Angel' and 'Rock Around the Clock'. You had Bob Dylan singing—a great example of someone who studied all the blues bands and knew all the blues songs and began to write in his own way and other writers did the same thing, writing about current politics. "

Beginning with "Tom Dooley" in 1958, the Kingston Trio had a series of hit singles in the late '50s and early '60s. The Highwaymen's first hit single was "Michael" in 1961, a number one hit on the AC and BB Hot 100 charts. Then they had a double-sided hit single, "Cotton Fields" "b/w" "The Gypsy Rover" in 1961 and "The Bird Man" in 1962, before fading out of earshot of folk music fans. Peter, Paul and Mary were a mainstay of folk music in the '60s and charted six top ten hits. The New Christy Minstrels, the Seekers, Joni Mitchell (born Roberta Joan Anderson), and Joan Baez also made their mark as folk groups or singers.

Bob Dylan (born Robert Zimmerman) began as a folk and blues music singer/guitarist/writer in the '60s, and often played folk rock music in the mid to late '60s. He started getting attention from NY critics while playing in cabarets there in 1961 and performed at his first Newport (Rhode Island) Folk festival in 1963. Dylan's genius as a songwriter produced nine highly acclaimed LPs in the '60s. He listened to Hank Williams, Little Richard, Woody Guthrie and Elvis and read poems by Dylan Thomas. Joan Baez introduced him at a '60s folk concert saying, "This is a young man who grew out of a need. He came to be, because things needed saying. He somehow has the ear of a generation. "Bob Dylan was popular music's poet who was heavily concerned with social activism in the early '60s. His songwriting was unparalleled in its sincerity and incisiveness, and his deep-rooted concerns about the many injustices people were suffering in our world (and still do) connected with many listeners.

From the start of their hold on young America, Bob Dylan loved the Beatles' sound, but he hoped they would start writing and playing songs that had a message, too. Promoter Al Aronowitz arranged for a meeting between Lennon and Dylan in New York in September 1964 after the Beatles played at the Paramount Theater. Dylan told Lennon that the Beatles needed to start writing songs with more meaningful lyrics and Lennon was all ears. Likewise, the Beatles' success influenced Dylan—after their meeting, he bought an electric guitar.

22

Folk rock music

♪

DYLAN MADE HIS FIRST PUBLIC "CROSS-OVER" FROM FOLK MUSIC to the new genre he helped create—folk rock music, when he played at the Newport Folk Festival in 1965. Folk-rock was the playing of folk music with rock instrumentation. Many folk music fans in the audience felt betrayed and booed when Dylan started playing his electric guitar, but he weathered the critics well and popular music was better off for it. At one of his concerts when he started playing folk rock and some of the audience booed, Dylan turned around to his bandmates and said, "Play it Loud!"

Dylan's folk rock game-changer, "Like A Rolling Stone" reached number 2 on the BB Hot 100 in 1965. In 2004, *Rolling Stone* rated it *number one* of the 500 greatest songs of all time based on a poll of 271 music industry professionals. Other Dylan folk rock hits include: "I Want You (1966)," "Just Like A Woman (1966)," "If You Gotta Go, Go Now (1967)," and "All Along The Watchtower (1967)." His hit single, "Lay, Lady, Lay" was originally written for the movie *Midnight Cowboy* but wasn't finished in time to be included in it. Considered country rock by some critics, "Lay Lady Lay" reached number 7 in 1969. Mark Knopfler of Dire Straits said in the mid-'90s: "When I was a kid at school, that's all I really wanted to be, was Bob Dylan.'"

The Byrds (also from Southern California) fueled the new folk-rock genre with their jangly electric guitar sound and their number one cover of Dylan's "Mr. Tambourine Man" and Pete Seeger's "Turn, Turn, Turn (To

Everything There Is A Season)" in 1965. The Mamas and Papas (first hit was "California Dreamin'" in 1965), Donovan (first hit was "Catch The Wind" in 1965), and Simon and Garfunkel piled up folk-rock hit singles in the '60s that were big successes on the BB Hot 100. Then came James Taylor in the early '70s.

Simon and Garfunkel wrote and sang about many basic feelings we had growing up, making their songs relevant to the everyday listener along with the fact their singing sounded so good. Their solos were warm and pleasing, and their vocal harmony as a duo left us spellbound. Some of their songs that felt so pertinent to many of us were: "The Sound Of Silence," "I Am A Rock," "My Little Town," "Homeward Bound," "Dangling Conversation," and "Bridge Over Troubled Waters." In "I Am A Rock," Simon and Garfunkel sang about someone committed to isolating themselves after a lost love and their insistence they don't need friendship because it causes pain. In "Bridge Over Troubled Water," they take an open compassionate stance, staying strong for a friend in need, telling them that they are on their side if things get rough and [especially] if friends can't be found. They insist they'll be "like a bridge over troubled water."

When we heard Simon and Garfunkel were breaking up in 1970, on the heels of the Beatles disbanding, it was very disturbing. It was mind numbing to think they would not be adding more songs as a duo to our "favorites" playlists after such a steady output of great music.

James Taylor's first hit single, "Fire And Rain" in 1970, was followed by his cover of "You've Got A Friend" that reached number one in the summer of 1971. It's surprising now to learn that the song's writer, Carole King, never released her original of "You've Got A Friend" as a single even though her recording of the song is on her top-selling LP *Tapestry*, released In February 1971. The only way King's fans could hear her version of "You've Got A Friend" was to buy *Tapestry* or hear it on FM radio.

In the Fall of '71, six of us walked across campus to the Varsity Grill on Route One in College Park, MD at 4pm on Fridays after our classes at University of Maryland. Ecstatic that the weekend was here, we'd settle in for our draft pitchers of beer and peanuts in the shell (drinking age was 21, so fake IDs helped). Among our favorite songs coming out of the Grill's great stereo system were Taylor's "Sweet Baby James," "Country Road," "Fire And Rain" and "You've Got A Friend." I thought Taylor's voice was the best I ever heard up to then—it made you wish you had a voice like him. Taylor's knack for singing at a pleasing pace, a soothing, easy to follow rhythm and a crystal-clear voice made him fun to sing along with (and it still does). Taylor issued "Sweet Baby James" as a single, but curiously, it failed to chart on the BB Hot 100. Did DJs in 1970 give it a short attention span? Still, the more his listeners heard "Sweet Baby James" on the LP, the more it became one of Taylor's fans' favorite songs.

Two songs Taylor wrote for his first LP, the self-titled Apple Records' *James Taylor*, sound as good today as his early hit singles, but those songs were largely unknown to popular music listeners after *James Taylor* was released in February 1969. His first single record, "Carolina In My Mind" appeared on *James Taylor*, but the single never received much playing time in the U. S. in 1969, placing on the Billboard BU chart for just two weeks. Taylor also penned "Something In The Way She Moves" for *James Taylor*, but it was never issued as a 45-record. Both songs and the LP were opportunities lost partly because Taylor was not able to promote his first LP much after it was released due to his hospitalization for drug addiction problems. Taylor's first LP did not receive much airplay in the U. S., but his growing legion of fans found out about it after *Sweet Baby James* (1970) and *Mud Slide Jim* (1971) became popular.

Fortunately, just before The Beatles gave up being a foursome, some other talented musicians stepped up to take over as a top-selling group. The folk-rock trio, (David) Crosby, (Stephen) Stills and (Graham) Nash issued their first LP in 1969, and another (*Déjà Vu*) with Neil Young, added to the group in 1970. In the mid- '60s, Crosby played with the Byrds, Stills and Young with Buffalo Springfield and Nash with the Hollies. They all sounded good as soloists, but their strong point was their vocal harmony. It was easy to put side one or two of these LPs on our turntables and let them play from beginning to end, uninterrupted.

23

Adult contemporary singles chart

♪

THE ADULT CONTEMPORARY (AC) SINGLES CHART, usually referred to as The Easy Listening Chart in the '60s, featured popular music hit records bought by adults, especially in the age range of 25 to 45 years old. In the early '60s onward, there were radio stations that wanted to play some current songs and separate themselves from being labelled a "rock and roll" station. Thus, *Billboard* established an "Easy Listening" chart for "softer" popular music. Many rock songs from the mid-'60s and later, had a harder sound, and a rougher edge to them and were less likely than mainstream pop to cross over to the AC chart. Even soul music seldom made it to the Easy Listening Charts in the '60s.

Top-selling artists who appeared often on the AC chart in the '60s included female vocalists: Barbra Streisand, Dionne Warwick, Petula Clark, Brenda Lee, Connie Francis, and Dusty Springfield. Some of the most popular male vocalists on the AC chart in the '60s were: Frank Sinatra, Andy Williams, Bobby Vinton, Nat King Cole, Tom Jones, Steve Lawrence, Robert Goulet, and Dean Martin. Singing groups who made their mark on the AC charts were Peter, Paul and Mary; The Lettermen; The Ray Charles Singers and The Vogues. They hardly ever played instruments, rather they were vocalists only. Bert Kaempfert's Orchestra and Herb Alpert's Tijuana Brass highlighted musicians rather than vocalists with their hits on the AC chart. Many of the same songs that these artists had on the AC chart also placed high on the BB Hot 100. This added to the large amount of mixing of genres and styles of popular music played on Top 40 radio on AM stations in the '60s. Once FM radio stations played more psychedelic rock and related genres and subgenres like southern rock in the early '70s, popular rock music became more separated from AC pop music on these stations.

24

Country (western) music

♪

C OUNTRY WESTERN MUSIC IN THE '60s grew out of hillbilly music (also called hick music), in part from musicians from the mountains of West Virginia, Virginia and the South in the 1930s. It spread to other areas in the U. S. by way of servicemen in WWII who hailed from southern areas steeped strongly in listening to country western and by white southerners creating a more widespread audience moving north and to California.

Roy Acuff was the most popular hillbilly singer in the '40s, known as The King of Country Music, singing in a hillbilly, twangy style. The singing cowboys—Gene Autry, Roy Rogers, Tex Ritter and "country's sweetheart," Patsy Montana brought the "western part" to country western and helped that term replace 'hillbilly" from the '30s to the '50s. Bob Wills (a fiddler) and His Texas Playboys played Western swing with his fiddle and the addition of horns and a call and response in a night club he opened in California after WWII.

Starting on October 20, 1958, BB combined radio airplay and sales to figure out a song's popularity on the Hot C&W sides (30 slots). The chart name was changed to "Hot Country Singles" on November 13, 1962 (still 30 slots), and that chart changed to 50 slots on January 11, 1964, and 75 slots on October 15, 1966. Then, on July 14, 1973, the chart changed to Hot Country Singles with 100 slots.

Country western songs appealed to many listeners who were proud to be working class whether it was on a farm or other blue-collar jobs in rural areas or suburban areas. Family, religion and patriotism were frequent subjects in country western songs and still are in the country and country rock genres. Truck driving songs were hugely popular in the '60s.

Following Patsy Cline's success in the early '60s, more women separated from being duos with men or part of a family group. They sang more openly about sex, too. Loretta Lynn had 17 top ten hits on the CW charts in the '60s and continued to chart hit singles in the '70s. She became a spokeswoman for many women who "got married too early or pregnant too soon. "

In the '60s, country western music had a loyal following of teens and adults in most rural areas and some songs crossed over from the country western (CW) chart to the BB Hot 100 and AC charts. Most teens in cities and suburbs preferred the BB Hot 100 and R&B chart songs, and they seldom listened to country music stations. This meant many city and suburban teens only heard country western tunes when they were crossover hits into the AC or BB Hot 100 charts. The biggest hit makers on the CW chart in the '60s included: Buck Owens (19 number one hits), Sonny James (12 number one hits), Merle Haggard (8 number one hits), Eddy Arnold (7 number one hits), Marty Robbins, Jim Reeves, Tammy Wynette, Loretta Lynn, and George Jones.

Some of the CW artists who crossed over to the BB Hot 100 in the '60s were Johnny Cash, Roger Miller, Glen Campbell, and Eddy Arnold. Claude King's "Wolverton Mountain (1962)" was number one on the CW chart an impressive nine weeks and stayed on that chart 26 weeks. It was a legitimate crossover hit for King, too, reaching number 6 and staying on the BB Hot 100 16 weeks, so I heard it often in my room and it played on mom's kitchen radio downstairs. Bobbie Gentry's "Ode to Billie Joe" reached number 17 on the CW chart and number one on the BB Hot 100 and stayed at the top spot for four weeks in '67. Roger Miller had several hits that made their mark on the BB Hot 100 including "Dang Me (1964)," "Chug-a-Lug (1964)," "King Of The Road (1965)," and "Engine Engine #9 (1965)." Glen Campbell's "Gentle On My Mind (1967)" paved the way for "By The Time I Get To Phoenix (1967)" which peaked at number 2 on the CW chart and two songs that reached number one on both the CW and BB Hot 100 charts—"Wichita Lineman (1968)" and "Galveston (1969)." Campbell's "Try A Little Kindness (1969)" reached number one on the AC chart and number 2 on the CW chart, no doubt helped by his playing of the song on *The Glen Campbell Goodtime Hour.*

25

Garage rock

♪

GARAGE ROCK MUSIC HAD ITS HEYDAY IN THE U.S. FROM 1964 through 1968. It usually featured white vocalists and musicians playing guitars, drums, tambourine and organ (not horns). These songs were up-tempo and urgent (except for the slower, more deliberate delivery of "Wild Thing"). It was based on a raw form of rock and roll coming from the perception that many such performers were amateurish and often rehearsed in the family garage. Signature songs for garage rock were "Wooly Bully (1965)" by Sam the Sham and the Pharoahs, "96 Tears" by ? and the Mysterians (it sold over a million copies by November 1966), "Wild Thing" by the Troggs (it was number 1 on the BB Hot 100 for two weeks in 1966), "Gloria" by Them (1965) and also Shadows of the Knight (1966), "7 and 7 Is (1966)" by Love, "Hanky Panky (1966)" by Tommy James and the Shondells, and "A Little Bit Of Soul (1967)" by The Music Explosion. For many listeners, "96 Tears" became a garage rock anthem. Rudy Martinez' lead singing was slightly off key and made "96 Tears" sound a little amateurish, but we still liked it because it gave us the impression that any one of us could learn to sing this one and many teen bands played it in their garage. Van Morrison's lead singing of "Gloria" by Them sounded brash like Martinez in "96 Tears" and Jamie Lyons in "A Little Bit of Soul."

While the Troggs came from England, most garage rock songs on the BB Hot 100 came from the U.S. More garage rock hit singles included:

102

"Louie Louie (1963)" by the Kingsmen, "Little Girl (1966)" by The Syndicate of Sound, the Standells' "Dirty Water (1966)," "Come On Down To My Boat (1967)" by Every Mother's Son and "Nobody But Me (1968)" by the Human Beinz. Originally, Sam the Sham intended "Wooly Bully" to be a tribute to the Hully Gully dance, but their record company's (MGM) legal department feared legal problems might occur because there was already a song issued with a similar title. "Wooly Bully" was named Billboard's number one song of 1965, even though it peaked at number 2 on the chart.

26

Bubble gum music

♪

BUBBLE GUM MUSIC BECAME POPULAR IN THE '60s, especially from 1967 through 1972. It had an upbeat sound that targeted preteens and teenagers with a "catchy melody, simple chords and simple harmonies." Back in the '60s, I thought this music was for pre-teens, but now if I hear it, I often let it play through and just categorize it as part of our '60s mix of songs. Bubble gum music that was played often on AM radio stations in the '60s included: Tommy Roe's "Hooray For Hazel (1966)" and his million-sellers, "Sheila (1962)," "Sweet Pea (1966)" and "Dizzy (1969)," and the Cyrkle's "Red Rubber Ball (1966)" and "It's A Turn Down Day (1966)." Tommy Boyce and Bobby Hart's "I Wonder What She's Doing Tonight? " and The Lemon Pipers' "Green Tambourine" sold over one million copies by 1968. In the late '60s and early '70s, Ron Dante was lead singer of the fictional Cuff Links with "Tracy" and the Archies' "Sugar, Sugar," and Joey Levine was the lead vocalist for the 1910 Fruitgum Co. —a classic name for a band that played bubble gum music. The 1910 Fruitgum Co. had three singles that sold over a million copies each—"Simon Says (1968)," "1, 2, 3 Red Light (1968)" and "Indian Giver (1969)." "Sugar, Sugar" was a heavyweight on the BB Hot 100 chart peaking at number one for 4 weeks and staying on the chart for 21 weeks (it also reached number one in Canada, the U. K. (for 8 weeks) and South Africa). Levine was also lead singer for the Ohio Express's "Yummy, Yummy, Yummy (1968)" and backup singer on

Crazy Elephant's "Gimme Gimme Good Lovin' (1969)." Then came Edison Lighthouse's "Love Grows (Where My Rosemary Goes)" in 1970. I know my mother (Rose Marie) liked when it played on her kitchen radio. Bubble gum music also sounds closely related to a subgenre sometimes called sunshine pop music that came, in part, out of Southern California from The Association and The Turtles, both highly successful groups on the BB Hot 100 for a few years in the late '60s.

27

Psychedelic rock

IN THE LATE '60s, PSYCHEDELIC ROCK (and psychedelic blues) with its colorful light shows exploded onto the popular music scene. Musicians had already been experimenting for a couple years with new sounds and often doing so while under the influence of LSD or other mind-altering substances. Psychedelic rock's loud, heavy-handed guitar and organ often had hard-hitting drums and a rash of experimental sounds with reverb, echo, wah wah pedals and the like (and usually no horns). Often, it had different instruments coming out of one speaker or the other or sounds revolving from one speaker to the other like the drum solo in parts of Iron Butterfly's "In-A-Gadda-Da-Vida."

"Psychedelic" was coined by English psychiatrist Humphrey Osmond in a letter to Aldous Huxley in 1956, when talking about "mind manifesting" effects of taking a pinch of LSD. Black lights, strobe lights, lava lamps, and Day-Glo (contained fluorescent pigments) art abounded wherever psychedelic music was played in the '60s, along with the drugs that bands and music listeners were often taking.

The breakout year for psychedelic music was 1967, when a cascade of trailblazing hit songs came our way—Jefferson Airplane's "Somebody To Love (April)" and "White Rabbit (June)," The Doors "Light My Fire (June)," Vanilla Fudge's "You Keep Me Hangin' On (July)," and Jimi Hendrix's "Purple Haze (August)" and "Foxey Lady (December)." The Beatles were important innovators of psychedelic music with "Tomorrow Never Knows" on *Revolver* in 1966, "Lucy In The Sky With Diamonds" on *Sgt Pepper's* and "Strawberry Fields Forever" on *Magical Mystery Tour* in 1967. In 1968, Cream's "Sunshine Of Your Love (January)" and "White Room (October)," Iron Butterfly's "In A-Gadda-Da-Vida (August)," and Steppenwolf's "Born To Be Wild (July)" and Magic Carpet Ride (October)" sustained the psychedelic craze and more psychedelic songs followed in 1969.

Still, plenty of other groups in the U. S. and U. K experimented with the genre and expanded its boundaries. The Strawberry Alarm Clock's soft psychedelic rock hit, "Incense And Peppermints (1967)" received widespread airplay on Top 40 radio stations, reaching number one for a week during its 16-week stay on the BB Hot 100. In the studio, the record's producer brought band outsider Greg Munford (just 16 years old) to sing lead and Greg's brush with fame was cemented. The beginning "bah (low note), bah (high note); bah (low note), bah (high note)," and the ending "sha la, la; sha, la, la; sha, la, la" by the chorus gave it a mellow, soft sound and the instruments were not nearly as loud as harder psychedelic rock, but the guitar and organ sounded a bit more psychedelic than garage rock. Pink Floyd's LP, *Piper at the Gates of Dawn* (1967) "featured a heavy use of echo and reverberation" and used automatic double tracking to add layers of echo to vocals and some instruments.

Some of the '60s' longest songs were the LP versions of "Light My Fire," "In A-Gadda Da Vida," and "You Keep Me Hanging On." Album versions of these songs helped pave the way for FM radio stations to start broadcasting album cuts and whole sides of LPs in stereo. Vanilla Fudge specialized in "extended rock arrangements of contemporary rock (and soul)" with long instrumental intros. Their self-titled *Vanilla Fudge* LP included psychedelicized covers of "Ticket To Ride," "People Get Ready," "She's Not There," "Eleanor Rigby" and "You Keep Me Hanging On. "

Music listeners were the benefactors of musicians in heavy competition with each other, frequently trying new instruments, gadgets and sound effects so they could record new sounds on their hit singles and albums. The Jimi Hendrix Experience (made up of Hendrix, Noel Redding and Mitch Mitchell) formed while Jimi was in London and recorded there, releasing *Are You Experienced* in the U. K. in May, and in the U. S. in August of '67. Cream (Jack Bruce, Eric Clapton (born Eric Patrick Clapp) and Ginger Baker) peaked in popularity in the U. S. and U. K. in 1967-68, with the *Dis-*

raeli Gears and *Wheels of Fire* LPs. Many U. S. fans only became aware of Cream's first LP *Fresh Cream* (released late in 1966) after hearing *Disraeli Gears* late in 1967 or in 1968. Clapton's guitar in *Disraeli Gears'* "Tales of Brave Ulysses," and Hendrix's guitar in "Burning of the Midnight Lamp" featured the wah-wah pedal. Hendrix loved using reverb and echo effects with his guitar, examples being his—"Love Or Confusion," "May This Be Love," "I Don't Live Today," and "3rd Stone From The Sun." We had never heard so much experimentation with electric guitar on one album, until we played Hendrix's *Are You Experienced*. Hendrix captivated audiences at his live concerts beginning in 1966 and 1967 and left his fellow musicians in awe. Carlos Santana said of Hendrix: "It was like going to a movie and changing from that small screen to cinemascope. That was Jimi Hendrix's music—even with the blues, it was wide. "Guitarist/vocalist Eric Clapton, bass guitarist/vocalist Jack Bruce and drummer Ginger Baker formed Cream in 1966. In short order, after their first hit single, "Sunshine Of Your Love" from *Disraeli Gears* they issued the hit singles "White Room" and "Crossroads" from *Wheels of Fire* and "Badge" before disbanding in '69. "Sunshine Of Your Love" stayed on the BB Hot 100 for 26 weeks, longer than any other hit single in the '60s. It was a rarity for any hit single to stay on the chart for five months, never mind longer, but listeners tired of this song much slower than most, or it enjoyed a steady stream of new listeners joining the bandwagon that bought the song during its chart run.

When Cream disbanded, Clapton and Baker joined vocalist/organist Steve Winwood and bass guitarist Ric Grech to form the short-lived blues rock group, Blind Faith, long enough to craft their self-titled album in 1969. *Blind Faith* featured Winwood's stellar vocals, especially on "Sea Of Joy," "Presence Of The Lord," and "Can't Find My Way Home" and became a number one best-selling LP in the U. S. and the U. K. Baker's raucous drumming on "Do What You Like" put him in the limelight and music listeners and guitarists loved listening to guitarists Clapton and Grech on each track.

Steppenwolf's "Born To Be Wild" and "The Pusher" gave extra life to the 1969 movie *Easy Rider*, starring Peter Fonda and Dennis Hopper. Fonda and Hopper cycled down the desert highway to the tune of "Born To Be Wild." They looked completely carefree, almost invincible, unlike later in the movie when everything unraveled. Goldy McJohn's freewheeling playing of his Lowery organ fitted with a Leslie Speaker became a trademark sound of Steppenwolf, especially in "Born To Be Wild" and "Magic Carpet Ride."

"Magic Carpet Ride's" 30-second lead guitar intro is still a favorite for many psychedelic and hard rock listeners.

The Doors followed "Light My Fire" on their first LP, with a hit single version that reached number one on the BB Hot 100 for three weeks. From the start, Jim Morrison was the band's lead singer and centerpiece during their live concerts. Always controversial for his behavior including bodily exposure, erotic gestures and modified lyrics, Morrison had a huge following of girl fans who were head over heels for him, pawing at him whenever he made a public appearance. Band member Ray Manzarek recalled: "Jim was influenced by [writer] Jack Kerouac and [poet] Alan Ginsburg. "Tom Petty looked back at the time when he first heard the Doors' music on the radio: "I thought the music was very dark and mysterious. I didn't know what to make of it. I thought the words were very good. You could tell right away, well we got a writer (Jim) here. "Listeners connected strongly with many songs on Doors' LPs that were never issued on 45s—"People Are Strange," "Love Me Two Times," "Roadhouse Blues," and "L. A. Woman." Guys identified with three more Doors hit singles—"Hello, I Love You (1968)," "Touch Me (1969)," and "Love Her Madly (1971)." How many times did guys feel like, "I'd really like to meet this girl, but I don't want to scare her off? ""Hello, I Love You" connected with those feelings. The Doors' "Touch Me" employed a bevy of horns and string instruments, a saxophone solo and an organ intro instantly recognizable today to any of us who played this song loud whenever it came on the radio or a turntable.

The British group, Procul Harum's long-term hit single, "Whiter Shade Of Pale" reached number one in the U. K. and number 5 on the U. S. BB Hot 100 in 1967. Sometimes referred to as psychedelic rock or baroque pop, it had a slow dance tempo; lead vocals with an R&B sound; and a prominent organ, piano, guitar and drums, but no horns. It has a "haunting" instrumental melody with odd lyrics, but it has endured longer than most '60s records, selling more than 10 million copies.

The First Edition's "Just Dropped In (To See What Condition My Condition Was In) (1968)" had a psychedelic edge with its lead guitar and choral refrain of backup singers with their distorted, quivering, echoing sound. "Just Dropped In" is a radical contrast to the sound that the band's lead singer Kenny Rogers adopted later as a solo country music hit maker of the '70s and '80s. His voice is much clearer in "Just Dropped In" than the raspy voiced Rogers of the '70s.

Donovan's "Hurdy Gurdy Man" (issued June 1968) and Tommy James and the Shondells "Crimson and Clover" (December 1968) and "Crystal Blue Persuasion (1969)" thrilled listeners of psychedelic and blues rock because we felt that those genres were gaining more refined, polished sounds. "Hurdy Gurdy Man" featured guitarist Jimmy Page with a psychedelic drone sound, and Donovan playing a tanbura and singing alternately with a quivering effect and an echo. For many teens, these records made it harder to decide whether to buy another soul record or a psychedelic record next. I assumed that great songs like these with a new psychedelic edge would keep coming from Donovan and Tommy James for years to come, but they did not. We had little appreciation then for the pressure these musicians faced and the difficulty they encountered in remaining fresh to continue producing new hits. "Crimson and Clover" featured a tremelo effect of the guitar and vocals creating those bizarre echo sounds that we loved to hear.

Elektra Records out of Los Angeles pushed the envelope for psychedelic sounds and their appeal in the commercial market in the late '60s. *The Zodiac: Cosmic Sounds*, employed drummer Hal Blaine and guitar bassist Carol Kaye from the Wrecking Crew; Bud Shank, a top flute performer and Paul Beaver an early expert on the Moog Synthesizer along with the deep baritone of narrator Cyrus Faryar to play phantasmagorical songs, one for each Zodiac sign. The album's back cover declared: "Must Be Played in the Dark" and I did, lights out. You didn't need any mind-altering substances to feel like you were listening to something "way out there" and other worldly. I still wonder what my mother and father thought when they heard that music coming from my bedroom. Elektra also issued David Peel and The Lower East Side's *Have a Marijuana*, mostly about marijuana and pot smokers' frustration with drug busting cops. "Up Against the Wall" had a loud whistle, with the police breaking into a room during a drug bust declaring 'Up Against the Wall'..."One dorm resident in University of Maryland's Ellicott Hall loved playing that song in the spring '70, with his speakers pressed against the window screen for everyone outside near the complex's dining hall to hear the song's recording of the cops' drug bust.

Some songs placed high on the BB Hot 100, but sounded bizarre to me because of the wildly distorted sound effects or the lyrics—"You're Gonna Miss Me (1966)" by the 13th Floor Elevators, "Pushin' Too Hard (1966)" by the Seeds, "Psychotic Reaction (1966)" by the Count Five, and "Get Me To The World On Time (1967)" and "I Had Too Much To Dream

(Last Night) (1966)" by the Electric Prunes. Some listeners considered them garage rock or psychedelic rock or a bit of both genres. The 13th Floor Elevators pushed the envelope of psychedelic music to new limits with their bizarre sound effects. Even their group's name was tongue and cheek because the frequent practice in the U. S. in the mid and late '60s was for high rise buildings to have a 12th and 14th floor, but buildings skipped 13th floor labels out of superstition for the number 13. Drummer Alban "Snoopy" Pfisterer of LA's psychedelic/garage rock group, Love, hammered his drums at such a frantic, relentless pace in "7 And 7 Is (1966)" that anyone watching the band live or hearing the song on radio wondered how it was humanly possible to play the drums that way. The Human Expression's "Love At Psychedelic Velocity (1966)" lit up the LA scene, too, with guitar and drums playing so rapidly, they sounded like the limits of human endurance. If nothing else, some of these songs were part of the overall "experiment" that rock was undergoing, making songs and sounds that were bridging the gap between genres old and new, between garage rock and rock and between garage rock and psychedelic rock.

Psychedelic rock was changing over to hard rock in the late '60s and early '70s. The U. K. 's Led Zeppelin issued their debut self-titled LP in January and *Led Zeppelin II* in October 1969. My brother Steve played Zeppelin's first album for me repeatedly and I was hooked enough to buy their 45-record, "Whole Lotta Love (1969)" from *Zeppelin II*. "Whole Lotta Love" (a million-seller) was one of the earliest hard rock songs to be a hit single on AM radio and made many music fans more aware of the group, spiking sales of *Zeppelin II*.

Grand Funk Railroad gave Led Zeppelin and other early hard rock bands competition in the late '60s and early '70s, before modifying their style to more mainstream rock in 1973, with "We're An American Band (1973)" and "The Loco-Motion (1974)," two number one hit singles. Jabber played Grand Funk Railroad's third album, *Closer To Home* for me when it was first released in the summer of 1970. The five and one-half minute single, "I'm Your Captain (Closer To Home)" had modest success peaking at number 22, but FM music listeners were entranced with the longer LP tenminute version. As was often the case, I had no interest in hearing the 45-record's shorter cover; I had to buy the album which was loaded with good songs. Shortly after, I saw Grand Funk Railroad Live at Cole Field House.

Led Zeppelin replaced The Beatles as Britain's most popular group on September 15, 1970 according to a *Melody Maker* poll. The Beatles released the singles "Let It Be" in March, and "The Long And Winding Road" in May, but did not produce any new material together in 1970.

Zeppelin fans felt both of their first two albums were loaded with great songs and no filler. Robert Plant's lead vocals, heavy lead guitar playing by Page and bass player/keyboardist John Paul Jones and drummer John Bonham went on to issue a string of top selling LPs in the 70s, but the group seldom released singles. Their mega hit song "Stairway To Heaven" was never issued as a single, but it was the most requested song on FM radio in the U. S. in the '70s. There was no song some of us in the fraternity would rather hear a live band play at our band parties than "Stairway To Heaven" in 1972-73.

28

Psychedelic soul

♪

PSYCHEDELIC GUITAR, LOUD DRUMS, ORGAN AND THE BEAT from R&B were all part of psychedelic soul. Diana Ross and the Supremes' "Reflections" was an early attempt by the Funk Brothers to psychedelicize Motown's soul sound with a Moog synthesizer in 1967. Sly and the Family Stone (five black and two white band members) were one of the earliest groups to play what became known as psychedelic soul with "Dance To The Music" and "Everyday People" in 1968, and "Stand" b/w "I Want To Take You Higher" and "Hot Fun In The Summertime" in 1969. The Chambers Brothers achieved short-lived success with their original "Time Has Come Today" and their psychedelicized "I Can't Turn You Loose" in 1968. The last two minutes of the Chambers Brothers' "In the Midnight Hour" from their LP, *The Time Has Come* is stirring fast dance music. Berry Gordy thought outside the box when he added Rare Earth (a band made up of three white members and no blacks) to his set of Motown groups. Rare Earth psychedelicized The Temptations' "Get Ready" and "(I Know) I'm Losing You" for two hit singles that peaked in the Top ten of the BB Hot 100 in 1970. They used psychedelic sounding guitar and organ with plenty of echo in the lead singer's vocals for "(I Know) I'm Losing You." The Temptations' versions were rousing three-minute fast dance songs and the longer versions by Rare Earth were good for listening, but not dancing. Although I liked the Temptations' original covers better, I liked Rare Earth's

113

remakes enough to see them live at Ritchie Coliseum at University of Maryland in 1971.

The Temptations stayed relevant longer than The Four Tops with top ten hits, in part because they made a set of crossover hits into psychedelic soul through songwriters Norman Whitfield and Barrett Strong (and producer Whitfield). This was not an easy decision for Berry Gordy and The Temptations because they still enjoyed popularity in the late '60s with their more standard soul sounds from "I Wish It Would Rain (1968)," "I Could Never Love Another (After Loving You) (1968)," "I Can't Get Next To You (1969)," and "Just My Imagination (Running Away With Me) (1972)." However, the psychedelic soul of the Funk Brothers' instrumentation and the Temptations' singing resulted in more good dancing songs—"Cloud Nine (1968)," "Runaway Child, Running Wild (1969)," "Psychedelic Shack (1970)," "Ball Of Confusion (That's What the World Is Today) (1970)," and "Papa Was A Rollin' Stone (1972)." All five of their psychedelic soul songs peaked in the top ten of the BB Hot 100.

Soul music brought black and white teens together on the dance floor of Perry Hall Senior High School (Baltimore County) in the late '60s.
Photo credit: From author's collection.

During the '60s we listened to our popular music by AM radio, vinyl 45-records and record albums (LPs) and author Mark Millikin had access to his dad's reel-to-reel tape player. *From the author's collection*

Soul music was often "king" in Mark Millikin's bedroom from 1964–1969 (list of soul songs on one of the author's reel-to-reel tapes, completed late 1967). *From author's collection.*

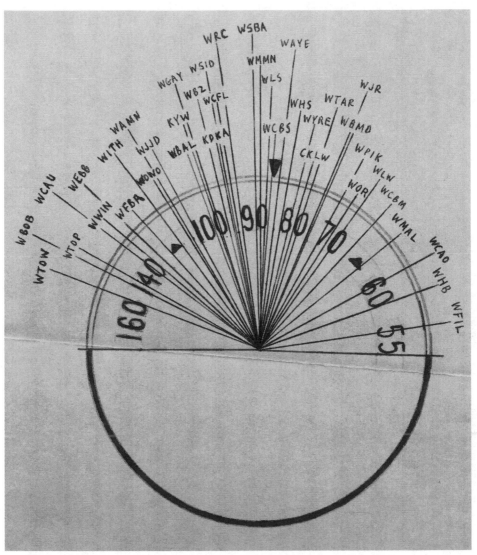

AM radio stations on Mark Millikin's desktop radio dial, 1967. *From author's collection.*

WCBS (NEW YORK)
WBAL (BALTIMORE) (1090)
WCAO (BALTIMORE) (600)
WLS (CHICAGO)
KDKA (PITTSBURGH)
WBZ (BOSTON) (1030)
CKLW (DETROIT) (800)
WHS (LOUISVILLE)
WCFL (CHICAGO)
WTOP (WASHINGTON) (1500)
WFBR (BALTIMORE) (1300)
WOWO (FORT WAYNE) (1190)
WITH (BALTIMORE) (1230)
WMMN (FAIRMONT, PA.)
KYW (PHILADELPHIA)
WJJD (CHICAGO)
WOR (NEW YORK) (710)
WFIL (PHILADELPHIA) (560)
WEBB (BALTIMORE) (1360)
WSID (BALTIMORE) (1010)
WYRE (ANNAPOLIS)
WRC (WASHINGTON)
WTAR (NORFOLK)

WGAY (WASHINGTON)
WAYE (BALTIMORE) (860)
WSBA (HARRISBURG) (910)
WAMN (ANNAPOLIS)
WTOW (BALTIMORE) (1570)
WHB (HARRISBURG)
WMAL (WASHINGTON)
WBOB (BEL AIR, MD.) (1520)
WPIK (WASHINGTON)
WCAU (PHILADELPHIA)
WBMD (BALTIMORE) (750)
WLW (CINCINNATI) (700)
WJR (DETROIT)

Key for the author's AM radio dial, 1967 (radio station call-letters, city and AM number). *From author's collection*

Michael's TV & Radio receipt for Mark Millikin, June 13, 1969 for one LP (probably Three Dog Night's first LP) and one 45-record (probably Jr. Walker and The All Stars' "What Does It Take (To Win Your Love)." *From author's collection.*

Advertisement for Michael's TV & Radio (Perry Hall Shopping Center) advertised in 1968 that it had "a large selection of all popular records—British, soul, and jazz." *From Hallmark, Perry Hall High School's newspaper, December 20, 1968.*

Soul WSID 45

101 ON EVERYONE'S DIAL
92.3 MC-FM

TITLE		ARTIST	LABEL	LAST WEEK

WEEK OF JANUARY 10th -16th 1965

#	Title	Artist	Label	Last Week
1.	My Girl	Temptations	Motown	3
2.	No Faith No Love	Mitty Collier	Chess	2
3.	Hold On To What You Got	Joe Tex	Dial	1
4.	Can You Jerk Like Me	Contours	Gordy	5
5.	A Change Is Gonna Come	Sam Cooke	RCA Victor	10
6.	You've Lost That Loving Feeling	Righteous Bros.	Philles	7
7.	It's Better To Have It	Barbara Lynn	Jamie	6
8.	Do Do Do Bah Ah	Bert Keyes	Clock	11
9.	The Name Game	Shirley Ellis	Congress	12
10.	Twine Time	Alvin Cash	Mar-V-Lus	15
11.	What Now	Gene Chandler	Cons.	4
12.	I Want To Be Your Everything	Manhattans	Carnival	18
13.	Finders Keepers Losers Weepers	Nella Dodds	Wand	16
14.	Voice Your Choice	Radiants	Chess	9
15.	Use Your Head	Mary Wells	20th Cen.	26
16.	Boy From New York City	Ad Libs	Blue Cat	22
17.	United	Jive Five	UA	27
18.	Come See About Me	Supremes	Motown	8
19.	Too Many Fish In The Sea	Marvelettes	Tamla	19
20.	How Sweet It Is	Marvin Gaye	Tamla	25
21.	Get Out	Harold Melvin	Landa	35
22.	I Fancy You	Charlie & Inez Foxx	Symbol	31
23.	Baby Don't You Go	Miracles	Tamla	
24.	He's My Guy	Irma Thomas	Imperial	-
25.	Blind Man	Little Milton	Checker	24
26.	Does It Really Matter	Flamingoes	Checker	17
27.	Seven Letters	Ben E. King	Atco	33
28.	I Know Why	Springers	Wayout	
29.	Are You Still My Baby	Shirelles	Scepter	38
30.	The Price	Solomon Burke	Atlantic	28
31.	Without The One You Love	Four Tops	Motown	13
32.	I Love You Baby	Dottie and Ray	Le Sage	-
33.	Camel Walk	Ikettes	Modern	-
34.	The In Crowd	Dobie Gray	Charger	-
35.	He Was Really Saying Something	Velvelettes	V.I.P.	-
36.	Always In Love	Joe Graves	TeeJay	44
37.	Warm and Tender Love	Joe Haywood	Enjoy	45
38.	I'm Over You	Jan Bradley	Chess	-
39.	Run My Heart	Baby Washington	Sue	-
40.	I Want You To Be My Boy	Exciters	Roulette	-
41.	Baby Don'cha Worry	Little Gigi-Vernon Harrell	Decca	-
42.	I Want My Love	Sir Joe-Maidens	Tonjo	-
43.	Taking My Time	Leroy Taylor	Shrine	-
44.	Danny Boy	Pattie La Belle	Parkway	29
45.	I'll Make It Up To You	Garnet Mimms	UA	-

The top 45 songs for WSID 1010 AM (also called 101 radio) in Baltimore, the week of January 10th–16th 1965. *From author's collection.*

29

Songs with a message

♪

TEENS AND 20-YEAR-OLDS ARE OFTEN MORE PENSIVE AND HOPEFUL about the world's problems and how they can help make changes before cynicism sets in as they become older. Frequent demonstrations and protests occurred on college campuses in the U. S. and other parts of the world in the '60s and early '70s. College student governments often sponsored speeches, especially related to the Vietnam War by activists (like Abbie Hoffman, Jane Fonda, Rennie Davis) on college campuses. Popular music in the '60s covered opinions pro and con about U. S. involvement in the Vietnam War and civil rights for blacks, but not much attention was given to women's rights in songs. Pete Seeger's "Turn, Turn, Turn" was made into a number one hit single by The Byrds in 1965, and the song's lyrics laid everything out on the table, pro and con about our life, our hopes and our fears. It was a wake-up call for teens to hear The Byrds sing about how there was a time for everything—there was a time to be born and another to die and a time to plant and another to reap, a time to kill and another time to heal, there will be laughing and crying, love and hate, and they sang at the end about a time for peace—they hoped it wasn't too late. This was a much different song in its theme and range of life topics on AM radio compared to most of our popular music songs we were hearing.

Popular music in the '60s included songs about the "generation gap" between teens and adults, an extension of those songs about teenagers' angst

115

in the '50s. The Who's "My Generation (1966)" personified the frustration many teens felt towards their parents and other adults while Merle Haggard's "Okie From Muskogee" typified the disdain many adults in the U. S. felt about teens and college students' behavior. In its 2004 survey, *Rolling Stone* ranked "My Generation" number 11, all time, reflecting the song's enduring importance despite the limited sales of the single. In The Leaves' "Too Many People (1965)," a local hit single in LA, they sang about the frustration of too many other people trying to run their lives. The Animals declared in "It's My Life (1965)" that it's their life and they can do what they want, and Mick Jagger sang in "Satisfaction (1965)" about how impossible it was to keep everybody happy in our lives by doing what they (including the man on TV) want us to do, instead of what we wanted to do. In "Anyway, Anyhow, Anywhere (1965)" The Who declared they could do anything—anyway, anyhow, anywhere they choose. It was a forceful declaration of independence by the younger generation.

Beginning with The Beatles and the ensuing British Invasion many teen boys in the U. S. began growing their hair longer copying the new hit-music acts, thinking if the teen girls like it, I better do it. The Barbarian's "Are You A Boy Or Are You A Girl (1965)" song title was an echo of what many teen boys heard from the adults around them. David Crosby's "Almost Cut My Hair" recorded by CSN and Young lamented the tug of war thoughts guys sometimes had about whether to cut their long hair, their "freak flag" (a visible symbol of their opposition to some of the "establishment's" values). Adults often judged a boy or young man by his hair length—clean vs. dirty, conservative vs. liberal, a conformist vs. a rebel. Surprisingly, in our Class of '69 yearbook photos of the guys at Perry Hall High School, most of us still had remarkably short hair in late summer of '68 when we took our senior class pictures.

Bob Dylan sang about many social injustices in his early LPs *Bob Dylan Freewheelin'* (1963) and *The Times They Are A-Changin'* (1964). He was disgusted with the status quo of many social issues and expressed heavy-handed frustration in his lyrics of "A Hard Rain's A Gonna Fall," "Blowin' In The Wind" and "Masters Of War" from *Freewheelin'*, and "The Lonesome Death Of Hattie Carroll," "With God On Our Side" and "Only A Pawn In Their Game" from *The Times They Are A-Changin'* LP. He warned Congressmen and parents in "The Times They Are A-Changin'" changes are happening, and you better come to grips with it, whether you like it or not.

Protests by teens in Los Angeles late in 1966, revolved around an early 10pm curfew that attempted to reduce traffic congestion caused by teens on the Sunset Strip. Buffalo Springfield was the house band for the Strip's Whiskey A-Go-Go nightclub and the group's Stephen Stills penned "For What It's Worth (Stop, Hey What's That Sound) (1967)" on the heels of teen protests objecting to the curfew starting in mid-November. They sang about a gun over there, battle lines being drawn, and young people speaking their mind, singing of songs and carrying signs. The curfew, protests and harsh treatment of teens by police fueled popularity "For What It's Worth" and made it one of the chief anthems for protests in the '60s and '70s, regardless of a protest's cause. "For What It's Worth" reached number 7 and stayed on the BB Hot 100 for 15 weeks in 1967, and *Rolling Stone* rated it number 63, all-time in 2004.

The Beatles' "Revolution (1968)" hard rock 45-record version and "Revolution 1 (1968)" their bluesy rock version on *The Beatles* LP responded to increased pressure on the Beatles to weigh in on The War and protests about various social injustices. The songs' writer John Lennon was not ready to join the bandwagon for protests in every instance, rather he "wanted to see a plan." He acknowledged we'd all like to change the world in one way or another, but many activists in the counterculture criticized The Beatles "Revolution" for being too noncommittal.

Protests about the Vietnam War at University of California in Berkeley, California spread to other campuses after the U. S. sent ground troops to Vietnam in 1965, and social protests kept increasing as the number of U. S. troops sent to Vietnam grew throughout the '60s. The U. S. fought the Vietnam War on the premise that we needed to contain the spread of communism in Southeast Asia, much like our rationale for being involved in the Korean War. Thus, many U. S. WWII veterans favored our military involvement in Vietnam and Southeast Asia in the '60s to maintain the boundaries between communism and democracies that existed after WWII.

The U. S. never suffered a direct attack on our soil related to the Vietnam War. Without such a rallying point, many younger U. S. citizens, especially those of the primary age who were subjected to the Draft or served in the War, did not feel justified about fighting a war in Southeast Asia in the 1960s. They were too young to vote and too young to drink a beer or other alcoholic beverages, but they were being drafted to serve in the military, often in the war. It was much easier for U. S. citizens to feel motivated about our involvement in a war after we suffered a direct attack like when we entered World War II following the U. S. being bombed at Hawaii's Pearl Harbor in 1941 by a Japanese sneak attack, and our attack on Iraq following the Taliban/Al Qaeda terrorist attacks on New York City and the Pentagon in September 2001.

Challenges facing new military recruits are always daunting, at times overwhelming, and often bring heavy loneliness even to those members who have been serving for months or years, even if participation in a War is not a certainty. In late '64, Bobby Vinton's "Mr. Lonely" began a 15-week run on the BB Hot 100, reaching number one for one week. He sang about never receiving a letter in the mail, wishing he had someone to call on the phone, and wishing he could go home. This song struck a chord with thousands of U. S. servicemen in late 1964, all of 1965 and beyond. All servicemen and women away from their families (and even their friends and hometowns) suffer tremendous loneliness at times so it's no wonder this became their anthem until they were discharged and able to go back home and stay there. Motown's The Monitors' "Greetings (From Uncle Sam)" was seldom played on mainstream pop stations in 1966, because it only reached number 100 on the BB Hot 100 and was on the chart for just one week, but we heard it on soul AM radio (it was on the R&B chart for nine weeks and peaked at number 21). Black U. S. military recruits loved the song because it identified the plight many youngsters felt who did not want to join the U. S. military or serve in the Vietnam War. "Greetings" included some loud orders from a drill sergeant and an appealing doo wop sound from the group's four vocalists.

After the Cuban missile crisis in 1962, when the U. S. was dangerously close to war with the Soviet Union, some homeowners bought underground bomb (fallout) shelters because we feared that a nuclear bomb could explode over the U. S. at any moment. The escalation of the nuclear arms race between the Soviet Union and the U. S. had no end in sight. For the next couple years, public school students had frequent air raid drills in the U. S. where we were told to crouch under our desks or go into the school hallway, get down on both knees, with hands over our heads, leaning up against the walls. Dylan's "Talkin' WWIII Blues (1963)" from *Freewheelin' Bob Dylan* talked about our paranoia of surviving a nuclear attack and being the only person still alive (and so did an episode of the TV show, *Twilight Zone*). It was another song that was seldom played on our radio in 1963, because it was not released as a single. The only music fans who heard "Talkin' WWIII Blues" were Dylan fans who bought *Freewheelin'*.

Songs arguing for and against War, and especially the Vietnam War, were strongly worded. Top 40 AM radio picked up on the strong feelings against and for the Vietnam War in Barry McGuire's "Eve Of Destruction" in 1965, and Sgt. Barry Sadler's "The Ballad Of The Green Berets" in 1966. The words to "Eve Of Destruction" that claimed there was no running away once a button was pushed [to start a nuclear war] felt close to home because we were already thinking about it and now a song was reminding us of it. McGuire also sang about the fear we had in the U. S. about Red China, while some whites showed so much hate towards blacks who were demonstrating for civil rights in Selma, Alabama.

Country western singer Johnny Wright and folk singer Phil Ochs sang in 1965 from opposite ends of the issue of whether we should be involved in another War or the Vietnam War. Wright's "Hello Vietnam (1965)" advocated enlisting for the U. S. military to serve in Vietnam, praised the virtues of patriotism, the prevention of the spread of communism, and preserving our democracy and way of life. Even "Hello Vietnam" pondered out loud if we would ever see the day when we no longer had wars to fight. Country music listeners identified strongly with Wright's stance, keeping it on the CW chart an impressive 21 weeks and number one for three weeks. I never heard it in 1965. It failed to cross over to the BB Hot 100, so it was seldom, if ever, played on AM radio other than CW stations. Like Dylan's "Blowin' In the Wind," Phil Ochs' "I Ain't Marching Any More (1965)" expressed total displeasure and a fed up feeling with all wars. His 45-record from his LP of the same name had little airplay on AM radio, because it never entered the BB Hot 100. Ochs sang of the native American Indians' plight, the expulsion of Mexico from California, the U. S. Civil War, WWII—the war that we hoped would end all wars, and the mushroom clouds from atom bombs dropped on Japan.

Plenty of '60s songs protested the War, but many of them were not played much on mainstream AM radio stations of popular music. Many popular music listeners did not hear Country Joe McDonald's (and the Fish) "I Feel Like I'm Fixin' To Die Rag" when it was released in '65, but we became more aware of their protest of the Vietnam War after they performed it at Woodstock in August '69. It was not played often on AM radio in '65 and '66. In "Take It Back (1967)" Cream's lead singer Jack Bruce declares, "take it back, take it (a draft notice or draft card) right out of here," because he didn't want to go where the streams were red; he wanted to[keep] sleeping in his own bed. Pete Seeger's "Waist Deep In The Big Muddy (1967)" warned of the danger of moving forward in the War without asking tough questions and was banned at first by CBS from being played on the *Smothers Brothers Comedy Hour* in late '67. After an appeal to CBS from the Smothers Brothers, Seeger played "Waist Deep" on a February 1968 broadcast of the show. Donovan sang in "The War Drags On (1965)" about a man named Dan in South Vietnam who was fighting for liberty for all, but there was plenty of blood, misery, and dying along the way. Donovan sounded very much like Dylan in his storytelling method, singing and playing acoustic guitar while also playing the mouth harp. The only way we heard that song was if we owned his LP *Fairytale* (1965). Scott McKenzie's (born Philip Blondheim) "San Francisco (Be Sure To Wear Flowers In Your Hair)" was often sung by Vietnam Veterans coming home and many followers of the counterculture and hippie movement on their way to the Haight-Ashbury district during the Summer of Love (1967). The song's writer, John Phillips, could have easily kept it for his own group, The Mamas and The Papas, making it another hit sandwiched between their "Creeque Alley" and "Twelve Thirty (Young Girls Are Coming To The Canyon)" in 1967. Instead, he gave it to McKenzie. It had a sound and lyrics of hope and promise and is still played often by baby boomers. Arlo Guthrie's "Alice's Restaurant Massacre" was largely a narrative issued with his *Alice's Restaurant* LP (1967) that mocked Arlo's draft board and the Vietnam War draft. "Alice's Restaurant Massacre" was much too long (over 18 minutes) to be on a 45-record, but it received some airplay in the late '60s on FM stations that were playing whole albums and album sides. Guthrie's LP and signature song became more popular in the early '70s as the Vietnam War dragged on and FM radio stereo stations played underground music and rock album sides more often.

I read some articles in the Baltimore *Sun* and watched some nightly CBS network newscasts about Vietnam War in the late '60s, but only on a scattered basis. I listened to portions of some broadcasts in English coming from Radio Hanoi, Radio Peking, Radio Moscow and the U. S. Armed Forces Network on my Hallicrafter's short-wave radio, but I didn't make a close study of the Vietnam War as it unfolded. I was sure there was plenty of propaganda coming from the three foreign stations, but what was the accuracy of the content from the U. S. Armed Forces Network broadcasts?

I don't remember any heavy coverage of the Vietnam War in our history classes at Perry Hall High School. Our teachers did not talk much about Vietnam, rather we were just told that we needed to avoid the Sino-Soviet (Red China/Soviet Union) sponsored spread of communism in the world at just about any cost. We didn't discuss the impacts of the Vietnam War on South Vietnam and North Vietnam's people.

In hindsight, if we had been tasked with a one or two-week assignment to summarize the newspaper and nightly news reports and then discuss the War and its impacts in class, it would have been useful for all of us. We might have heard some classmates talk about what their family or close friends currently serving in Vietnam were saying in their letters home if we had class discussions. People in the U. S. who had a father, mother, brother, sister, son or daughter serving there were on pins and needles and many of them watched the newscasts with understandable worry and fear, but many other U. S. citizens passed over those newscasts quickly and just hoped President Johnson would work towards a negotiated peace settlement soon. Jim Morrison and The Doors expressed their distraught in "The Unknown Soldier (1968)" over the frequent lack of emotion we felt and expressed nightly when we watched news coverage of the War. If we didn't know the dead and dying and others suffering permanent disabilities personally, we didn't stop to think about their military service very much or their ultimate sacrifice—they were like men without a name, unknown soldiers.

By the end of 1967, U. S. military servicemen and women in Vietnam had suffered over 20,000 deaths, not to mention the thousands of deaths of South Vietnamese citizens and military forces and of North Vietnamese citizens and military, and the worst was yet to come. North Vietnam's Tet Offensive launched throughout South Vietnam at the end of January 1968, was devastating in terms of casualties for both sides and an eye opener for President Johnson and his chief commander in South Vietnam, General Westmoreland. Still, they continued to deceive the American people about our chances of winning the War. CBS News correspondent Walter Cronkite was hunkered down in Hue during the Tet offensive reporting from there for nightly telecasts. Cronkite was the most trusted national newscaster by millions of U. S. TV viewers for his sincerity and lucid nightly commentaries, so his assessment after returning to the U. S. was a turning point in swaying more Americans to oppose the War. Cronkite concluded that the Vietnam War was unwinnable for the U. S., that we had tried our best to defend South

Vietnam and help establish a democracy there, but we had not succeeded, and it was time to accept that fact and seek a negotiated peace settlement with North Vietnam.

Just days later, Martin Luther King, Jr. was assassinated in early April in Memphis, Tennessee by a lone white gunman, James Earl Ray, and America's cities went into a convulsion of riots. Blacks' frustration with racism and suppression by whites had been simmering like a powder keg and Dr. King's assassination was the final flash point for massive riots and burning and destruction of property in hundreds of U. S. cities and towns. Many blacks finally lost all hope of economic advancement in society and acceptance by whites. For many whites and some blacks in the U. S., Dr. King represented the best approach for blacks to finally gain a better quality of life, fairer treatment and equal opportunities, even though many whites were often ignorant about how difficult that would be, with so many Jim Crow laws in various states. Still, some blacks held out hope for better days ahead for their race and many whites and blacks hoped for an end of the Vietnam War when Democratic presidential candidate Robert F. Kennedy gained momentum in the polls in April and May. We were dealt another severe blow when Robert Kennedy was assassinated in Los Angeles in early June 1968. It felt like our country was coming apart at the seams. I remember thinking in the back of my mind during April-May, "I surely hope no one will ever attempt to assassinate Robert Kennedy, especially on the heels of his brother, President John F. Kennedy and Martin Luther King, Jr. 's lives being taken in that horrific manner." Then it happened again. The new song, "Abraham, Martin and John" written by Dick Holler captured the hopeless feeling we had after MLK's and RFK's deaths at the hands of assassins. Dion was the first mainstream artist to record the song and it reached the BB Hot 100 in October 1968, selling over a million copies. Smokey Robinson and the Miracles issued a cover of "Abraham, Martin and John" in July '69, that was on the BB Hot 100 and R&B charts for six weeks.

The gigantic rift between Federal government policy (pro Vietnam War) and antiwar protestors came to an ugly climax at the Democratic Convention in Chicago in late August 1968. During the Convention, antiwar protesters gathered at Grant Park and decided to march to the streets outside of the Convention, but they were beaten back by Chicago police and Federal and state officers deployed by Mayor Richard Daley. We witnessed on national TV newscasts, unarmed protesters being beaten by police, a game-changing event for many Americans who became more outspoken against the War after the Convention. Two songs in *Chicago Transit Authority* admonished the "establishment" for the police brutality at the Convention—"Prologue, August 29, 1968" and "Someday, August 29, 1968." It was the first of many times that the band Chicago sang about the hopelessness they felt about War.

In the face of growing opposition to the War by 1969, CW singer/songwriter Merle Haggard (and The Strangers) took up the cause of defending our country's freedom and criticized college students for protesting the War in his hit single "Okie From Muskogee." Rural areas in the U. S. where country western was often the favorite popular music genre were usually strongholds for patriotism and loyalty to our country that translated into defending our freedom at any cost. It was the overriding objective, no matter what the other factors were in a war like the Vietnam War or the Korean War or any other. "Okie" placed number one for four weeks, stayed on the CW chart for 16 weeks and was Haggard's only CW hit single in the '60s that also made it to the BB Hot 100. It peaked at number 41 and was on the BB Hot 100 for 14 weeks in 1969, so I heard it on mainstream AM popular music stations in Baltimore.

I witnessed college campus unrest first hand in May 1970, at the University of Maryland in College Park, MD. Protests erupted there and on college campuses nationwide after President Nixon announced that the U. S. was expanding its Vietnam campaign into Cambodia to disrupt North Vietnamese supply lines. On May 1, over 1,500 students at University of Maryland vandalized the armory where ROTC classes were held and the following day, Kent State student protesters burned down the ROTC building there. The nationwide college campus protests escalated after the U. S. Army National Guard fired on protesters at Kent State (Ohio) University, killing four students and wounding over 50 others on May 4. Several days later, over 440 college campuses nationwide, including the University of MD at College Park ended their spring semester early to avoid further unrest (we had the option of keeping the grade we had so far in a class or taking a final exam). Shortly after, Neil Young wrote "Ohio" and CSNY released it in July asking, "how many more [will die during social protests]?" Unlike many songs of the '60s and early '70s, the lyrics of "Ohio" and their meaning were crystal clear. Many college students and others wondered, "how could this killing of unarmed students happen?"

Other musicians continued to release songs that criticized war in general and fueled the antiwar movement against the War in Vietnam. Edwin Starr's "War (1970)" criticized the uselessness, hopelessness and sadness coming from war, singing that war was good for nothing, destruction of innocent lives, causing heartbreak to thousands of mothers' eyes, and "a friend only to the undertaker." Marvin Gaye's "What's Going On (1971)" cried out about all the mothers crying, brothers dying, and the answer was not to escalate. Gaye reasoned that "only love can conquer hate." Chicago's "It Better End Soon (1970)" on *Chicago II* called out for an end to all war, and they became more despondent in *Chicago III*'s (1971) "When All the Laughter Dies In Sorrow," "The Approaching Storm" and "Man vs. Man = The End."

On July 1, 1970, Tom N., Mike A., Joe F., Tom D. and I watched the draft lottery being drawn on TV for boys born in 1951. I qualified for a draft deferment because I was a full-time college student enrolled in a degree program. If we gained a high enough draft number out of one to 365, we might not have to enlist in the U. S. military even if we were not in college. If we had a low enough number and we were not in college, we would have to enlist or be drafted. Generally, if you had a draft number less than 100, you would be drafted and if you had a number higher than 300, you were "safe." Two screened drums with capsules were used, one with birthdates and the other with draft numbers. When they pulled out the date of my birthday and then number 31, I was not happy. Draft boards would start with number 1, record who had the corresponding birthdays in their area for that number and send draft notices to guys with the lowest draft numbers first. By this time, I was not in favor of our involvement in Vietnam. I believed we were losing the War and would have too much difficulty maintaining a democratic government there even if we did "win" the War. It was a hard pill to swallow for Americans because we were used to winning Wars. A few of us in the group were off the hook, but a couple guys drew low draft numbers with their birthdays and were not attending college, nor planning to attend. Fortunately, the guys I was closest too who enlisted did not have to serve in Vietnam, so they did not suffer injury or death there. Tom Douglass's dad, Bill (a WWII veteran) told me in 2018, "The Vietnam War was a war full of politics. It was awful what that war did to our country. A draft system with the conditions that existed in the early 1970s was unfair to young men from poor families who had no chance to get college deferments. "

Pop musicians sang about blacks' civil rights matters in the '60s at a time when the Civil Rights Act in 1964 and the Voting Rights Act of 1965 were signed into law, but many state-by-state Jim Crow laws were still in place. Dylan sang in "Only A Pawn In Their Game" about black activist Medger Evers' death and how southern politicians and deputy sheriffs manipulated poor southern white people to "kill blacks without [feeling] pain [guilt]," with the attitude, well they [authorities] told me to do it. Sam Cooke's "A Change Is Gonna Come" wasn't released until after his death at age 33 in December 1964. Cooke's original version was voted the 12th best song ever by *Rolling Stone Magazine* in 2004, and Otis Redding, Aretha Franklin, and Three Dog Night, among others, recorded excellent covers of the song. Cooke's original version was a mainstream hit on the BB Hot 100 and the R&B chart, in part because he was locked in place as one of popular music's top-selling artists and his song was less direct than the hard hitting "Backlash Blues (1965)" by Nina Simone (born Eunice Waymon). "Backlash Blues" was never played on stations relying on the BB Hot 100 or BB Top 40 and seldom played on soul stations so most teens and older popular music listeners never heard it. Simone taunted the white establishment for its treatment of blacks—lower wages, higher taxes, and taking our sons off to War. The Impressions' "Keep On Pushing (1964)," "We're A Winner (1968)," "This Is My Country (1968)," and "Choice Of Colors (1969)" (written by Curtis Mayfield) and James Brown's "Say It Loud - I'm Black And I'm Proud (Part 1) (1968)" championed black pride and an urgent need to push forward in the blacks' civil rights movement. Neil Young wrote and sang in "Southern Man (1970)" about racism towards blacks in the South—burning crosses and bullwhips cracking. Lynard Skynard took exception to Young's criticism in "Sweet Home Alabama" telling Neil that southern man didn't need Neil around [in the South].

Some '60s songs made general wide-sweeping appeals for people to open their minds and hearts and try to accept and get along with everyone. The Youngbloods' "Get Together" asked us to try to love one another and Sly and the Family Stones' "Everyday People" asserted the need for people of all colors and backgrounds to get along better with each other. The Youngbloods' "Get Together" placed much better on the BB Hot 100 in 1969 (peaked at number 5 and was on the chart for 17 weeks) than its first release in 1967 (peaked at number 62 and was on the chart for 8 weeks). The song was released in various forms many times by other popular music recording artists before The Youngbloods, but never with the success of The

Youngbloods' second release. The Impressions' "People Get Ready (1965)" and Cat Stevens' "Peace Train (1971)" sang about the hope for people getting along with each other much better and achieving peace throughout the world. The Rascals' "People Got To Be Free (1968)" lamented the large number of people around the world who were suppressed and had little or no freedoms.

Zager and Evans' "In The Year 2525 (1969)" had the somber theme of eventual doom for mankind, but was a smash hit in spite of its lyrics. Their one-hit wonder reached number one on July 12, and it stayed there for six weeks. I never cared for the song because of its lyrics, but obviously many listeners liked it and bought the 45-record. The song was a stark contrast to the peppy, very uplifting "Aquarius/Let The Sunshine In" by The 5th Dimension, the other 6-week number one song of 1969, that started its run as number one three months earlier.

John Lennon's Plastic Ono Band's "Give Peace A Chance (1969)" and John and Yoko's sit-ins and bed-ins asked all of us to simply give peace a chance. What would it hurt, they implied? Their ideals sounded appealing to many listeners, but it was hard to embrace their hopefulness due to the unevenness in the world, the large difference between so many millions of people who did not have enough to eat and little reason for healthy self-esteem, compared to the excesses a much smaller portion of the world's people enjoyed.

Lennon's "Imagine (1971)" asked us to try to imagine that there is no heaven or hell, no countries (to fight or die for), no possession, just people living in peace. He made us pause and think about our values. When he sang about imagining no heaven and no possession and asking listeners, "I wonder if you can? "I thought I certainly hoped there was a heaven after life on earth and I would not want to live without many of my prized possessions. I wondered, "did my love of material things make me a bad person? "

There was very little voice given to women's rights in popular music in the '60s, even though Betty Friedan's book, *The Feminine Mystique* was published and The National Organization of Women (NOW) was formed in 1966. Both Frieden's book and NOW were finally bringing more attention to the unfair treatment women received in and outside the workplace in the U. S. Before *The Feminine Mystique*, Helen Gurley Brown wrote *Sex and The Single Girl*, published in 1962. Brown encouraged women to become financially independent and experience sex before marriage. Three years later, Brown became editor of *Cosmopolitan* magazine. Helen Reddy's "I Am Woman" helped sustain the feminist movement in 1972. Some of the lyrics in songs by Lesley Gore, Aretha Franklin, Carole King and Helen Reddy made some strides in a long uphill climb speaking up for women's rights and feelings and a calling out for better treatment of women by men.

When we listened to The Temptations' "Ball of Confusion (That's What The World Is Today)" in 1970, it reminded us of widespread problems that many of us seldom witnessed in mostly white suburban areas in the U. S. It made us realize again how good our lives were compared to so many other people. It sounded like the world at large was in deep trouble. The Temptations sang about segregation, integration, gun control, kids were growing up too soon, and politicians who were claiming more taxes will solve everything. Today, all the same categories of social issues exist, but some progress has been made on most of these issues since 1970.

Occasionally, a song in the '60s derided the use of drugs or at least the dangers associated with some drugs. Paul Revere and the Raiders' "Kicks (1966)" warned that using drugs to escape reality "will get you nowhere"— You'll still have to deal with reality when you come down or off your high. "Kicks" reached number 4 on the BB Hot 100 and stayed on the chart 14 weeks so its lyrics were a frequent reminder because it was played so often on AM mainstream popular music stations. All of us understood the song's message. Rex Garvin and the Mighty Cravers sang about the hallucinations LSD users might suffer in "Believe It Or Not (1967)," but it did not receive much air time in the U. S. due to its failure to appear on the BB Hot 100. The First Edition's "Just Dropped In (To See What Condition My Condition Was In (1968)" warned against taking LSD and was strewn with lyrics depicting a person in an obvious state of confusion having many contradictory thoughts.

Diana Ross and the Supremes' "Love Child (1968)" and the Temptations' "Papa Was A Rollin' Stone (1972)" tackled the issue of neglected children left behind by one or both parents. Living life in the suburb like I did with mom and dad in a new home with a middle-class income, I was not aware of the plights many youngsters faced, except through songs like "Love Child" and "Papa Was A Rollin' Stone." I don't recall discussing these issues in our high school social studies classes and these topics should have been front and center. Only in the summers of '69, '70 and '71, when I worked in Baltimore and rode by car with dad through poverty-stricken areas of town did I start seeing the outside living conditions of many blacks living there.

Rachel Carson became our chief spokesperson on pollution of our natural environment caused by pesticides and other poisonous chemicals with her groundbreaking book, *Silent Spring* in 1962, and U. S. Senator Gaylord Nelson founded the First Earth Day on April 22, 1970. Events on the First Earth Day at over 2,000 U. S. colleges and universities supported environmental protection. Joni Mitchell lamented in "Big Yellow Taxi (1970)" that paving paradise with a parking lot and a swinging boutique had its down side—the loss of some beautiful natural settings and "sometimes you don't know what you've got till it's gone." Chicago sang about the rapid rate of environmental destruction in "Mother" and played a series of loud and then louder sounds of the industrial world in "Progress? " on their *Chicago III* (1971) album. The Beach Boys sang about manmade pollution of our water in "Don't Go Near The Water" and trees dying in "A Day In The Life Of A Tree" with its funereal organ on their *Surf's Up* (1971) album.

30

Instrumentals

♪

INSTRUMENTALS WERE VERY POPULAR IN THE '50s AND '60s. The Percy Faith Orchestra issued a much more robust and appealing cover of "The Theme From 'A Summer Place'(1960)" than Hugo Winterhalter's version for the movie *A Summer Place* in 1959. Faith's cover remained number one on the BB Hot 100 for nine weeks, the longest stretch at the top spot for an instrumental. Clarinetist Acker Bilk's "Stranger On The Shore (1962)" reached number 2 on the BB Hot 100, and stayed on that chart for 21 weeks. Even more impressive, it was number 1 on the AC chart for seven weeks. It stuck with me even as a pre-teen because it spotlighted the clarinet, but it had a lonely, somber feel to it that I didn't enjoy at age 11. I categorized it as a song that adults liked. Pete (born Roddis Franklin) Drake (And His Talking Steel Guitar) issued the popular "Forever" in 1964, reaching number 25 and staying on the BB Hot 100 for 11 weeks. His use of a talk box attached to his steel guitar (the guitar looked a bit like an organ because it laid flat and he sat down when he played it) was a forerunner of Peter Frampton's widely popular songs that used a talk box with his guitar in the '70s.

Some instrumentals of the early '60s had more of a rock and roll sound. The Ventures and a few other groups played mostly guitar and drums in the late '50s and early '60s, and instrumentals in the mid-'60s often used organs, horns and string instruments. The Ventures' "Walk, Don't Run (1960)" and

their reprise, "Walk Don't Run '64" were their biggest hit singles until "Hawaii-Five-O" in 1969 for that TV show's theme song.

Two songs highlighted the organ and were among the most upbeat up-tempo instrumentals of the late '50s and the '60s. Dave "Baby" Cortez's "The Happy Organ" reached number one on the BB Hot 100 in 1959. Walter Wanderley's organ and the song's beat in "Summer Samba (So Nice) (1966)" spurred many dancers to move their feet to the cha cha cha and samba. Astrud Gilberto added her sultry voice to another version (title switched to "So Nice (Summer Samba)" with Wanderley in 1967.

Singer Astrud Gilberto and tenor saxophonist Stan Getz's "The Girl From Ipanema (1964)" strongly appealed to popular music listeners in the U. S. in 1964, reaching number one on the AC chart for two weeks, and number 5 on the BB Hot 100. "The Girl From Ipanema" a Brazilian bossa nova song, was a worldwide hit that won the 1965 Grammy Award for Song of the Year. It is believed to be the second most recorded popular song, behind The Beatles (McCartney's) "Yesterday." Astrud's voice was so light and sexy, and so distinctive on "The Girl From Ipanema" that we easily recognized her when we heard her. We still do. As a young teen I had never heard a woman's voice like hers and it cast a spell on me. It still does.

Other instrumentals in the '60s that had an easy listening sound and placed high on the AC chart included: Ramsey Lewis Trio's "The In Crowd (1965)" and "Hang On Sloopy (1965)," The Sounds Orchestral's "Cast Your Fate To The Wind (1965)," Ramsey Lewis's "Wade In The Water (1966);" Paul Mauriat's "Love Is Blue (1967)," Mason Williams' "Classical Gas (1968)" and Young-Holt Unlimited's "Soulful Strut (1968)." Popularity of some of these instrumentals was especially strong with adults, often reaching number one on the AC chart.

Barbara Acklin recorded "Am I The Same Girl" at Brunswick Studios before record producer Carl Davis removed her voice and added a piano to make the instrumental version called "Soulful Strut" by Young-Holt Unlimited. Acklin's vocal version was a minor hit single in early 1969, but Young-Holt's instrumental was a major hit single starting in late 1968, reaching number 2 on the AC chart and number 3 on the BB Hot 100 and RB charts, selling over a million copies.

Herb Alpert and the Tijuana Brass was the most popular instrumental group in the '60s and had over 30 hit singles, starting with "A Taste Of Honey" in 1965. Alpert's omnipresent trumpet on radio, records and TV

sounded so good to us that he inspired many a budding musician to learn that instrument, much the way the Beatles, The Byrds and other guitar playing groups inspired new guitar players. In an interview in mid-1966, Alpert characterized his sound as having "jazz, folk, rock, Dixie and a little mariachi or Mexican street band blended into one." "Tijuana Taxi" and "The Work Song" were two of my favorites, but his number one songs on the AC chart after "A Taste of Honey" were: "Casino Royale," "A Banda," and "This Guy's In Love With You" (Herb made a weak stab at singing in this one). "Tijuana Taxi" and "Spanish Flea" could pull you out of a funk lickety-split!

Some of Alpert's instrumentals had such wide appeal that they were used in a commercial or as a theme song on a TV show. Alpert re-recorded his "Mexican Shuffle" as "The Teaberry Shuffle" at the request of the Clark Gum Company and Clark used it in its commercials for Teaberry Gum (had a similar flavor to *Big Red*). A patron in a bank, a football player running downfield with a ball, and a guard *a la* Buckingham Palace, all unwrapped a piece of gum, stuck it in their mouths and happily did quick 5-second shuffles. TV watchers nationwide enjoyed the shuffle and we imitated it, sometimes around our friends and often when no one else was around. Alpert's "Spanish Flea" was played on TV's *The Dating Game* starting in December '65 as the "Bachelor's Theme" whenever a new bachelor was being introduced. *The Dating Game* also used "Whipped Cream" to introduce the bachelorette questioning the males, and "Lollipops And Roses" when she met her date. In the late '60s, during batting practice before Baltimore Oriole games at Memorial Stadium, it *seemed* like slugger Boog Powell walloped more practice home runs during Alpert's "The Work Song." Who knows? Could that song have put Boog in a peppy happier mood and that home run swing followed?

Soul instrumentals had widespread popularity in the '60s, and some were important dance staples for teen bands at dances, including Alvin Cash & The Crawlers' "Twine Time (1965)," Alvin Cash & The Registers' "The Philly Freeze (1966)," the Bar-Kays' "Soul Finger (1967)," and Cliff Nobles and Co.'s "The Horse (1968)." Its invigorating beat made "The Horse" the most popular instrumental dance song of the '60s. Hugh Masekela's "Grazing In The Grass (1968)" was number one on the BB Hot 100 for two weeks and number one on the R&B chart for four weeks. Soul instrumentals that reached number two or three on the R&B chart were King Curtis's "Soul Twist (1962)" and Cannonball Adderly's "Mercy, Mercy, Mercy (1967)." King

Curtis's (Curtis Ousley) band had several other hit instrumentals on the R&B chart in the '60s including: "Soul Serenade," "Memphis Soul Stew," and "Ode To Billie Joe." His best hit single for dancing the boogaloo and shing-a-ling was "Memphis Soul Stew (1967)." I played this 45-record over and over in my room, admiring the song's horns and raucous dance beat.

The Stax Records house band, Booker T. and the MGs, had six top ten hits on the R&B chart in the '60s. Group leader Booker T. Jones usually played organ and the group's baseline foursome also featured drums and guitars, with the addition of horns and piano (sometimes Isaac Hayes) on some of their studio recordings. "Green Onions (1962)" was their top-seller, and my favorites were "Hip Hug-Her (1967)," "Soul-Limbo (1968)" and "Time Is Tight (1969)."

Unlike Booker T. and the MGs, Motown's house band, the Funk Brothers, was not in the limelight in the '60s by design by Berry Gordy. The Funk Brothers' talent and essential role in the achieving the high quality and success of the Motown sound finally received overdue recognition in the movie *Standing in the Shadows of Motown* (2002). The introduction to the Funk Brothers movie said: "They played on more number one records than the Beatles, the Beach Boys, the Rolling Stones and Elvis Presley combined. "When they weren't playing for Motown recording sessions, the Funk Brothers often scattered into smaller groups or singly and played jazz at various nightclubs in Detroit. The music they heard and played outside of Motown was often the basis for some of their ideas for the rhythm and beats they used at Motown.

"Music to Watch Girls By" became an anthem for many young and older guys watching girls anywhere in 1966 and 1967. Bob Crewe's studio musicians, the Bob Crewe Generation, recorded the instrumental, "Music To Watch Girls By" late in 1966 and it went to number 2 on the AC Chart number 15 on the BB Hot 100. Guys were already familiar with a brief version of the tune that began as "backing music" for a Diet Pepsi TV ad in 1965. The commercial narrator said, "The girls that girl watchers watch, drink Diet Pepsi Cola with only one calorie." Crewe's "Music To Watch Girls By" built on the idea the T-Bones used when they re-worked a jingle of an Alka-Seltzer TV commercial into the hit instrumental, "No Matter What Shape (Your Stomach's In)" that reached number 3 on the BB Hot 100 in 1966. Andy Williams made "Music To Watch Girls By" into a vocal, thanks to lyrics by Tony Velona. Williams' hit peaked at number 2 on the AC chart, and only reached number 34 on the BB Hot 100 in '67, but it was the head turning video that was accompanied by Williams' song that baby boomer men still recognize. Millions of young and older men's jaws dropped while watching movie star males who were hypnotized at the sight of the video's star ladies' (Natalie Wood, Ann-Margret, Diana Rigg, Janet Leigh and Sharon Tate) walks, wiggles, dance gyrations and bending over showing their backside. The video fit the lyrics and the girls' walks fit the song's beats.

The advantage of a well-played instrumental is it allows us to focus more on the instruments than we often do for songs with vocals, but when we add vocals to an instrumental it often adds to our listening pleasure. When the Buckinghams added lyrics to "Mercy, Mercy, Mercy (1967)," the Classics IV put words to Mike Sharpe's (born Michael Shapiro) "Spooky (1967)," and the Friends of Distinction sang their vocal of "Grazing In The Grass (1969)," those hit singles appealed to me more than the original instrumentals because now they had a story line, however brief. The words to the Buckinghams' "Mercy, Mercy, Mercy" and the Classics IV's "Spooky" made us think about girls in our lives who fit those songs—now we had visuals in our minds for these hit singles that we didn't have when we heard the instrumentals. These vocal covers are still three of my favorite '60s songs. I am surprised years later that I was impressed enough with Mike Sharpe's (born Michael Shapiro) saxophone instrumental of "Spooky" to record it off the radio onto a reel-to-reel tape in early '67. It was only on the BB Hot 100 for 7 weeks and peaked at number 57, and it did not make the R&B chart, so it was not played often on AM radio.

The Friends of Distinction's cover of "Grazing In The Grass" is more up tempo than Hugh Masekela's instrumental and one of the most uplifting songs ever recorded for popular music. Lead singer and lyrics writer Harry Elson sang about how mellow it is grazing in the grass with the sun beaming down between the leaves, and birds darting in and out of the trees. He sang about grazing in the grass being a gas, and how everything is so clear you can see it and so real you can feel it.

31

Vocals—the human instrument

THE BEST-SELLING POPULAR MUSIC no matter the genre is usually a great collaboration of vocals and musical instruments. Great voices (often called the purest musical instrument) follow a song's melody with perfection, blending the song's lyrics with instruments to project emotion that connects with listeners' thoughts and feelings. There was the baritone of Jim Morrison; the raspy soulful singing from Wilson Pickett and Otis Redding; and the falsetto of Eddie Kendricks, Smokey Robinson and Frankie Valli. Some singers are equally competent whether in the studio or on stage (like Redding and McCartney). Some of the greatest singers are the ones who project emotion on a grand scale like Aretha Franklin, Otis Redding, Elvis Presley, Barbra Streisand, and Ella Fitzgerald.

Everyone's voice is unique and popular musicians' voices are often instantly recognizable like Frank Sinatra, Bill Medley, Bryan Adams, Rod Stewart, Smokey Robinson, Otis Redding, Aretha Franklin, and Neil Young. "They are personal and allow a truly authentic singer to resonate with their listeners," said singer Annie Lenox. The Rascals' Felix Cavalierre recalled during his time with Atlantic Records in the '60s: "When Aretha was on Atlantic, I used to go to the sessions. I used to kind of stick my head in there to hear this artist, you know who was phenomenal. She'd get better and better recording a given song. "

Vocalists (and their musicians) are often very adept at projecting moods.

Ray Charles, Aretha Franklin and Otis Redding appealed to us because they sounded very sincere and often projected urgency in a song if its lyrics called for it. Ray Charles' sincerity in "Georgia On My Mind" and "I Can't Stop Loving You," among others, is poignant. Likewise, Aretha's emotions in "I Never Loved A Man (The Way I Love You)" and "(You Make Me Feel Like) A Natural Woman" and Otis's sincerity in "I've Been Loving You Too Long" and "Try A Little Tenderness" seeps through us when we listen to them. Adele's anger over the end of her relationship with her boyfriend in "Rolling In The Deep (2011)" and John Lennon's anger at his mother and father in "Mother (1970)" are palpable.

I used to wonder as a teen, "who were the girl singers in the background of most of the Four Tops' songs?" They were the Andantes, Motown's most widely used background vocal group. They added a richness, another layer of appealing sound to the Four Tops' songs and some Jimmy Ruffin and early Marvin Gaye songs that was missing when the Four Tops, Ruffin and Gaye did live performances that weren't lip synced. Before they made their mark as hit makers on their own, Martha and the Vandellas and The Supremes provided background vocals for other Motown artists. In Marvin Gaye's "You're A Wonderful One" the Supremes sang the simple, but pleasant chorus "you're a wonderful one," Martha and the Vandellas sang "pride and joy" and "baby boy" in "Pride And Joy," and Gladys Knight and the Pips sang the chorus "You, you, you…" while Marvin sang the other lyrics in "You." The Temptations songs seldom had girl groups for background vocals (except The Andantes on "It's Growing"), but they really didn't need them because they had their own group of five. Smokey Robinson recalled, "I used to call them the Five Deacons, because they had that church harmony. Awesome. Melvin was my way, way, way down on the bottom and Eddie was way, way, way up on the top, and all of those harmonic sounds in between them. Those brothers could really 'blow'. "

Vocal groups varied their sound by using different members for the lead vocals for different songs. The Beatles changed their sound by using George or Ringo as the lead singer on some of their songs rather than Paul or John. Ringo sang lead vocals in about one song per record album: "Boys," "I Wanna Be Your Man," "Act Naturally," "Honey Don't," "Yellow Submarine," "With A Little Help From My Friends," "What Goes On," and "Octopus's Garden." George sang lead on most of the Beatles songs he wrote like "Taxman," "If I Needed Someone," "I Want To Tell You," "My Guitar

Gently Weeps," "Here Comes The Sun," and "Something." The Temptations varied their sound by switching lead vocalists for different songs. Eddie Kendricks sang lead on "The Way You Do The Things You Do," "Beauty Is Only Skin Deep," "Get Ready," and "You Can Depend On Me." David Ruffin sang lead on "My Girl," "Ain't Too Proud To Beg," "(I Know) I'm Losing You," and "All I Need." Ruffin and Kendricks traded off the lead vocal on "You're My Everything" and on a rare occasion Melvin Franklin or Paul Williams sang lead on a song. This variation of lead singers and the switch to psychedelic soul for some of their late '60s and early '70s songs kept them fresh to listeners' ears.

Vocal sounds like vowels or syllables, rather than lyrics, show off vocal versatility, dress up many songs with extra layers of sound, and often make a song more fun for listening or doing a sing-along. The variety of possible sounds seems almost infinite, and one wonders where the idea for many of them come from. Sometimes singers conjure up a sound called "scat" vocals—vocal improvisations that are often wordless vocables, nonsense syllables that use the voice as [another] instrument. As far back as 1926, Louis Armstrong sang "scat" vocals in the jazz song "Heebie Jeebies." He and Ella Fitzgerald often used scat vocals in many of their jazz songs. Jim Morrison played with scat vocals in "Roadhouse Blues (1970)" and some of us enjoyed singing along with his syllables he sang to the song's beat.

Popular music in the '50s and '60s was loaded with vocal sounds (other than words) like "bah dah dah dah dah; na, na, na, na na; yip, yip, yip. Barry Mann's "Who Put The Bomp (1961)" paid tribute to all those vocal sound effects that music lovers loved to hear and sing-along with. He sang about how those sounds helped make the singer's "baby" fall in love with him – the bomp, bah, bomp, bah, bomp; the rama, lama, ding, dong; the bop, shoo, bop; and the dip, da, dip, da, dip. Frankie Ford's "Sea Cruise (1959)" has "ooh we; ooh we, baby; ooh we; ooh we, baby…" In The Marcels' cover of "Blue Moon (1961)," their bass singer sang variations of "bom, ba, bom, ba, bom; dip, da, dip, da, dip; and dang, da, dang, dang, ding, da, dong—blue moon. " The Mills Brothers' "Cab Driver (1968)" has the happy-go-lucky sounding, "du, du, dooby, du; du, du, dooby, du…." In "He's So Fine (1963)" The Chiffons sang in part, "do-lang, do-lang, do-lang;" "do-lang, do-lang." The chorus in Wilson Pickett's "Land Of 1000 Dances" and the Beatles' "Hey Jude" is laced with, na, na, na's. "Na, na, na's" were prominent again in Steam's "Na Na Hey Hey Kiss Him Goodbye (1969)."

Today's record producers often use Auto Tune, an electronic method of changing a recording's voice for pitch correction. If this method becomes more standard over time, would voices in songs start sounding more alike and less recognizable and unique? If this happens then the enjoyment of popular music will take a big step backward. Not only do all the different human voices give us a wide variety of appealing sounds, but the ability to recognize different voices is another aspect of popular music that makes it appealing to its listeners.

32

Vocal harmony at its best

♪

GOOD VOCAL HARMONY was a trademark of many doo wop groups in the '50s and early '60s, and it continued in popular music with Motown's vocal groups and several duos in the '60s. Motown's The Temptations, The Supremes, The Four Tops, The Miracles, Martha and the Vandellas, and The Marvelettes excelled in vocal harmony. Popular music fans still admire the vocal harmony of Motown's group singers, Marvin Gaye and Tammi Terrell and four male duos that made some or all of their hit singles in the '60s—the Everly Brothers, the Righteous Brothers, Simon and Garfunkel and Sam and Dave.

Two "mixed" groups associated with popular music's California Sound, the Mamas and the Papas (two women and two guys) and the 5th Dimension (two women and three guys) had harmony that reached perfection. The Mamas and Papas' "California Dreamin'," and the 5th Dimension's "Aquarius/Let the Sunshine In" showcased their vocal harmony sound that also made their other songs so appealing to listen to. Both groups had slow tempo serious songs and more upbeat up-tempo songs that were popular hit singles.

Four more California groups, the Beach Boys, the Byrds, The Association, and The Turtles gave us a long list of hit songs with great vocal harmonies. The Beach Boys' "Surfer Girl," "In My Room," and "God Only Knows" stand out as three of their best songs for vocal harmony, and the Byrds' "Mr. Tambourine Man" and "Turn, Turn, Turn (To Everything There

Is A Season)" epitomized their great vocals. The Association's "Along Comes Mary," "Cherish," "Windy," and "Never My Love," and the Turtles' "You Baby," "Happy Together," "She'd Rather Be with Me" and "Elenore" were hit singles because they excelled at vocal harmony. Music fans often sang along with these songs trying to blend in with a group's harmony.

The Beatles' "And I Love Her" and "Because;" Crosby, Stills, and Nash's "Suite: Judy Blue Eyes" and "Helplessly Hoping;" and CSN and Young's "Carry On," "Helpless" and "Our House;" are joyful to listen to, because of their superb harmony. We never tire of them. These songs still sound like vocal perfection that we try to imitate in sing-alongs as we drive down the road almost 50 years later.

In the early 70s, The Doobie Brothers and The Eagles issued many songs we relished partly because of their outstanding vocal harmony. The Doobie Brothers' *Toulose Street* (1972) featured "Listen To The Music" and "Jesus Is Just Alright With Me." The Eagles' excellent vocal harmony plays out in "Take It Easy (1972)," "Peaceful Easy Feeling (1972)," "Tequila Sunrise (1973)," "Lyin' Eyes (1975)," and "New Kid In Town (1976)." I am still baffled that "Tequila Sunrise" only reached number 64 on the BB Hot 100 in 1973.

Like many other popular hit singles in the '60s, The Mamas and Papas "California Dreamin'" and the Lovin' Spoonful's "You Didn't Have To Be So Nice" used polyphonic texture. Both songs had different voices overlapping, meaning the lead singer(s) were about halfway through a verse when the back-up singers began an overlapping same or a similar verse. I remember being surprised how good that sounded to us as young popular music listeners and realized that was part of the reason those songs grabbed me. The Lovin' Spoonful's "You Didn't Have To Be So Nice (1965)" vocal layering sound inspired The Beach Boys use of polyphony in their hit song, "God Only Knows (1966)." The Mamas and Papas' "California Dreamin' (1966)" used the simultaneous sound of the male duo (John Phillips with Denny Doherty) and female duo (Mama Cass and Michelle Phillips) vocals, sometimes overlapping the same verse and sometimes different verses, yet all of it sounds very appealing. At other times in "California Dreamin'" they caught up with each other and emphasized their impeccable harmony. They used the same techniques again in their second million-selling single, "Monday, Monday (1966)" (their only number one song).

33

Duos and duets

♪

I N THE LATE 50's AND EARLY '60s, the Everly Brothers were the dominant duo artists. Then came several more extremely gifted male duos—The Righteous Brothers, Simon and Garfunkel and Sam and Dave in the '60s. But why weren't there any successful female duos? Following Paul (Ray Hildebrand) and Paula's (Jill Jackson) duet "Hey Paula" that reached number one in 1963, male/female duos became highly popular in the '60s, including Sonny and Cher (originally they recorded as Caesar and Cleo in 1963), Peaches and Herb, and Marvin Gaye with several different women at Motown Records, especially Tammi Terrell (born Thomasina Montgomery). Peaches (Francine Barker) and Herb Fame issued the hit singles "Close Your Eyes," "For Your Love" and "Love Is Strange" in 1967 and several other hit singles in the '60s, but the Motown duets reigned supreme.

Gaye's success as a soloist in the early '60s was one of the chief reasons that Motown's soul sound rose so quickly in popularity. Still, Berry Gordy decided to pair Marvin with various Motown female stars, beginning in 1964, while still featuring Marvin as a solo performer, too. Gaye's popularity didn't miss a step as both his solos and duets throughout the '60s became hit singles, including many number one songs. Gaye recorded "What's The Matter With You Baby" b/w "Once Upon A Time (1964)" with Mary Wells and the very popular "It Takes Two" with Kim Weston in early '67. Many music fans felt that the popularity of "It Takes Two" meant more hits were on the way from Gaye and Weston, but Kim Weston fell out of favor with Gordy over royalties issues and he abruptly switched gears and paired Gaye with Terrell beginning with their May 1967 hit, "Ain't No Mountain High Enough" and "Your Precious Love" a few months later. Gaye and Terrell's duets soared in airplay time on radio and jukeboxes with five of their songs peaking at number 3 or better on the R&B chart from 1967-68. Their duets "Ain't Nothing Like The Real Thing" and "You're All I Need To Get By" in 1968, were number one R&B hits. Great love duets by male/female duos convince you they are in love with each other when you see them perform one. Gaye and Terrell conveyed that in their videos and live performances.

Motown preferred the "head over heels in love" duets, while Stax's Otis Redding and Carla Thomas bantered back and forth in "Tramp (1967)" a fun-loving duet. Much to our amusement, guys would take on Otis's lines in "Tramp" when we heard the song on the radio and girls would sing Carla's lines when they listened to the song. It would have been a treat to watch Otis and Carla tease and torment each other while performing "Tramp," but this was the era before music videos became more commonplace. About the time of Otis and Carla's "Tramp," I wondered what about a duet between Otis and Aretha? Only years later did I learn Otis was contemplating a duet with Aretha not long before he died at age 26.

The BB Hot 100 chart had songs from many genres, so it was rare for soul songs to place as high or higher on the on the BB Hot 100 as they did on the R&B chart. "Tramp" peaked at number 26 and Gaye and Terrell's "Ain't No Mountain High Enough" peaked number 19 on the BB Hot 100 in 1967. They both seemed wildly popular to me in Baltimore, because I listened to soul stations at least half the time that year. "Tramp" reached number 2, and "Ain't No Mountain High Enough" reached number 3 on the R&B charts, so soul stations played them every hour.

In 1968, Motown raised the duo/duet scene up a notch. Always the innovator, Berry Gordy released the LP *Diana Ross and The Supremes Join with The Temptations* late in 1968, along with their *TCB* TV special. Their biggest "duet" hit single from the album was "I'm Gonna Make You Love Me" which peaked at number 2 on the BB Hot 100 and R&B charts. It was rich in layers of vocals and listeners made it a platinum hit single.

34

Upbeat songs

♪

WHILE THE REASONS WE PLAY MUSIC VARY WIDELY depending on the mood or setting we are in, often we're simply in the mood for some songs that put us in a happy mood or help keep us in one. Upbeat songs often appeal to us for listening, or dancing or singing along or a combination of two or all three of these reasons.

Amid all the troubles and turmoil of the '60s, we were happily bombarded by a barrage of upbeat songs that had deep, positive long-lasting effects on us. Some of our best upbeat songs for listening in the '60s included: "Do Wah Diddy Diddy," "Do You Believe In Magic," "Daydream," "Groovin'," "Good Vibrations," and "It's A Beautiful Morning." Others included "A Girl Like You," "Grazing In The Grass," and "Aquarius/Let the Sunshine In" and three songs from *Blood, Sweat & Tears*—"Smiling Phases," "More And More," and "You've Made Me So Very Happy." Some of The Beatles' upbeat songs of the '60s included: "Good Day Sunshine," "All You Need Is Love," "With A Little Help From My Friends," "Birthday," "Ob-La-Di, Ob-La-Da," and "Here Comes The Sun." Many up-tempo songs that were great for dancing also felt upbeat to listen to, including: Spencer Davis's "Gimme Some Lovin'," Otis's "I Can't Turn You Loose" Archie Bell's "I Just Can't Stop Dancing," Tommy James' "Mony Mony," and Sam the Sham's "Wooly Bully."

Largely forgotten today in most of the U. S., except California and

Arizona, The Turtles' "You Baby (1966)," "Happy Together (1967)," and "She'd Rather Be With Me (1967)" epitomized a feeling of absolute euphoria we felt if we were in a relationship with a girl or guy that was at its peak. You were sitting on top of the world. "You Baby" sang about a guy's love for his girlfriend who "believes in his wildest dreams and craziest schemes." He thinks about her all day and night in a happy exuberant way, not in the manner of worry or insecurity. "She'd Rather Be With Me" sang about the ultimate feeling you hoped to have, an unshaken confidence that she wanted to be with you, rather than anyone else.

If we heard one of those songs as a teen or older in the '60s, or hear one of them now, they will enhance a good mood you're already in or steer us towards one. "Do Wah Diddy" has that upbeat tempo that also has easy-to-remember lyrics starting with: "There she was just a walking down the street, singing, Do Wah Diddy Diddy dum diddy doo..." The Friends of Distinction sang about the sun, beamin' between the leaves and birds darting in and out of trees and they frequently used the popular term "dig it." Although it doesn't appear in some versions of the lyrics listed for "Grazing In The Grass," the singers belt out an ecstatic "Whewwww!" [or "Whooo-oooh!"] several times during the song and its effect on us if we imitate it is exhilarating. Try listening to it while riding down the road on a sunny day. It's loud, exuberant and fun, and it makes you want to corral some friends who can belt out "Whewwww!" with you along with the song as it plays again.

"Do Wah Diddy" "Grazing In The Grass," "Daydream" and "It's A Beautiful Morning" have always been some of my favorite upbeat songs since they were hit records, despite 50 more years of popular music songs being issued since then. Even in 2018, I don't tire of hearing them. They are soothing, so relaxing and sometimes invigorating and bring a smile to my face. The themes in those songs are timeless—happily watching a girl while walking down the street; enjoying the sun, birds singing in the trees, and the green grass; a good day for daydreaming walking down the street; and fresh air on a beautiful morning.

35

Summertime and sunshine

♪

I T IS NO SURPRISE THAT OTHER THAN SONGS ABOUT LOVE, some of the most recurring themes in music are summertime, sunshine and the beach. Many of us have always associated summer with vacation, the beach, being out of school, cookouts, picnics, riding in a convertible with the top down, and music blaring out open car windows. If we worked a part time or fulltime job in the summer, we still heard music more than during the school year, often staying up later at nights during the weekdays.

We saw fewer different teens daily in the summer compared to school days, but in Perry Hall we had teen gathering places like the shopping center, local driving around the few daytime and night time hangouts, and Teen Center on Saturday nights. In the early '60s, few families had air conditioning and many families did not have it until the late '60s. We were outside more in the summertime than pre-teens, teens and adults are now.

We heard those summer hit songs more often than we heard our favorites during the school year, and we still connect them with summer because that is when our memories were imprinted with them. Some of the songs that still trigger "that was summertime" when I hear them are: "Heat Wave (1963)," "Surfer Girl (1963)," "Under The Boardwalk (1964)," "G. T. O. (1964)," "House Of The Rising Sun (1964)," "Satisfaction (1965)," "California Girls (1965)," "Like A Rolling Stone (1965)" and "Down In The Boondocks (1965)." Later, others included, "Little Girl (1966)," "Summer In

144

The City (1966)," "Light My Fire (1967)," "Ode To Billy Joe (1967)," "Brown-Eyed Girl (1967),""Whiter Shade Of Pale (1967),""Hurdy Gurdy Man (1968)," "Hello, I Love You (1968)," "Born To Be Wild (1968)," and Sweet Caroline (1969).""Summer In The City" had the sounds of the city— car horns beeping, a jack hammer throbbing. In "Dancing In The Street," Martha and the Vandellas called out for a dancing party, announcing that summer is here, the time is right for dancing in the street –sweet music play- ing everywhere will prompt swinging, swaying and records playing. They were right on target with the occasional pool parties that had all of that. Mungo Jerry sang "In The Summertime (1970)" about the hot weather in the summertime, the need to have a drink and drive and find those women who were always on your mind. Nat King Cole sang in "Those Lazy-Hazy- Crazy Days of Summer" about drive-ins where kids often didn't watch the movie that much with all that "kissing in the cars" and soda, pretzels and beer (at all those picnics and cookouts). Other popular, upbeat songs that mentioned sunshine or the sun were the Beatles "Good Day Sunshine" and "Here Comes The Sun." In Harrison's "Here Comes The Sun," the Beatles sang about smiles returning to people's faces and it seemed "like years since the sun was here."The Lovin' Spoonful sang in "Daydream" about "blowing the day to take a walk in the sun. "

Lucky summer vacationers all over the U. S. had those ocean or lake resorts to go to. Baltimoreans had beach vacations at Ocean City, MD or Rehoboth Beach or Bethany Beach, DE., or Wildwood, NJ or Virginia Beach,VA. We had live band dances at the Pier Ballroom near the southern end of Ocean City's boardwalk where *Ripley's Believe It or Not Museum* now resides.The Beach Boys and the Rolling Stones and other groups' hit singles poured out from the boardwalk's pizza shops' jukebox speakers. Nothing compared to the beach and boardwalk for the girls watching boys and the boys watching the girls. (When I said to a teen boy flipping pizza dough at Tony's Pizza on the O. C. boardwalk in 2002, "I bet you love this job? " he said,"This is the best job in Ocean City, maybe anywhere" as he looked out at the girls walking by on the boardwalk.)We vacationers thought we died and went to heaven when we were there. Other lucky teens worked there all summer.The Drifters sang in "Under The Boardwalk" about that board- walk food aroma being so good you could "almost taste the hot dogs and French fries." For many of us beachgoers to Ocean City, MD that song con- jures up the smell of Old Bay seasoning and apple cider vinegar served with

Thrasher's Fries there with long lines then, and long lines still formed there in 2018.

Songs about summer and the beach and others that mention that happy ingredient, sunshine, often placed high on the BB Hot 100 chart. The Drifters' "Under The Boardwalk (1964)" was the number one R&B song for three weeks, the Lovin' Spoonful's "Summer In The City (1966)" was number one for three weeks, Sly and the Family Stone's "Hot Fun In The Summertime (1969)" was number two for two weeks, and Mungo Jerry's "In The Summertime" peaked at number 3 in 1970.

36

Novelty and comedy songs

♪

THE '50S AND '60S ALSO HAD THEIR SHARE of novelty and comedy songs that provided listeners with some honest-to-goodness fun. These songs were often played when we were with friends and family, but we surely enjoyed them even when we were alone. Some of the songs had off-the-wall themes. David Seville's (born Ross Bagdasarian) "The Witch Doctor" known by some as the "ting tang walla walla bing bang song," was popular in 1958, with an 18-week stay on the BB Hot 100, including three weeks at number one. Sheb Wooley's "Purple People Eater" was number one on the BB Hot 100 for 6 weeks in mid-1958. People often joined in singing with this record when it played on the radio and over time it has become one of the classic favorites every Halloween. Gary Paxton's "Alley Oop (1960)" (issued under the recording group name, The Hollywood Argyles), was on the BB Hot 100 for 15 weeks, including one week at number one and was on the R&B chart for 9 weeks. Paxton's "Alley Oop" was based on a caveman who had starred in a syndicated comic strip of the same name beginning in 1932. Lonnie Donegan's "Does Your Chewing Gum Lose Its Flavor (On the Bedpost Over Night) (1961)" had an 11-week run on the BB Hot 100 and it peaked at number 5. My mother enjoyed this quirky song's lyrics when it played on her kitchen radio in Randolph in 1961, so she let it play through. Bobby "Boris" Pickett and the Crypt-Kickers' "Monster Mash" was released in September 1962, and it reached number one for

147

two weeks in October just before Halloween. The "Monster Mash" featured Pickett's carbon copy imitation of Boris Karloff's voice. Pickett lip-synced his song on Dick Clark's *Bandstand* and the song was featured in October 1965 on *Shindig!* with Boris Karloff. It's been a staple song of Halloween every year since '62 and it still appears on Halloween CDs and greeting cards that have recorded music (i. e., part of a song). Allan Sherman's "Hello Mudduh, Hello Fadduh (A Letter from Camp)" made it to the HT 100 chart in 1963, and the AC chart in 1964, and it connected with many youngsters like me who spent a weekend or week at summer camp those two years. Parents were often glad to see one of their children go off to camp, but then they worried about their children much of the time they were away from home. The Detergents' "Leader Of The Laundromat (1964)" was a parody of The Shangri-Las' "Leader Of The Pack." The lead singer met his new girlfriend at the laundromat, but her shirts always turned out brown. His dad finally told him he had to find a new laundry, so the singer had to tell his girlfriend that they were "through." It rose all the way to number 19 on the BB Hot 100, but only lasted 8 weeks. Like many novelty songs it was funny at first, but listeners tired of it quickly. Jonathan King's "Everyone's Gone To The Moon" in 1965, made us stop and think what it would be like to wake up to a world deserted, except for one of us. We knew that scientists felt certain there was no oxygen to support life on the moon, but some of the lyrics in King's song were eerie because they made it easy to relate to the circumstances of "no one being around" after a nuclear attack, a fear we still had because of the Cold War between the U. S. and the U. S. S. R. Napoleon XIV's "They're Coming To Take Me Away, Ha-Haaa! (1966)" made it on the BB Hot 100 and peaked at number 3, but it was only on the hit chart for six weeks. The singer chastised his former lover for leaving him because he was losing his mind and on his way to the funny farm where the men (workers) wore white jackets. Ray Stevens had a series of novelty songs, the most popular being "Ahab, the Arab (1962)," "Gitarzan (1969)" and "The Streak (1974)." "The Streak" was released on the heels of a frenzy of streaking (nude runs) by college students at various campuses nationwide from 1972-1974.

We sang along with parts of some songs like "The Witch Doctor" and "Hello Muddah, Hello Fadduh" or the whole song like, "The Name Game (1964)." Shirley Ellis's (born Shirley Elliston) "Name Game" reached number 3 and stayed on the BB Hot 100 for 14 weeks. Pre-teens and teens loved memorizing and singing along with Shirley's rhyming in "The Name Game." We even added our own set of names to the song's original name list that lengthened the song as much or as little as we wanted.

Eddie Byrnes and Connie Stevens issued "Kookie, Kookie (Lend Me Your Comb) (1959)" during Stevens' starring role on *Hawaiian Eye* and Byrnes' popularity as "Kookie" on the TV show, *77 Sunset Strip*. Their appearance on *Bandstand* (on YouTube) in 1959, shows that Byrnes' popularity with teen girls was soaring at the time. While Byrnes and Stevens lip-synched their parts, any sneer, grin, or look by Byrnes their way prompted many girls in the studio audience to scream and hold their heads like they hurt in much the same way many girls acted at Elvis Presley concerts. The song was a spin-off of Byrnes' character on the TV show where he was obsessed with combing his hair and played a parking valet and a private investigator. For some reason that maybe only girls can explain, his hair combing excited them, drove them wild. It didn't hurt that Byrnes exuded "cool" in the way he cocked his head while combing his ducktail haircut, and his grin excited them. Byrnes' effect on the girls was no different than Nancy Sinatra's effect on the boys (and there are countless other examples). When Nancy sang her "These Boots Are Made For Walkin'" on her video with several other girl dancers in 1966, she oozed sexy, cute and cool to the point that guys thought, "I wish she would walk all over *me*, wow!"

Other comedy/novelty songs played in one way or the other with that familiar love theme. Ernie K–Doe's "Mother–In–Law (1961)" depicted some guys' mother–in laws being a real-life nightmare, and Joe Tex's "Skinny Legs And All (1967)" sang about some guys avoiding that girl with the skinny legs (while many guys in real life loved them). Herman's Hermits surprised many listeners when their single, "Henry The VIII, I Am (1965)" made the BB Hot 100, and it peaked at number one for one week. In this song the singer's name is Henry and he just got married to the widow living next door who had already been married seven times before and every former husband's name was Henry. It was another song that peaked high, but only lasted on the hit chart for ten weeks. It did not have staying power compared to some songs that were on the BB Hot for up to 18 to 25 weeks.

37

Christmas songs

♪

RECORD COMPANIES AND RECORDING ARTISTS recognized throughout the 20th century that Christmas created a large seasonal market for music to celebrate the holiday. Some Christmas songs of the '50s were so popular that more songwriters, recording artists and companies felt compelled to make their mark on the holiday in the '60s. In the '50s and '60s, we heard Eartha Kitt's "Santa Baby (1953)," Barry Gordon's "Nuttin' For Christmas (1955)," Bobby Helms' "Jingle Bell Rock (1957)," Elvis Presley's "Blue Christmas (1957)," The Chipmunks (with David Seville's) "The Chipmunk Song (1958)," The Harry Simeone Chorale's "The Little Drummer Boy (1958)" and Chuck Berry's "Run, Run Rudolph (1958)" on mainstream popular music stations. I don't remember ever hearing The Drifters' cover of "White Christmas (1954)" on AM radio in the '50s or even in the mid-60s at Christmas time, except on soul/R&B AM stations in Baltimore in 1967-68. It instantly became my favorite version of "White Christmas" and still is. Its doo wop sound was peppier, much more fun to listen to, and sing along with when it came on the radio compared to other covers of the song. When I was seven years old in Randolph (suburb of Boston) in 1958, mom and dad instantly realized how much my brothers and I liked "The Chipmunk Song" on the radio and bought the 45-record. We played that record enough for three or more weeks so that my mother was relieved when it was time to put it away until next Christmas.

Some late '50s and early '60s Christmas songs had a rock and roll or R&B sound to them while others were more mainstream pop music favored by our parents. Chuck Berry's "Run, Run Rudolph (1958)," Brenda Lee's "Rockin' Around the Christmas Tree (1960)," and Bobby Helms' "Jingle Bell Rock (1960)" built on the growing craze over rock and roll since the mid—'50s. If anyone in the music industry including music critics were asked in the '60s, do you think these songs will still be popular 50 years from now at Christmas, what would they have said? R&B singer Charlie Brown's "Please Come Home For Christmas (1961)" had a doo wop sound and received little airplay on white mainstream popular music stations while building a heavy following by black listeners of black radio stations.

Other popular Christmas songs in the '60s did not fit the rock and roll or R&B genre, but many adults liked them because they were released by artists who often had hit records on the AC chart. Nat King Cole's cover of "The Christmas Song (Chestnuts Roasting On An Open Fire)" was originally subtitled "Merry Christmas To You" and was first recorded by the Nat King Cole Trio in 1946. Cole re-recorded it in 1961 (that's the version that has been played on the radio and on most Christmas LPs ever since then). Two of Andy Williams' most enduring Christmas songs "It's The Most Wonderful Time Of The Year" and "Happy Holiday/The Holiday Season" were issued in 1963. Other '60s Christmas songs that still received heavy airplay in 2017 included Frank Sinatra and Bing Crosby's "We Wish You The Merriest (1964)," Burl Ives' "Holly Jolly Christmas (1964)," Percy Faith and His Orchestra and Chorus "We Need A Little Christmas (1966)" and Jose Feliciano's "Feliz Navidad (1970)." It seemed any recording artist worth their salt released one or more Christmas LPs that occasionally had songs that have had staying power. The album, *A Christmas Gift for You* (from Phil Spector) (1963) featured the Ronettes, The Crystals, Darlene Love, and Bob B. Soxx and The Blue Jeans, and has remained a staple of radio stations at Christmas for over 50 years.

38

Songs about things we did in the '60s

♪

OPULAR MUSIC'S THEMES OR LYRICS are often historical because many songs center around sayings or concepts or ways of doing things that were part of life when a song was written. In a sense, many of them become mini audio time capsules. So, it's no surprise that some of those topics in the '60s and early '70s bring back memories of the way we lived, things we did or popular sayings we used then. If those fads or ways of living are no longer commonplace today, they raise questions for younger people hearing those songs. Sonny and Cher's "The Beat Goes On (1967)" rattled off "current" things like the term "supermarket"—a new term for the larger food or grocery stores, electric baseball scoreboards (replacing the hand operated ones), boys still marching off to War (Vietnam), mini-skirts, and teeny boppers. Sayings and words of the '60s that found their way into song titles and songs included: "groovy," "feelin' groovy," "cool," "sock it to me baby," "uptight," "out of sight," "whip it on me," "a love in," "make out," "make up," "break up," "soul," "soul man," "it's a gas" and "the beat goes on." In the late '60s, "peace," "can you dig it," "far out," and "psych out" abounded.

As preteens and teens, before we had our driver's license, we often walked up and down the street to go somewhere, get some fresh air or just see some other teens. My family lived in a sweet spot for teenagers off Carlisle Avenue in between Ebenezer Road and Joppa Road in Perry Hall. We had Belair Road and Perry Hall Elementary School and the first Perry Hall High School (just east of the elementary school), about one-fourth of a mile to our west, the second Perry Hall High just one-half mile to our southeast, and the best teen hangout spot of all, Perry Hall Shopping Center about one-fourth of a mile to our west. I collected subscribers' payments for the *Baltimore Sun* as my first paying job, so I met many of our neighbors on my route near our house. Knowing the family names and meeting many of the parents made me feel more connected to the neighborhood. Girls constantly walked the neighborhood, boy watching, and the boys did the same, girl watching.

We liked those songs in the '60s about guys ogling a girl, or girls watching a guy walking down the street. It's no wonder some of those girls seemed to wiggle while they walked, on purpose. The Crystals' "He's A Rebel" and The Shangri-Las' "Give Him A Great Big Kiss (1965)" gave the girls a chance to sing-along with a song about a girl ogling a guy. Bruce Channel sang in his number one 1962 hit "Hey! Baby" about seeing his baby walking down the street. The R&B group, The Jellybeans (wow what a name!) sang "I Wanna Love Him So Bad" in 1964 about a guy living in a girl's neighborhood who looks so good and how she wished he would let her make him happy. Peter and Gordon sang in "I Go To Pieces" about seeing his former girlfriend comin' down the street and the sight of her making him feel shaky and weak. Manfred Mann sang in "Do Wah Diddy Diddy" about a girl walking down the street, snapping her fingers and shuffling her feet, singing, "Do Wah Diddy Diddy Dum Diddy Do." Roy Orbison sang in "Oh, Pretty Woman" about a woman walking down the street that he'd like to meet who surprised him by stopping, turning around and walking back towards him (to meet him). The song's drum beat felt just like a teens' brisk pace of walking. The Box Tops' 17-year old lead singer Alex Chilton sang in "Cry Like A Baby" about how he passed his former girlfriend on the street, and she just walked on by, and his heart just fell to his feet, and he began to cry. Many guys liked The O'Kaysions' "Girl Watcher" for its brash opening admission, "I'm a girl watcher!" We related to the bit about "here comes one now," and the singer "got rid of his toys and adopted a new pastime." Lead singer Donny Weaver asks the girl to walk a little slower, asks her if she knows she's putting on a show and to please walk a little closer. He sang about all the things teen guys were thinking. The Sir Douglas Quintet sang about a girl walking down the street in "She's About A Mover (1965)" and Tommy James and the Shondells sang about a girl "walking on down the line" in "Hanky Panky (1966)." Guys loved listening and singing along to songs about girl watching. We couldn't get enough of it.

I still picture those walks I took like they just happened weeks or months ago, sunny walks on Carlisle Avenue, Ebenezer and Joppa Roads. In the shopping center's stores, Gino's fast food restaurant and Berg's Farm Dairy we saw different girls all the time. Often we could not call friends on the phone in the '60s because of the limited time we could use our family's house phone. Our mothers might be using it, or we sometimes stayed off the phone to keep it open for an incoming call. Walking up and down the street was a way to reach out, find and talk with others, not social media. Because almost all teens today have their own smartphones for constant texting and calling, they probably don't walk the streets as much as teens did in the '60s. Now that texting is taking over our smartphones, teens are calling each other less even though most of them have their own phone; just a few years ago they were calling each other more often until texting became more popular.

Sometimes we wrote or received a letter in the late '50s and the '60s, but it is seldom the way teenagers (or anyone else for that matter) communicate now. Songs that were about receiving or writing a letter were, Gladys Knight and the Pips' "Letter Full Of Tears (1961)," The Marvelettes' "Please Mr. Postman (1961)," Presley's "Return To Sender (1962)," The Beatles' "P. S. I Love You (1964)" and The Box Tops' "The Letter (1967)." We had hand-delivered letters passed along to us by a girlfriend in school or if we were separated long distance for a while, boyfriends/girlfriends exchanged letters in the mail. I had a close girlfriend still in high school when I was a freshman in college in '69-'70 and I lived one and one-half hours away from her, seeing her once or twice most weekends. Back then, long distance calls were a rarity because they were expensive, and e-mail and texting did not exist, so we usually wrote one letter to each other, each week. For younger readers of this book, try to imagine life without email and texting and not being able to send a message, note, text or email and receive a response within minutes or at least during the same day. We waited many days for a letter to arrive and when it did, it might be the highlight of our day.

In the early '60s, many families had one phone that was a party line, meaning we shared use of a phone line with one or more other subscribers or families. It was almost impossible to resist listening in on someone else's phone call on a party line at least once when we were preteens or teens. Any noise you made or loud noise in your house in the background would let the people know on the line you were eavesdropping, and that ended that misbehavior.

By the mid –'60s, party lines were dropping out of use, but teens had to share their home phone with the rest of their family. There was no privacy when we made a call from home, so guys from my neighborhood often used the pay phone (with a glass enclosed folding door for privacy) in Perry Hall Lanes bowling alley in our shopping center. For a dime, you could make a local call to a girl, but if no one was home you couldn't leave a message. There were no answering machines yet. To make matters worse, many times a line began to form outside the pay phone within minutes of the start of your phone call. You better have some of your conversation rehearsed to maximize your call and avoid that dreaded air space when no one was talking on the call. Pay phones were scattered everywhere in shopping centers, gas stations and some stores, but most of them were not enclosed in booths so there was little privacy. All this meant we used phones a lot less then, and we listened to music a lot more than teens do now.

Back in the '60s we often asked the telephone company's operator for assistance on long distance calls. Chuck Berry's "Memphis, Tennessee (1958)," Jim Croce's "Operator (That's Not The Way It Feels) (1972)" and the 5th Dimension's "The Girls Song (1970)" all made pleas to the telephone operator to help them place their calls.

We memorized phone numbers routinely in the '60s. Of course, now they are stored in our mobile phones. Two similar songs placed high on the BB Hot 100 and R&B charts and had similar easy-to-remember phone numbers. The Marvelettes sang "Beechwood 4-5789" in 1962, telling a guy he can call her any time. Wilson Pickett followed with "634-5789 (Soulsville)" with a different melody and lyrics in 1966, telling a girl all she had to do was pick up a telephone and dial 634-5789.

Recently, social behavior trends sometimes change quickly. In just the past few years, teens and many people in their 20's and 30s are spending much more time listening to music on their smartphones. Just a few years ago they were listening to their playlists on handy portable iPods or another MP3 player.

39

Censorship of some songs' lyrics or banning some songs from airtime

♪

CENSORSHIP OF SOME SONG'S LYRICS or banning the playing of some songs from a radio station was prevalent in the '60s. Peter, Paul and Mary alluded to it in their hit single "I Dig Rock And Roll Music (1967)" when they sang about "saying it, but the radio won't play it, unless they lay it between the lines." Compared to today's looser standards for what is allowed visually and by audio on TV, movies, and radio, the reasons some songs were banned or censored by radio stations or TV in the '60s seem very trivial. As in any era, radio station and TV show producers were often acting within the range of the ways songs were "rated" subjectively at the time.

Sometimes, radio programmers or TV producers worried about a theme or how the song would affect teenagers. Ray Peterson's "Tell Laura I Love Her (1960)" was banned by some radio stations, possibly because it was "too sad," a song about a guy dying in a car accident while racing. The Everly Brothers "Wake Up Little Susie (1957)" was banned by some radio stations because a boyfriend/girlfriend fell asleep together in a car and were late getting the girlfriend home. Bobby Darin's "Splish Splash (1958)" was banned by some stations because it implied brief nudity as a guy walks out of a bath and into a party in the next room. The Shangri-Las' "Leader Of The Pack (1964)" was banned by ABC-TV and some stations in Great Britain because they felt the song glorified motorcycle gangs. The Who's "My Generation (1966)" was banned from playing on some radio stations in the U. K. because

157

they feared people who had stuttering problems would be offended by lead vocalist Roger Daltrey's stammering in parts of the song, sounding like a speech impediment. Some radio stations banned Barry McGuire's "Eve Of Destruction (1965)" because the song opposed the U. S. government's stance on the Vietnam War and made some listeners fearful that nuclear war was imminent. The Christian Anti-Communist crusade claimed, "the song tried to instill fear and hopelessness." Chicago's Mayor Richard Daley tried to ban radio stations from playing the Rolling Stones' "Street Fighting Man (1968)" during student demonstrations outside Chicago's Democratic National Convention in August 1968.

TV show and radio station producers in the '60s often balked at playing songs that contained words or phrases that appeared to refer to drug use. Some radio stations banned the Byrds' "Eight Miles High" in 1966, because radio programmers thought the word "high" was referring to "getting high from taking drugs." Before Jim Morrison and The Doors appeared on *Ed Sullivan* on September 17, 1967, the Show's producers asked Morrison to sing, "Girl we couldn't get much *better*, instead of much *higher* while they played "Light My Fire." When Morrison sang, "Girl we couldn't get much higher" anyway, The Doors were banned from future *Ed Sullivan* shows. Some stations banned the playing of the Beatles "Lucy In The Sky with Diamonds" because it fit the acronym of LSD and "sounded like a song that drug-enhanced listeners would enjoy." Some BBC stations banned "A Day In The Life," claiming the song contained explicit drug references. The Supremes pre-recorded "Stoned Love" for the *Merv Griffin Show*, but CBS-TV cut it from being aired in November 1970, because it feared possible drug connotations of the word "stoned" in the title and song's lyrics. The lyrics of the song do not give any hint of drugs, but paranoia was widespread among many parents and other adults about drugs and the drug culture in the mid and late '60s and the '70s.

Songs that were considered too explicit about sex were often banned by stations or censored so that lyrics had to be changed before they would be played on the radio or on TV. Some radio stations refused to play the Kingsmen's "Louie, Louie" because part of the lyrics sounded like, "At night, in bed I ... her again, (and the F word), all night and day." Rather than reduced airplay sinking the song's sales, young teen boys were often on the hunt for the "Louie, Louie" 45 in record stores so we could hear the song and try to decipher the lyrics. In late '63-early '64, it was number two on the BB Hot 100 for six weeks, and number one on the R&B chart for six weeks. Not long after the Rolling Stones' blockbuster hit "Satisfaction" was released in the U. S., some radio stations banned it, at least for a while due to "sexually suggestive lyrics." The ban by some radio stations had little effect on record sales of "Satisfaction." It was on the BB Hot 100 for 14 weeks and number one for four weeks in 1965 and remains the Stones' top selling single of the '60s. Them's (including Van Morrison) original version of "Gloria" used "and then *she comes to my room*," the trigger point for many radio stations banning Them's version of "Gloria." Them's version did not receive much airplay in 1965, peaking at number 71 and clinging to the BB Hot 100 for 7 weeks. The Shadows of the Knight's "Gloria" did much better on the BB Hot 100 in 1966 (peaking at number 10 and staying on the chart for 12 weeks), by replacing "and then she comes to my room" with "and then *she calls out my name*." Ed Sullivan did not like the connotations for teens of the Stones' "Let's Spend the Night Together (1967)" and insisted that the Stones replace the song's title when that phrase appeared in the lyrics with "Let's spend some time together" on Sullivan's January 15, 1967 show. Mick Jagger complied with Sullivan's censor, but Mick rolled his eyes while singing "spend some time together." Two years later, Jagger was not asked to alter any lyrics of "Honky Tonk Women" when singing that song on *Ed Sullivan*. Chuck Berry's live version of "My Ding-A-Ling" was banned from many U. S. radio stations in 1972, for reference to the male body part/sexual organ, but it didn't seem to affect the record's sales too much. Some record buyers figured, if I can't hear on radio, I'll buy it. "My Ding-A-Ling" stayed in the BB Top 40 for 12 weeks and was number one for two weeks.

40

Album covers, record labels, and group names

♪

Record album covers became more of an art form in the '60s, than in the '50s, and are part of the reason for the mild comeback of vinyl records in the 2000s. Album covers had a shine, an appeal all their own. Sometimes there was enough information on the back cover to lure one into buying the record. It was a ritual we enjoyed at every record store, flipping through the large LPs in alphabetical order, by band or singer, looking for something current or new and sometimes an older one that we wanted to buy. The 12-inch square cardboard album holders were big and easy for the eyes to look over. Try reading the back of many CD covers today!

Meet The Beatles! Whipped Cream and Other Delights, Disraeli Gears and Sgt. Pepper's Lonely Hearts Club Band had LP covers from the '60s that are etched in my memory the most. Each one had a special appeal to it. Cream's Disraeli Gears is my favorite one—Fluorescent pink, purple, orange and yellow splashed on the faces of Jack Bruce (in the middle) flanked by Eric Clapton and Ginger Baker, surrounded by a myriad of more pink, purple, orange, blue, yellow and green on ornamental trim of flowers, architecture, wings and the word CREAM. Meet The Beatles! had the four handsome portraits of John, George, Paul and Ringo on the cover and Sgt. Pepper's had the hodge-podge "group photo" of the Beatles (past and present versions) standing, surrounded by many U. S. celebrities we recognized and many British celebrities we could not identify. Herb Alpert's Tijuana Brass's *Whipped Cream and Other Delights* had that beautiful woman mostly covered in whipped cream staring at us.

Many other LP covers that were first issued 45 to 50 years ago, are still instantly recognizable, even if we did not own them. Among them are: The Beatles' *Rubber Soul, Revolver, Abbey Road* and the *White Album*; The Byrds' *Mr. Tambourine Man*, and Cream's *Wheels of Fire*. A few more eye-catching LP covers were the Jimi Hendrix Experience's *Are You Experienced*, the Rolling Stones' *Let It Bleed* and *Sticky Fingers* LPs, Derek and The Dominoes' *Layla and Assorted Other Love Songs*, and Led Zeppelin's first album cover with the zeppelin.

When I walked into Michael's TV & Radio each week from mid-1965 to mid-1966, the first album cover I looked for was *Whipped Cream*. Many guys—teens and older, did the same thing. How could you not look for that beautiful sexy girl covered in whipped cream? We all wished she was looking at us. Much later, we learned she was model Delores Erickson who was three months pregnant, covered in shaving cream. Many of us wouldn't dream of buying the record and taking it home with that cover, but at least we could look at it safely in Michael's. When it finally left Michael's wall of current hit albums because it was no longer on the top seller's list, I was shocked. Well, I was devastated.

Sgt. Pepper's 1967 album cover gave us plenty to think about. Listeners loved having all the album's songs' lyrics on the back cover (it was considered a huge bonus and likely the first time that had been included on an album cover). Many teens wondered, "Did the album's name, and the Beatles dressed in Sgt. Pepper's garb next to the four wax figures of the 1964-like Beatles mean they were renaming themselves 'Sgt. Pepper's'? Who were all the celebrities on the front cover? "Beatles fans studied the cover and tried to identify the colored and black and white photos of over 60 celebrities standing there with the Beatles. It was a motley group mostly from show business, philosophy, and politics. The Beatles in the center are dressed in Sgt. Pepper's garb, looking proud and dignified. The four wax figures of the Beatles on one side look sad and dull, heads looking down at the ground where "BEATLES" in red flowers looks funereal.

George Harrison's first LP, *All Things Must Pass*, after the Beatles disbanded, had a front cover that is also embedded in my mind. On the album's black and white cover, George sat on a stool in an open field with four gnomes lying sideways on the grass surrounding him and looking up at him. Some of us who owned the album or just viewed the cover in a record store figured it represented George now free of the Beatles, looking back at days of the foursome, but content sitting there looking at them.

Popular music listeners from the late '50s to the early '70s still identify certain record labels with hitmakers from those years. Each of us have different or similar associations with record labels depending on the 45s and LPs we and our parents owned. The RCA Victor label (the dog listening to "His Master's Voice") reminds me of Elvis, Sam Cooke and Neil Sedaka. Seeing a Columbia Records label reminds me of The Byrds, Gary Puckett, Simon and Garfunkel, and Paul Revere and the Raiders. Capitol Records (with the orange and yellow swirl) makes me think of The Beatles, The Beach Boys, and Nat King Cole. Atlantic Records takes me back to the Rascals, Aretha Franklin and Ray Charles. Volt Records conjures up Otis Redding for me and Stax Records with that small stack of 45s on the label makes me think of Eddie Floyd and Sam and Dave. Vee-Jay Records reminds me of some of the early Beatles and 4 Seasons hit singles. The Beatles' Apple Records had one of the most clever and cool record labels for their 45s and LPs. The label became iconic and very easy to remember with Side One being an image of the outside of a green (granny smith) apple with that side's music info on it. Side Two's image was an apple cut in half with the fresh white inside being the background for that side's song information. We played the records so often that those record label images became imprinted/embedded in our early memories.

While there were some comical or quirky names of popular music groups and songs in the '50s, it became more commonplace in the '60s. In the 50s some of these songs were in the novelty category, like "The Purple People Eater" or we had The Trashmen of "Surfin' Bird" fame. In the '60s groups' names were often variations of a common word's spelling like Beatles, Byrds, Human Beinz, or Kozmic Blues. We liked having the odd, offbeat names too, like Creedence Clearwater Revival, The Who, The Troggs, The Lovin' Spoonful, ? and The Mysterians, Canned Heat, The Guess Who, The Kinks, The Zombies, and The Yardbirds. Many of the groups with offbeat or bizarre names played psychedelic or hard rock including: Iron Butterfly, The

Thirteenth Floor Elevators, The Strawberry Alarm Clock, Steppenwolf, Moby Grape, Grateful Dead, The Electric Prunes, and The Velvet Underground. What might an electric prune look like or what did that mean? What was a Trogg? Most of us didn't know the group shortened its name to Troggs from Troglodytes (cave men).

41

Rock and roll heaven

THE '60s AND EARLY '70s WERE STREWN WITH PREMATURE DEATHS of popular music stars, many during the peak of their careers. Poor health, plane or car accidents, shootings and drug overdoses were often to blame. Music fans' pop music listening pleasure suffered when Sam Cooke died of a gunshot wound in 1964, at the age of 33, and Nat King Cole died from lung cancer at age 45 in 1965. Cooke and Nat were two of my mother's favorites and her sadness over their deaths was palpable. My mother talked about their deaths with dad and her sadness over losing them, otherwise I would not have known about their deaths because I seldom read the newspaper at that age except for the sports pages. Thus, when The Drifters' lead singer Rudy Lewis died of a heart attack (a suspected heroin overdose) in May 1964, I was not aware of it. The Drifters quickly brought back their former lead singer Johnny Moore for them to record "Under The Boardwalk (1964)," one of my favorites that summer, which first placed on the BB Hot 100 in June.

A few years later, I was more tuned in to national and international news, so I was shocked along with many other R&B/soul music fans when Otis Redding and four members of the Bar-Kays died, when his private plane crashed in December 1967. Now I knew how my mother felt when Cooke and Nat King Cole died, and how a large contingent of rock and roll fans felt in February 1959, when Buddy Holly (22), Richie Valens (17) and the Big Bopper (28) died in a plane crash, and in April 1960 when Eddie Cochran (only 21 years old) died in a car crash. Likewise, country western and popular music fans were devastated when Patsy Cline (30 years old) died in a plane crash on March 5, 1963.

Only 26, Otis had finished recording "(Sittin' On) The Dock Of The Bay" just a few days before his death. Being a big fan of his music, I wondered what could have been—how many other hit songs would he have compiled over the next few years if he hadn't taken that plane flight? Redding was in the prime of his career as a songwriter and singer. He did great covers of other groups' songs, changing the sound of those songs to suit his style. He was also an "idea man" of recording music, willing to step out of his original comfort zone of R&B/soul just before his death to record "The Dock Of The Bay." There was more of the same coming from Otis, had he not died so suddenly and so young. He wanted badly to go to the top of the BB Hot 100 and his success with "The Dock Of The Bay" would have kept him on that path of songwriting had he lived longer. A few days after Otis's death, I made a run to Michael's TV & Radio in Perry Hall Shopping Center and bought Redding's recent album release, *History of Otis Redding*, as if time was running out to get a copy. I didn't have any of his hit songs on vinyl yet, so this LP was a treasure trove of soul music. We didn't know about Redding's up and coming hit single, "Dock of the Bay"—it was issued a month later.

Motown's Frederick "Shorty" Long and Chess Records' Billy Stewart died very young from boating or car accidents. Long had some mild success as a singer/songwriter with "Devil With A Blue Dress On," "Function At The Junction," and "Here Comes The Judge" in the '60s, but he died in a boating accident on the Detroit River in June 1969, at the age of 29. Billy Stewart died in a car accident in January 1970, at age 32. He had 11 R&B chart hits in the '60s including, "I Do Love You," "Sitting In The Park" and "Summertime."

Tammi Terrell's death at age 24 (March 1970) from a brain tumor ailment stunned popular music listeners and was a great loss for soul music lovers. Tammi and Marvin Gaye had seven hit single duets in the BB Top 40 from 1967 to 1969, but she began having problems as early as October 1967, when she collapsed in Marvin's arms while they were performing at Hampden-Sydney College. Several operations during the next couple years were unsuccessful in treating her cancer.

Jimi Hendrix died from an overdose of sleeping tablets, *Vesparax* in

September 1970, Janis Joplin died of a heroin overdose exacerbated by alcohol a few weeks later, and Jim Morrison died of a drug overdose that caused heart failure in July 1971, while taking a break from the Doors. We alternated between feeling numb about the parade of deaths and hoping the barrage of lost musicians would stop for a while. Many of rock's biggest, most important performers in 1967 and beyond, had slipped away from us. Young music fans had to face up to the dark side of the performing arts industry—plenty of stress, fatigue and risky behavior and decisions when it came to drugs and alcohol.

We lost several more popular music hitmakers in the early 1970s. King Curtis died at age 37 in August 1971, when he was stabbed during an argument with two drug dealers he discovered outside his apartment in New York City. Jim Croce died at the age of 30 in a plane crash in September 1973. His hit single, "Time In A Bottle" was another posthumous number one song in December 1973, after Redding's "The Dock On The Bay" in 1968, and Joplin's "Me And My Bobby McGee" in 1971. Bobby Darin died of heart failure in December 1973, at the age of 37 and Mama Cass died of a heart attack at age 32 in July 1974, after completing a two-week singing tour in England.

The loss of so many musicians when they were young and at the peak of their popularity weighed heavily on their fellow musicians, too. Morrison sang in "Runnin' Blue" about "poor Otis" being dead and gone, and the need to find the dock on the bay. Don McLean referred to the 1959 plane crash that killed Buddy Holly, Richie Valens, and the Big Bopper as "the day the music died" in "American Pie (Parts I and II) (1971)." The Righteous Brothers dedicated their single, "Rock And Roll Heaven" in 1974 to Hendrix, Joplin, Morrison, Redding, Croce and Darin. Medley and Hatfield hoped "there's a rock and roll heaven" and concluded, if so, "well you know they have a hell of a band." They sang about Jimi giving us rainbows, Janis taking a piece of our hearts, and Otis bringing us to the dock of the bay, told us to "sing a song to 'Light My Fire'" because it was good way to remember Jim [Morrison].

Often when we hear their songs, we feel a touch of sadness even 40 years later. We "miss" them. They were only a few years older than me and my classmates. Each of these musicians had a unique presence on stage which only added to their appeal among fans. Because their posthumous hits were number one songs, we couldn't help but wonder, "what if they had lived longer? "Redding's "The Dock On The Bay," Joplin's "Me And My Bobby McGee," Croce's "Time In A Bottle" and "I'll Have To Say I Love You In A Song" are still favorites for many listeners. It can easily be argued that a posthumous hit's popularity is boosted because we feel sentimental about the recent death of the song's recording artist, but many critics and fans agree that Redding's, Joplin's and Croce's posthumous hits are among their best songs. We didn't *know* them, but we know their music and love it, and we wish they had lived a lot longer.

42

The interplay of popular music with courtship

♪

OUR SUCCESS OR FAILURE IN COURTSHIP is very important to our overall psyche and happiness, so it's surprising how much we stayed away from this subject in classes in junior high school, high school and college in the '60s and early '70s. Love relationships, premarital and marital, should have been a topic in health classes required at each of those levels of schooling. During new love relationships, we are on a three-month ride of high strung emotions, sometimes painful, but often euphoric. We don't understand that initial chemistry between us and someone else, but it sure feels good most of the time. Then, a relationship levels out a bit, probably because our bodies can't handle the high adrenaline that goes along with anxiety and excitement forever, and we find at least a few things about each other we do not like and decide whether they are minor enough to tolerate over the long run.

The most recurrent theme of popular music was love and courtship. Our '60s music gave us advice and often commiserated with us, and we often heard what we wanted to hear, interpreting the lyrics to suit our hopes and dreams. The tricky part about relying on different songs' lyrics was that it often did not apply to us because relationships were often a lot more complicated than the simple theme covered in a song.

There were plenty of songs about a love relationship going well or feeling sky high in the beginning. It's what everyone wanted (if they were willing to take a chance). While the heartbreak that came with a breakup was awful, the euphoria that came with a good relationship made many teens try again after suffering a love gone bad. Some of our '60s songs that praised the euphoria of a great (often new) relationship included: "Heaven Must Have Sent You," "My Girl," "My Guy," "Sunny," "How Sweet It Is (To Be Loved By You)," and "Your Precious Love." Others included "She'd Rather Be With Me," "(You're Love Keeps Lifting Me) Higher And Higher," "Ain't Nothing Like The Real Thing," "Can't Take My Eyes Off You," and "You've Made Me So Very Happy." Sometimes songs gave music part of the credit for making a relationship go well or just help make people happier like in "Do You Believe In Magic," "I Dig Rock And Roll Music," "I Can Hear Music," and "Listen To The Music."

Popular music in the '60s included many songs about the heartache of being the one on the short end of betrayal or a break up. The feeling you had when you lost your girlfriend/boyfriend because they wanted to move on or had already found someone new was gut wrenching, heartbreaking. The first day of a break up is the longest day of your life and the next few days aren't easy, either. Truly, you feel like your world is ending. Almost everyone goes through it at least once. Some go through it many times. If you lost or were losing someone you would rather have kept, listening to AM radio was a bit challenging at times. If some songs with lyrics about a "break up" were hit singles when you broke up with someone, we often tied them with a bad place and time in our life and changed the dial whenever it came on the radio for months, and sometimes years to come. Songs like "You've Lost That Lovin' Feelin'," "(I Know) I'm Losing You," "The Tracks Of My Tears," "Ask The Lonely," "What Becomes Of The Brokenhearted," "7 Rooms Of Gloom," "Over You," and "My Whole World Ended (The Moment You Left Me)" became radio dial changers for some listeners if we had just broken up with someone, or favorite songs for others who did not lose a boyfriend/girlfriend during the song's run on the hit charts.

Without social media in the '60s, we relied more on listening to our music to fill our time, even after a relationship "break up" than teens do now, because we spent more time "alone" without friends who were not readily available. This made songs like Simon and Garfunkel's "I Am a Rock," the Beach Boys' "In My Room," and Martha and the Vandellas' "In My Lonely Room" solitary fallbacks for us who were lonely while we listened to them, but maybe it was better than total silence.

Other songs expressed relief that a relationship was over or about to end or asked their love partner to let them go. Among them were Dylan's "Don't Think Twice," The Byrds' "I'll Feel Whole Lot Better," Glen Campbell's "By The Time I Get To Phoenix," and The Eagles' "Already Gone (1972)." The Beatles' "She's Leaving Home" was about a mother and father's sadness when they read an early morning note their daughter wrote before she left home during the night to move out and start a new life. "She's Leaving Home" and "By The Time I Get To Phoenix" both had a somber sound with the slow tempo, string instruments and sadness in McCartney's and Campbell's voices. The Byrds' up-tempo sound along with lyrics in "I'll Feel A Whole Lot Better" made it clear that a guy was relieved and even happy that he was finally leaving a girl who had two-timed him. The Supremes' "You Keep Me Hanging On" had a beat and guitar riff that sounded like an SOS message giving the song a sense of urgency. Diana Ross's voice and the other Supremes sang the song with that same rush, that same frustration with that boy or man who was the target of the song.

We've always valued honesty and faithfulness as one of the most important traits our love partner can have for obvious reasons. This is especially true once the initial crush or three-month honeymoon period of a relationship is over. The Castaways' "Liar, Liar (1965)," The Knickerbockers' "Lies," The Beatles' "No Reply (1964)," and Derek and The Dominoes "Tell The Truth (1970)" sang about the frustration the singer felt because their love partner or former love partner told lies or was not telling the truth. Nancy Sinatra sings in "These Boots Are Made For Walkin'" that she's sick and tired of her two-timing, lying boyfriend and her boots that were made for walkin' are ready to walk all over him. She's had enough already. More than a few listeners identified with the frustration in those songs while others hearing them were relieved we weren't dealing with it.

Often guys loved when girls, or girls loved when guys they were pursuing, were a challenge. The "hard to get" approach and unpredictability of someone you were trying to make your boyfriend or girlfriend made it more exciting, especially in the beginning of a relationship. The Classics IV's "Spooky," and The Eagles' "Witchy Woman" personified the fun, but eerie feeling that went along with the territory of a girlfriend or boyfriend who was unpredictable. Marvin Gaye's "Ain't That Peculiar (1965)" sang about how he loved a girl even though she hurt him more and more.

In the '60s, sometimes we heard through friends that our

boyfriend/girlfriend had found someone new. Often what we heard was true or parts of a story were true and parts of it were not. It was like the exercise in a classroom when a teacher told the first student in the first row a short sentence and one by one the rest of the students passed along the sentence to the next one until it reached the last student in the room. By the time the sentence reached the last person of twenty or so students, and the final student repeated it out loud, the sentence had changed radically. We were often surprised and embarrassed how fast girlfriend-boyfriend news traveled. Sometimes, within a few days everyone seemed to know about it, but it traveled slower than in today's world of texting and other social media. The trouble with the grapevine then and now, is if a story is wrong, it can still spread just as rapidly as the truth and then it's difficult to undo the false rumor for a while. The Temptations' "It's Growing (1965)" sang about how quickly a story could change, "like the tale by the time it's been told by more than one—it's growing." "I Heard It Through The Grapevine" epitomized what we were up against if we heard bad news that was accurate, by word of mouth instead of directly from our girlfriend or boyfriend. Gladys Knight and the Pips' cover of the song was from the girl's point of view. It was on the BB Hot 100 and R&B charts seventeen weeks beginning in late '67 (it reached number 2 on the HT chart and was number one for six weeks on the R&B chart). Then, Marvin Gaye sang the song from the guy's point of view in 1968 (it stayed number one on the BB Hot 100 and R&B charts for seven weeks). In The Eagles' "Already Gone (1974)," the singer begins the song by saying he heard people talking just the other day and they heard "you're gonna put me on the shelf," prompting him to beat her to the punch and leave her first.

Teens were often frustrated when their parents passed off strong feelings they had for a boyfriend or girlfriend as simply infatuation or a teenage crush. Parents sometimes said, "you have strong feelings now, but you'll see, it will pass." In "Teenage Crush," Tommy Sands sings about how they (parents) call his feelings for a girlfriend a [typical] teenage crush, it won't last. Ricky Nelson sang in "Teenager's Romance" about how they (parents) say we don't have the right to decide for ourselves. He insisted teens' love feelings for each other could be just as strong and real as anyone who was older. Proof for that lies in some of my high school classmates—out of a graduating group of about 440 members in 1969, at least sixteen are still married to their high school boyfriends/girlfriends 49 years later, and they're proud of it.

Teen's had to deal with their boyfriends' or girlfriends' parents. A boy's mother was sometimes protective, but his parents often didn't meet a new girlfriend right away, rather it was often if the guy and girl had been dating for a while, then a guy's parents finally met his girlfriend. In Smokey Robinson's "Shop Around (1961)," his mother advised him to make sure that his girl really loved him, was true to him and "not to get sold on the very first one." And there was the anxiety and uncertainty Bobby Taylor and the Vancouvers sang about in "Does Your Mama Know About Me? (1968)." Guys had to deal with their girlfriend's fathers and mothers more often, especially the nerve-wracking first time meeting them when picking up a girl for their first date, much the way it was portrayed in the 2000 movie *Meet the Parents*. Some of those girls' fathers were every bit as intimidating as the grim-faced *Meet the Parents'* Robert DeNiro. Guys strongly valued the approval of their girlfriends' parents and a girl's mother could be a guy's best ally. The best that most guys could hope for from most girls' dads was that they felt neutral about a boyfriend. Dads usually took a longer time than mothers to warm up to their daughters' boyfriends (it might not be much different today). In The Lovin' Spoonful's "Did You Ever Have To Make Up Your Mind? ," a girl's father sees a boy confused about whether he favors his new found girl friend or her older sister and the girls' father tells him to go home and make up his mind.

Many parents in the '50s and '60s set an 11 or 11:30 pm curfew for their teen daughters to be home from a date. The penalty for missing a curfew could be severe. Two of my high school girl classmates said the worst restriction they could suffer was being forbidden from going to Teen Center. It's no wonder so many girls' parents didn't want their daughters still out on a date at midnight or later. Songs about midnight were plentiful in the '60s, including Pickett's "In the Midnight Hour (1965)"—that's when his "love would come tumbling down" and "he'd do all the things he told her." Eric Clapton proclaimed in "After Midnight (1970)" they would "do things to cause talk and suspicion, and "find out what it's all about." The Grassroots sang in "Midnight Confessions (1968)" about a guy finally telling a girl how he felt at midnight, telling her about how much he loved her, even though she was already wearing a ring.

Some songs were more direct, often getting right to the point about the singer's wishes from his girlfriend or her boyfriend. Sometimes their chief hopes or demands were in the song's title like, Jr. Walker telling the object of his affection, "Pucker Up Buttercup," Mel Carter singing "Hold Me, Thrill Me, Kiss Me." The Lovin' Spoonful sang in "Wild About My Lovin'" that a girl better "bring it" with her if she wanted to be his girlfriend. Tommy James and the Shondells' "I Think We're Alone Now (1967)" sang about that frequent obsession that teenage boyfriend-girlfriend couples felt —the need to get away from everyone, especially parents, at night, in the dark when anything sexual could happen. The song took you "there," putting the sound of crickets chirping and hearts beating (drum beating) without any other sounds near the end of the song. It made you want to go there with her or him, as soon as you could, tonight if possible!

Songs often advised us to be patient and things would work out for the better. "Too Many Fish In The Sea" told us: not to waste time on a girl (the Young Rascals' version) or guy (the Marvelettes' cover) who doesn't love you. This song just made good common sense and we thought it must be true, but if we were in a one-sided relationship, or right on the heels of a breakup we had a hard time believing we'd find another boyfriend/girl-friend who would measure up to the one we had or were about to lose. A girl's mother in "You Can't Hurry Love" told her to slow down and relax and not look so hard and fast for that new love. It will come, "it's a game of give and take." The message was, loneliness won't last forever.

Guys talked about girls all the time just like girls talked about guys— we seemed almost obsessed with it. Girls tended to be more open and honest with their closest friends and guys were often more private about their deep-down feelings, putting on a front like everything was okay, smooth sailing, even when it wasn't. Guys seemed more embarrassed about sharing doubts, misgivings, and true feelings. It's no surprise that many guys identified with Simon and Garfunkel's "I Am a Rock."

If we were in a love relationship that was one-sided and not healthy to stay in, we often held on because our love or attraction for that other person was too strong to let go. Some '60s songs covered that dilemma, with Mo-town leading the way. Many teen lovers (and older) on the wrong side of a relationship identified with "Ain't That Peculiar," "Ain't Too Proud To Beg," "This Old Heart Of Mine (Is Weak For You)," "I Can't Help Myself," and "You Really Got A Hold on Me" when they heard them at Teen Center or on the radio.

Some songs advised guys to stop putting so much importance on how good looking a girl was and connect with a girl's personality, dependability and loyalty. But where were the songs with the same theme about guys sung by women? These songs served as a warning—beware, those good-looking girls are an instant magnet (they always have been and always will be), but you better put plenty of stock in who they are, what kind of person they are. Jimmy Soul went so far as to say in "If You Wanna Be Happy (1964)" to never make a pretty woman your life, rather get an ugly girl to marry you. The Temptations warned in "Beauty Is Only Skin Deep (1966)" that "if you're looking for a lover, don't judge a book by its cover."

Guys often thought it was admirable, macho or the safe thing to do (emotionally) by "playing the field" and not staying loyal to just one girl, or not staying in one place too long. Yet, girls who did the same were instantly labeled with a bad reputation (another unfair double standard for women in the '60s). Dion's "The Wanderer (1961)," Jr. Walker's "(I'm A) Road Runner (1966)" and The Bob Seger System's "Ramblin' Gamblin' Man (1968)" made it sound acceptable for guys to play the field and be on the run, and Dion's "Runaround Sue (1961)" chastised a girl who did the same. The Eagles' "Take It Easy (1972)" continued the trend that it was okay for guys to be on the move and have more than one girl interested in them.

Sometimes we just didn't know where to begin or how to jump-start a new relationship with someone we liked or had a crush on. The Temptations sang about that dilemma in "I Can't Get Next To You" and Jr. Walker and the All Stars wrestled with it in "What Does It Take (To Win Your Love)."

Songs often asked for forgiveness or one more chance. The Temptations sang about it in "All I Need" and "(Loneliness Made Me Realize) It's You That I Need," and The Chairmen of the Board's 'Give Me Just A Little More Time" and Stevie Wonder's "Signed, Sealed Delivered, I'm Yours" asked for more time or another chance. The Buckinghams' "Hey Baby (They're playing Our Song)" implored a guy's former lover that we should get back together, after all, that's where we belong. Robert Knight pleaded with his former lover who he neglected to give him another chance in "Everlasting Love."

Sometimes we took too long to let someone know how we felt about them, and now someone was in front of us in the cue to win her or his heart. They were just too much in demand—others were literally waiting in line to swoop them up. The Soul Survivors sang in "Expressway To Your Heart" that he had been trying to get to her for a long time, but his timing was off because there were too many competitors for her heart—it was like rush hour, way too crowded.

Some songs sang about the euphoria we felt if our former lover was giving us another chance. The Box Tops "The Letter" and Edwin Starr's "Twenty-Five Miles" sang about the high energy excitement they felt when their former lovers asked them to come back home, and the intense urgency they felt whether it was getting a plane ticket right away or to start making that long walk home. They felt a need to act fast before she changed her mind. Dave Clark Five's "Come Home (1965)" sang that there was only one thing he wanted to do and that was to come home, "as long as I know, I'm coming to you."

Songs about girls who were sixteen or seventeen were a recurring theme in popular music because that's when many girls came into full flower. Often the three-month period between the end of one school year in June and a new one the following September was enough time for a girl's appearance and confidence to change markedly. We didn't see some girls during summer break and were amazed how much they changed by the time school re-started. Some of the best-selling singles about girls this age, were: Chuck Berry's "Sweet Little Sixteen (1958);" The Crests' "16 Candles (1958)," Sam Cooke's "Only Sixteen (1959)," and Ringo Starr's "You're Sixteen (1973)." Girls observed the same changes with many teen boys in that short period of time. I don't recall any songs recorded from a young teen girl's point of view about teen boys looking a lot older after just a few months passed by.

Guys who were seniors in high school often dated a girl in the eleventh or tenth grade, and they still do for that matter. They rarely dated a girl in ninth grade and dating a girl four years younger was taboo. A few songs lamented from the guys' point of view, about the frustration they felt if they were attracted to a girl who they felt was too young for them to date, but songs covering the frustration that a younger girl felt when she wanted to date an older guy are hard to find. Many of the older baby boomers heard the Coasters' "Young Blood" on the radio in 1957, and how "he" couldn't get her out of his mind. Bobby Vee and the Strangers issued "Come Back When You Grow Up" in 1967, with that earlier '60s sound of the Elvis look-a-likes and the same message as Steve Lawrence's "Go Away Little Girl (1963)." John Sebastian wrote "Younger Girl" in 1965, for the Lovin' Spoonful's debut album *Do You Believe in Magic*, but the band never released it as a single. Both the Critters and the Hondells cherry-picked "Younger Girl" from the LP *Do You Believe in Magic* and issued singles in 1966, with modest success on the BB Hot 100 peaking at number 42 and number 52, respectively. The Lovin' Spoonful's version has always sounded better to me. It would have been a good B-side for the groups' first hit single, "Do You Believe In Magic" or a hit single of its own. Sebastian sang about the age difference not being important in a few more years, but for the time being it was. Still, he kept thinking about that "younger girl" and couldn't get her off his mind. Gary Puckett and the Union Gap's "Young Girl" peaked at number 2 for three weeks in 1968, and it was on the BB Hot 100 for 15 weeks, selling over a million copies. Puckett told the young(er) girl to (please) get out of here before he had time to "change his mind" and try to be with her. He was afraid they would "go too far" and declared his love for her was "way out of line. "

On the flip side of the age and gender difference issue, many guys who were my tenth-grade classmates in high school marveled at the beauty, personality and maturity of some of our school's senior girls, who were generally off limits for sophomore guys to date or pursue as a girlfriend. Fifty years later, when David, Jabber and I looked together at our high school yearbook from our sophomore year for few minutes, we pointed out many of those senior girls who we admired or had a crush on. I'm not aware of any songs that covered the theme of teen guys admiring slightly older teen girls.

Some guys and girls in their late teens or their twenties were as interested in a potential girlfriend or boyfriend's money as they were the person themselves, or they were just obsessed with money. Before he frequently wrote songs for Motown artists with Norman Whitfield (especially for The Temptations), Barrett Strong's "Money (1960)" placed high on the R&B chart at number 2 and was on that chart 21 weeks (it also peaked at number 23 and stayed on the BB Hot 100 for 17 weeks). He sang about that old saying that "the best things are life are free," but he figured you can keep them for the birds and bees, because they don't pay the bills. Above all, he wanted money. In "First I Look At The Purse (1965)," the Contours sang about how some fellas look at the eyes, nose, size, clothes, smiles, legs, hairstyles or the waist but the song's singers looked at the purse, first. They were obsessed with money. Johnnie Taylor sang in "Cheaper To Keep Her (1973)" that if you're thinking of two timing your wife, you better think again. Wait till you're in front of the judge!

In the Rendezvous Inn in College Park, MD in 1972-73, college guys and girls played a cover (but not Kane's Cousins' 1969 version) of "Take Your Love And Shove It" on the jukebox when they were on the short end of a love affair gone bad. Often, as soon as it started playing, some of us sitting there drinking a beer, caught a glimpse of the song player, looked at each other and just nodded, "yep, there's another one [busted up couple]!"

Songs in the late '50s and early '60s often zeroed in on a kiss or kissing while avoiding any mention of intercourse, but when the late '60s came, anything about making love/intercourse was fair game. We went from J. Frank Wilson's "The Last Kiss (1964)" and Brian Hyland's "Sealed With A Kiss (1962)" to Wayne Fontana and The Mindbenders' "Game Of Love (1965)" and Jewel Akens' "The Birds And The Bees (1965)." Then came The Rolling Stones' "Let's Spend The Night Together (1967)" and "Honky Tonk Women (1969)" and Led Zeppelin's "Whole Lotta Love (1969)." While the titles were mildly suggestive, there were no explicit lyrics in "The Game Of Love" and "The Birds And Bees." The theme in "Let's Spend The Night Together" was more direct and the lyrics in "Honky Tonk Women" and "Whole Lotta Love" were more explicit. Along with the song's lyrics, "Whole Lotta Love's" sound effects (Robert Plant's moaning and groaning and the guitar and drums) simulated a sexual climax. Long before *Viagra* and *Cialis*, Howard Tate's "Look At Granny Run, Run (1966)" told the story of grandpa getting a "brand new pill." The doctor told grandpa, "son, you ain't over the hill," and now grandpa can't sit still—look at granny run, run, because grandpa's chasing her over the hill.

43

Musicians competing and learning from each other

♪

MUSICIANS ARE ALWAYS LISTENING TO EACH OTHER, hoping to learn a few new ideas or approaches for their own music, and they listen to a wide variety of songs for their own pleasure. Keith Richards summed it up in a nutshell, "Anything you ever heard comes out in what you play." Musicians depended more on their own record collections in the '60s, because they didn't always have other media to play a song on demand like we have now. The Rascals' lead singer Felix Cavalierre recalled the importance of 45-records to musicians in the '60s: "Nowadays, you have places where you can study this music, but back then, we learned from playing our 45s. Those records in those days were like gold [to us]. George Harrison had many of his favorite 45-records on his own jukebox in late 1965, including many R&B songs (four 45s by Otis Redding, three by Booker T. and The MGs, two by Joe Tex, and at least one each by James Brown, The Miracles, The Four Tops and Jackie Wilson).

Sometimes singers sang about some of their peers they admired. Writing "Sweet Soul Music," Otis Redding rattled off several soul singers and one of their hit singles, each, for singer Arthur Conley to salute: Lou Rawls and "Love's A Hurtin' Thing," Sam and Dave and "Hold On! I'm A Comin'"; Wilson Pickett and "Mustang Sally," and Otis Redding and his "Fa-Fa-Fa-Fa-Fa-Fa-Fa." "Sweet Soul Music" also asserted that "James Brown was the king of them all." Likewise, Dyke and The Blazers reeled off Ray Charles, James Brown, Johnnie Taylor, Aretha, Nancy Wilson and Pearl Bailey as examples of premier soul performers of the day in their 1969 hit single, "We Got More Soul."

Musicians often based at least a portion of their next song's sound on a recent hit single they liked, or they often openly declared they were on a mission to top a new group's hit single or album. Brian Wilson wrote surfing lyrics for "Surfin' U. S. A." to the rhythm and melody of Chuck Berry's "Sweet Little Sixteen" for the Beach Boys' first top ten song in the BB Hot 100 it in 1963. Driving down Los Angeles' Sunset Boulevard in 1963, Wilson heard the Ronettes' "Be My Baby" on the radio for the first time, pulled over and had a fit over the song. Instantly, he knew he had to find a way to use those layers of sound by the song's producer Phil Spector in his next recording. In short order, Brian used some of the musicians from the Wrecking Crew who played on "Be My Baby" for his new song, "Don't Worry Baby." On our local jukeboxes in Perry Hall, we heard "Don't Worry Baby" as often as the 45 record's A-side, "I Get Around." Likewise, Wilson was inspired to up the ante in his production of "Good Vibrations" in 1966, because he admired the sound of the Righteous Brothers' "You've Lost That Lovin' Feelin' (1965)" (another Phil Spector production). Meanwhile, Mike Love based "Good Vibrations'" lyrics on the popularity of psychedelic music coming out of San Francisco and Los Angeles.

The Beatles' *Rubber Soul* inspired the Beach Boys' Brian Wilson so much that he labored long and hard and put his band mates through torture before finishing his response, *Pet Sounds*. To some, *Pet Sounds* had a warmer and more inspirational sound than *Rubber Soul*. "Wouldn't It Be Nice," "Sloop John B," and "God Only Knows" took the Beach Boys away from surfing and cars at a time in their career when a change in their sound and themes of their songs kept them relevant. "Good Vibrations" was also recorded during the *Pet Sounds* sessions and was released as a single, but not included in the album. By some accounts from the Beach Boys they spent over 90 hours re-recording "Good Vibrations." In 2004, *Rolling Stone* ranked it the sixth greatest song of all time.

In turn, the Beatles had high praise for *Pet Sounds*. Paul McCartney recalled: "We loved the Beach Boys. It was a bit of competition across 'the pond'. So, we listened to *Pet Sounds* and I said, "Listen to what they're doing here. So, we did *Sgt. Peppers*." Just a few days after *Sgt. Peppers* was released,

Jimi Hendrix played *Sgt. Pepper's* intro/theme song from that LP at his next live performance. Talk about promoting the album!

The Beatles *Sgt. Pepper's* sent shock waves through the popular music recording industry and popular music listeners everywhere. Roger Waters of Pink Floyd recalled: "We were driving off to a gig in an old Zephyr Four. And *Sgt. Peppers* came on the radio for the first time. And we pulled off onto the side of the road [to listen to it]. And I remember we just looked at each other [Like, wow, the Beatles did it]. That's the kind of thing we should be trying to do. "Waters added, "You know I couldn't wait to hear the songs again. Suddenly, there was an album that was like a theatrical production. But here were songs that were about our hopes and fears, an album about life and our feelings. In that sense, the album opened up Pandora's Box for everybody." Roger Daltrey said: "The way George Martin had musically put that [*Sgt. Peppers*] together, I thought, where do we go from here? "Two years later, the Who issued a legitimate answer and show stopper, the rock opera, *Tommy*.

The sound of the orchestra in The Beatles' "Hey Jude" (and probably in the earlier, "A Day In The Life") impressed Mick Jagger and prompted him to use The London Bach Choir in "You Can't Always Get What You Want," the B-side of the Stones' hit single "Honky Tonk Women." How many buyers bought this 45-record in part because of the B-side? As is often the case with B-sides for 45 records, it's hard to measure the role a B-side's popularity plays in a hit single's record sales. The single of "You Can't Always Get What You Want" was slightly less than 5 minutes long without the Choir's intro; the longer LP cut on *Let It Bleed* included the intro. Most listeners I knew, liked the LP cut better.

After Otis Redding co-wrote "Respect" in 1965, he recorded a raucous version that we loved to dance to when soul bands played it at Teen Center. Its rapid rhythm/beat for dancing helped it reach number 4 on the R&B chart and made it "a must, to be on the dance floor" if that was your scene. White stations did not play it often and it suffered a disappointing peak of number 35 on the BB Hot 100. Then Aretha Franklin recorded "Respect," after modifying the words with her sisters who sang the chorus, and she made it an anthem for the ladies and a number one hit on the R&B and BB Hot 100 charts in 1967. It remains a contender for the all-time greatest soul song (in 2004, *Rolling Stone* ranked it the number five greatest song of all time). Inspired by the Beatles' *Sgt. Peppers*, and songs he heard from the

Association and others at the Monterrey Pop Festival, Otis re-examined his style and wrote "(Sittin'On) The Dock of the Bay" with some help from Steve Cropper.

Paul McCartney was inspired by The Lovin' Spoonful's "Daydream" when he wrote "Good Day Sunshine" and based "Back In The U. S. S. R. " partly on advice from The Beach Boys' Mike Love. Paul played an early version of "Back In The U. S. S. R. " on guitar for Mike Love in India in 1968, while they both took a Transcendental Meditation course from the Maharishi Mahesh Yogi. Love liked what he heard, but suggested Paul add something about the girls of the U. S. S. R. much the same way the Beach Boys sang about girls in "California Girls." McCartney liked Love's idea and mentioned the "girls" of U. S. S. R. —after all, "girls" from everywhere have a universal appeal to guys.

After James Taylor auditioned with Peter Asher and Paul McCartney for Apple Records in 1968 with his song, "Something In The Way She Moves," it became one of the tracks on his Apple Records album *James Taylor*. Not long after, George Harrison used "Something in the way she moves" as the opening line in his hit song "Something" in 1969, but he gave no songwriting credit to Taylor for "Something." Taylor shrugged it off and never made a big deal out of the issue. Harrison's argument "all music is borrowed from other music" has been troublesome when court actions are lawsuits challenging the lack of songwriter credits. Bright Tunes Music, the publisher of the Chiffons' "He's So Fine" sued Harrison in court for plagiarism in 1971, because the melody of "My Sweet Lord" and "He's So Fine" was the same and they were not receiving any royalties for Harrison's song. Judge Richard Owen of the U. S. District Court found in favor in 1976 for Bright Tunes, that Harrison had subconsciously copied "He's So Fine" for "My Sweet Lord. "

Recording artists sometimes watched each other in awe. The first time that Eric Clapton and Peter Townshend saw Jimi Hendrix play guitar in England in 1967, Jimi's skills and showmanship caused plenty of concern because he was raising the bar for guitar players everywhere. Townshend said after seeing Hendrix "there was a helluva lot of pain (smiles) because in the presence of him you felt small and you realized how far you had to go. And I think Eric Clapton was really shaken, and I think we both wondered, "Oh God, what has happened to us? The tornado called Jimi Hendrix. "Mama Cass (born Ellen Naomi Cohen) of the Mamas and Papas was blown away

singing of "Ball And Chain" at the 1967 Monterey Pop Fes-
the Festival shows Cass sitting in the audience, spellbound
Janis and just saying, "Wow!" when Joplin held some of her
longer notes. Likewise, Michele Phillips watched Janis and said, "I was
amazed that this white woman was singing like Bessie Smith. "When Otis
Redding played at the Festival, Janis Joplin couldn't wait to sit in the front
row to see and hear his performance. Otis and Janis had similar gritty styles
of singing soul, so she identified with his songs and how he sang them. A
year later, a *New York Times* critic said that the influence of Aretha Franklin
and her sisters and Otis "was readily apparent" in Joplin's performance at
New York's Anderson Theater.

44

Human element sounds

PLENTY OF SONGS IN THE '60s HAD HUMAN ELEMENTS, other than voices, like hand clapping, finger snapping, whistling or even foot stomping that made the song sound better and they became a signature part of the song. These were sounds any of us could do without a musical instrument when we heard these songs. The Temptations' "My Girl (1965)" and Brenda Holloway's "When I'm Gone (1965)" opened with a simple snapping of a finger and guitar licks that sound like an essential part of those songs now. The Four Tops used a snapping of the finger throughout "Baby I Need Your Lovin' (1964)" to set the song's beat at a slightly slower tempo than the finger snapping in The Tymes' "So Much In Love (1963)."

Some '60s songs used hand clapping *a la* gospel music or even foot stomping like another percussion instrument. Some of Motown's songs that used rhythmic hand clapping were: Marvin Gaye's early hits, "Pride And Joy (1963)," "Ain't That Peculiar (1965)," and "Your Unchanging Love (1967)," and The Temptations' "The Way You Do The Things You Do (1964)" and "I Truly, Truly Believe (1968)." The Beatles' "I Want To Hold Your Hand (1964)" had rhythmic clapping that some fans did when they heard the song. Hand clapping sounds peppy and natural as the songs' beat setter at the beginning of The Angels' "My Boyfriend's Back (1963)." The foot stomping sound at the beginning of the Supremes' "Where Did Our Love Go" is an attention getter, setting the pace for the rhythm and beat of the song.

The whistling fadeouts at the end of Lovin' Spoonful's "Daydream (1966)" and Otis Redding's "(Sittin' On) The Dock of the Bay (1967)" feel like essential ingredients of the songs. Now that we're used to them and they sound good with those songs, they wouldn't sound right without them. "Daydream" has a ten-second whistle fadeout at its song's end and "The Dock Of The Bay" has a 15-second fadeout. Even if we're not whistlers, we like the whistling at the songs' ends and often try to whistle along with them whenever we hear them. In one of the outtakes of "The Dock Of The Bay" on the more recent album *Remember Me*, Otis tried to whistle near the song's end, failed miserably, and chuckled at the end along with a giggling Sam "Bluzman" Taylor who said, "You'll never make it as a whistler. "The story goes that Taylor did the whistling for the hit single version.

45

How did they make that sound?

♪

P HIL SPECTOR USED MEMBERS OF THE WRECKING CREW MUSICIANS, or-
chestral strings, and many vocalists and echo effects for his "Wall of
Sound" on records by The Crystals, The Ronettes, Darlene Love and
The Righteous Brothers in the early and mid- '60s. His loud, layered, clear
vocals and instruments amplified teens' feelings about a boyfriend or girlfriend as we drove down the street or heard those songs at home. Ronnie
Spector and Darlene Love's vocals were high powered, and Bill Medley and
Bobby Hatfield upped the ante for vocal perfection in "You've Lost That
Lovin' Feelin'." Spector wanted records that were "little symphonies for the
kids" and "came across well over AM-radio and jukeboxes" and he succeeded. His early '60s music made a sound that stood out compared to most
other songs until imitators came along. We heard a similar sound using echo
for the vocals in the Shangri-Las' (two sets of sisters) 1964 hits, "Remember,
Walkin' In The Sand" and "Leader Of The Pack."

Listening to Spector's records was addictive; we played his 45-records
repeatedly at home. It was hard to get our fill of The Righteous Brothers'
"You've Lost That Lovin' Feelin'," a testament to the strong feelings we had
for a girlfriend or boyfriend or the hope of having one soon, even at the
age of 13 or 14. We were surprised we were identifying with these songs so
strongly that we associated with older teens and adults only a few months
or years earlier.

Spector was compulsive in many ways and one of the most blatant examples was when he recorded "He's A Rebel" in Gold Star Recording Studios in L.A. The Crystals were in New York, but he gave them credit for the song because they already had a couple hit records. The actual singer was Darlene Love (born Darlene Wright).

On Junior Walker's "Shotgun," it sounded like they recorded a gunshot at the beginning of the song. Instead, someone kicked an amplifier—that's all it took to jump start the song. The story for the vocal for "Shotgun" was that when Jr. Walker and his "All Stars" (musicians) were ready to begin recording the song their session singer did not show. Berry Gordy told Jr. Walker that he needed to come up with a singer quickly, so Walker sang lead himself, trading back and forth between singing lead and playing tenor saxophone. "Shotgun" went all the way to number one on the R&B chart. It's heavy combo of drums and bass guitar in the intro and a rapid join-in of Walker's sax sprang dancers onto the floor like a James Bond car's ejection button.

I never thought about it much at the time, but the Beatles used only a string quartet for "Yesterday" (1965) and a string octet for "Eleanor Rigby" (1966). Once you're aware of this, it's easy to listen to "Yesterday" and "Eleanor Rigby" and hear that no drums are being played by Ringo, nor any guitars by John, Paul or George. That is what gave these songs a more subdued sound than most of the other Beatles' songs. "Yesterday" and "Eleanor Rigby" came along during the early stages of George Martin and the Beatles creating records with sounds not normally employed on popular music records. McCartney came to Martin after a dream and talked about a new song ("Yesterday") he was writing in his head, "I dreamt about it and I must have pinched it from someone. Have you ever heard it? " and Martin said, "No," to Paul's delight. Early on, probably in 1963 or 1964, Martin strongly recommended that Lennon and McCartney (in that order) always be listed as the songwriters for any Beatles songs except those written by George Harrison. So, Lennon is listed as a cowriter even though he had no role in writing "Yesterday." While Paul is the only singer on "Yesterday," along with no instrument being played by his bandmates, it has always been listed under "the Beatles" since Day One.

Popular music became much louder in the '60s when bands emphasized electric guitars and amplification. Speakers kept getting larger prompting Roger Daltrey to liken it to a lighthearted version of a [nuclear] arms race. Phil Spector's layers of sounds (more guitars, organs, horns, vocalists) and other record producers who used The Wrecking Crew increased a song's loudness. The rich sound of the extra layers by The Wrecking Crew in songs like "Midnight Confessions," "MacArthur Park," and "Aquarius/Let The Sunshine In," seeped through us more, amplifying the rousing uplifting sensation we felt.

Many songs' intros are imprinted in our musical memories just waiting to be triggered again. Opening guitar riffs for '60s songs are instantly familiar for many baby boomers—"My Girl," "You Really Got Me," "The Way You Do The Things You Do," "I Feel Fine," "Day Tripper," "Satisfaction," "I Can't Help Myself," "But It's Alright," "You Keep Me Hanging On," and "I Think We're Alone Now." Opening piano notes in Aaron Neville's "Tell It Like It Is" and Three Dog Night's "One," the first few synthesizer notes in The Supremes' "Reflections," and the opening drum beats of The Temptations' "Ain't Too Proud to Beg" spur us to name those tunes right away when we first hear them (much like the radio show *Name That Tune* that began in the 1950s and later aired on TV).

Various guitarists started using the Fuzztone unit and wah wah pedal in the mid-'60s. Eric Clapton used the "wah wah" pedal for his guitar on Cream's "Tales Of Brave Ulysses" and Keith Richards used a Fuzz-Tone distortion device for his guitar on "Satisfaction." Tommy James said of the Stones' Satisfaction: "That really was a moment that changed everything. That's when the Stones became the number one rock and roll band (In 2004, *Rolling Stone* ranked "Satisfaction" the second greatest song of all time). McCartney used a fuzz box on his bass guitar for the sound on the Beatles' "Think For Yourself." We listeners loved the variety of sounds—the fact that even the guitar sounds were different broadened the appeal of various hit records.

Before magnetic tapes, artists were recorded live and the mechanical process was etching grooves onto a shellac disc. Magnetic tape provided better fidelity and allowed you to manipulate sounds. Les Paul and his wife, Mary Ford, were among the first musicians to use multitrack recording. Paul recorded his wife singing over multiple recordings of her voice using a standard *Ampex* tape machine. She added a tenor voice among other voices. When future guitarist Jeff Beck's mother said to him: "You shouldn't listen to this music. It's fake. It's one guy tricking us. " Beck said, "That's it. That's the music for me. " The Beatles used 4-track recording for *Rubber Soul* and automatic double tracking, reverse tapes and vari-speeding on *Revolver*. Magnetic tapes enabled artists/producers the chance to edit, overdub, cut and splice recordings. George Martin recalled: "You can cut, edit, slow down, or speed up a tape. You could put in backwards stuff. "In *Dark Side of the Moon*, Pink Floyd used noise generators and oscillators and 16-track recording allowed overdubbing to their heart's content," said Roger Waters.

The Beatles revolutionized how music was made in the studio. "In 'Rain' some music and voices are playing backward," said Chuck Granata. The Beatles experimented with sounds again on "Tomorrow Never Knows." George Martin recalled: "'Tomorrow Never Knows' had no harmonies, but it featured a continuous drone. "Giles Martin explained: "The Beatles made tape loops that sounded like seagulls. " Engineer Geoff Emerick further explained, "at 1:30 [minute interval] a Leslie (revolving) speaker kicks in." Harrison first played the sitar on "Norwegian Wood (This Bird Has Flown)," then "Love You Too," and "Within You Without You." In *Revolver's* "Tomorrow Never Knows" George Harrison plays the Indian tambura, a long-necked stringed instrument related to the guitar. By the time *Sgt. Pepper's* was recorded, McCartney said, "Things had advanced so much since the mono days. Now we could use a symphony in 'A Day In The Life'."

In the mid and late '60s and early '70s, synthesizers (for example the Moog synthesizer) became more popular—sounds often imitated a piano, a Hammond organ, flute or vocals. Some synthesizers in the '60s looked like a control board for telephone operators. The Who used a synthesizer on "Baba O'Riley (1971)" and the wildly popular, longer version of "Won't Get Fooled Again (1971)."

Tommy James and the Shondells made big waves with their new sound using 16-track equipment on "Crimson And Clover" in early '69. They set a tremelo effect on the guitar to the song's rhythm, and near the end of the song converted the vocal to a tremelo effect (described by *Wikipedia* as a "lush, warm and roundly pulsing sound"). The microphone was plugged into the *Ampeg* guitar with tremelo turned on to the output from the amplifier. Many of us at the time had no idea how they did it, but we liked what we heard and wanted to hear more.

46

Our popular music of the early '70s

♪

T HE '60S OFFERED AN EXPLOSION OF NEW GENRES and the late '60s had better quality sound on stereophonic record albums and hit singles. In the late '60s, some FM stations started playing a mix of psychedelic and hard rock songs that weren't played much if at all on AM radio. We heard the LP versions of The Doors' "Light My Fire" The Chambers Brothers' "Time Has Come Today," and whole sides of Led Zeppelin's LPs, The Beatles' *White Album* and Hendrix's *Are You Experienced*.

Many popular music listeners of the '60s were in their late teens or twenties in the '70s and were looking for a new playlist of songs with more hard rock in the mix. Record albums' popularity kept growing along with the increasing number of FM radio stations playing more rock music in the early 1970s. When the Federal Communications Commission required separate programming on AM and FM outlets with a common owner beginning on January 1, 1967, many FM stations switched over to classical music programming. By mid-1971, classical music on many FM stations in New York City and elsewhere was giving way to pop-music formats much to the delight of hard rock and underground music fans and to the chagrin of classical music lovers.

We were listening to clear stereo from FM radio receivers with a much better quality of sound than AM radios. Later, Steely Dan memorialized the listening pleasure we felt in their tribute to FM-stereo pop music: "FM (No

Static At All) (1978)." Everyone in my fraternity in the early '70s had good quality stereo receivers and large speakers. My roommate, Bill and I celebrated my new stereo receiver, turntable and speakers by throwing the old record player out the window onto our parking lot out back (and quickly retrieved it for a final toss into the dumpster).

We heard rumors about a Beatles break up as early as 1968, but we were not aware that John told the other group members around the time *Abbey Road* was released that he was leaving The Beatles. John released "Give Peace A Chance" under The Plastic Ono Band in July 1969, and "Instant Karma" in February 1970, before and after *Abbey* Road's release so many Beatles fans felt like a break up was already underway. The Beatles released the hit single, "Let It Be" in March 1970, and Paul announced on April 10 that he was leaving the Beatles. A month later, The Beatles released their *Let It Be* LP and the single "The Long And Winding Road." For some heavy-duty Beatles fans, "The Long And Winding Road" sounded a bit melancholy, because some of the lyrics for many of us seemed to relate to the Beatles' breakup. The lyrics and chorus of "Let It Be" conveyed more of a settling feeling, a general hope that things will be alright.

The likelihood of The Beatles remaining disbanded were further cemented when Paul McCartney filed suit in a London Court on December 31, 1970, to end the partnership of the band members and asked for an accounting of assets and income. At that point it was estimated they had sold 250 million records.

We wondered, which members of The Beatles would record good hit songs as solo artists? How would they measure up to songs they wrote and recorded when they played together? Music critic Don Heckman wrote in September 1971 that Lennon's "Imagine" and McCartney's *Ram* LP along with some of their earlier solo efforts gave us an idea of the individual strong-points the two offered when they collaborated as members of The Beatles. He reminded us that McCartney was the stronger composer and Lennon the better lyricist and concluded their "survival as solo performers" depended on whether they could strengthen their relative weaknesses. He called McCartney's music during his early solo efforts "superb" and his lyrics were "either obscure or cutesy" and Lennon's music had become "almost totally verbal—at the cost of his music." Still, it turned out that we had the treat of hearing an impressive number of good songs from each of them in the early '70s, if the measure of good songs is record sales. George and John usually wrote more serious-minded lyrics and Paul and Ringo's songs were more lighthearted.

It didn't take long for us to find out how George Harrison would fare as a recording artist, post-Beatles. Harrison came into full flower without the other Beatles with his album, *All Things Must Pass* in late 1970. He became a regular user of the slide guitar and collaborated with Eric Clapton, Delaney and Bonnie, and Billy Preston along with other musicians who Joe Cocker employed in his live tour and album, *Mad Dogs and Englishmen.* When we first heard *All Things Must Pass* we were impressed with the remarkable clarity of sound that was in part due to co-producer Phil Spector's Wall of Sound technique. It was a joy to hear George's voice again—so clear, song after song—"I'd Have You Anytime," "My Sweet Lord" (a number one hit single), "Isn't It A Pity," "If Not For You," "Behind That Locked Door," and "Beware Of Darkness" being some of the LPs' best cuts. A few years later, his "Give Me Love - (Give Me Peace On Earth) (1973)" also reached number one.

McCartney issued 12 hit singles from 1971 through 1974, and steadily released more hit songs in the late '70s and early '80s. He had one number one hit, "Uncle Albert/Admiral Halsey" in 1971, before three more million-sellers with the band, Paul McCartney and Wings, "My Love (1973)," "Live And Let Die (1973)" for the *James Bond* movie, and "Band On The Run (1974)."

For John Lennon, it seemed like more of a mixed reaction by his listeners. Many fans liked the early new songs by John and Yoko Ono, but some Beatles fans did not. Lennon's Plastic Ono Band's "Give Peace A Chance (1969)" turned out to be a forerunner of many of his songs after The Beatles disbanded. Lennon's most notable early 70's singles were "Instant Karma (We All Shine On) (1970)" and "Imagine (1971)" that both reached number three, and "Power To The People (1971)" that reached number 11 and "Mind Games (1973)" that peaked at number 18.

Ringo enjoyed better success away from The Beatles in the early '70s than some Beatles fans expected. Three of his singles sold over a million copies each: "It Don't Come Easy (1971)," "Photograph (1973)," and "You're Sixteen (1973)" with the latter two reaching number one on the BB Hot 100. Ringo's more lighthearted, upbeat sound likely helped his records' sales. While many popular music listeners are deep thinkers, many record buyers want to play a record or song at home that has a pick-me-up feeling.

Paul Simon hardly missed a beat with his solo career going in high gear in the early'70s, while Art Garfunkel only charted a few hit songs on his own. Simon's early '70s hits, "Mother And Child Reunion (1972)," "Kodachrome (1973)" and "Loves Me Like A Rock (1973)" all landed in the Top five of the BB Top 40 and his 1976 LP *Still Crazy After All These Years* spawned a single of that name and the number one hit single, "50 Ways To Leave Your Lover."

Joe Cocker's *Mad Dogs and Englishmen* was a live two-day show at New York City's Fillmore East that was released in August 1970. We felt Cocker's exuberance and enthusiasm in his covers of "The Letter" and "She Came In Through The Bathroom Window" and his blues medley of "I'll Drown In My Own Tears" / "When Something Is Wrong with My Baby" / "I've Been Loving You Too Long. " His riveting performance and the layers of sound from his live music and loud band made *Mad Dogs* a popular party LP.

Eric Clapton's group, Derek and the Dominoes was formed in mid-1970 and issued *Layla and Other Assorted Love Songs* in November 1970. We heard their LP on FM radio and my brother Steve loaned me his cassette copy of *Layla and Other Assorted Love Songs*. I played that cassette on dad's Sony player with Koss Pro headphones and couldn't get enough of it. The LP's sales were slow at first, but critics routinely gave it high marks and it has remained a very popular rock and blues LP. Among the LP's more enduring songs with many blues and rock music fans are "I Looked Away," "Bell Bottom Blues," "Key To The Highway," "Tell The Truth," "Layla" and "Little Wing."

Creedence Clearwater Revival followed up their six top forty hit singles in '69 with six more in 1970 and three more in 1971. Sometimes called rock and roll or country rock, their songs often referred to settings we associated with rural or country living—"Proud Mary," "Green River," "Down On The Corner," "Lookin' Out My Back Door" and "Sweet Hitch-Hiker." In all, they issued five gold records and five platinum records.

Carole King's (born Carol Klein) *Tapestry* issued in February 1971, catapulted her from a songwriter with some credits as an arranger/singer to a top-selling songwriter/arranger/singer with a very appealing, soothing voice. Like other record stores throughout the U. S., our college bookstore at University of Maryland, couldn't keep the album in stock. Beginning with *Tapestry*, King was the spokesperson and heroine of teen and college girls, in a big way. You might not hear *Tapestry* too often coming out of a guy's dorm or frat room if he was by himself, but if his girlfriend was there, he might be playing *her* copy that she brought over. *Tapestry's* thoughtful tunes alternated between the slow-paced haunting "So Far Away" and medium-paced "It's Too Late" to the sped up "I Feel The Earth Move" and "Smackwater Jack." King also added her own covers of "Will You Still Love Me Tomorrow," "You've Got A friend," and "(You Make Me Feel Like) A Natural Woman." The album had no filler. Her double A-sided "It's Too Late" b/w "I Feel The Earth Move" was number one on the BB Hot 100 and the AC charts for five weeks. How many millions of girls in a happy or new relationship put "I Feel The Earth Move" on their turntable, cranked up the volume, romped around their room, and sang along with it in glee?

Pop-folk singer guitarist Cat Stevens (born Steven Georgiou; in 1979 he took the Muslim name Yusuf Islam) had a run of hit singles in 1971 ("Wild World," "Moon Shadow," and "Peace Train"), 1972 ("Morning Has Broken" and "Sitting"), 1973 ("The Hurt"), and 1974 ("Oh Very Young" and "Another Saturday Night"). His best albums were his real bread winners—*Tea for the Tillerman* (1970), *Teaser and the Firecat* (1971), and *Catch the Bull at Four* (1972). Watching Stevens perform on PBS for his 50th anniversary tour, "In The Cat's Attic" in 2017, brought me back to the Theta Chi fraternity house where I heard those wonderful songs most often.

Rod Stewart's *Every Picture Tells a Story* (released in May 1971) contained "Maggie May," "(Find A) Reason To Believe," "Mandolin Wind" and a gritty fast-paced cover of "(I Know) I'm Losing You" using all the members from his group Faces. It was a mix of rock, country soul, the blues and folk music. The first time I heard the album along with its signature song "Maggie May," my B&O Railroad coworker, Mike Householder took me to a summertime party in June 1971, in Baltimore where I knew no one. Carly Simon's "You're So Vain" played on the stereo when we first walked in and by coincidence looked into a large mirror on the wall. The party's song list was mostly early '70s music. Stewart's *Every Picture Tells a Story* lifted me and made me feel more at ease at a party full of strangers. That's what music we enjoy does for us sometimes. "Maggie May" was number one on the BB Hot 100 for five weeks. Stewart's follow up LP, *Never A Dull Moment* was almost as good. Issued in July 1972, it included "You Wear It Well" and another party favorite, Stewart's cover of Sam Cooke's "Twistin' The Night Away. "

Elton John's (born Reginald Kenneth Dwight) success on the BB Hot 100 skyrocketed starting in the early '70s, with his albums, *Tumbleweed*

(1970), *Madman Across the Water* (1971), *Honky Chateau* (1972) and *Goodbye Yellow Brick Road* (1973), and platinum hit singles "Crocodile Rock (1972)," "Goodbye Yellow Brick Road (1973)," "Bennie and the Jets (1974)," and "Philadelphia Freedom (1975)." Elton's success stems from his ability to write both good ballads and popular fast tempo songs.

I bought Steely Dan's *Can't Buy a Thrill* in early '73 on the strength of its hit singles "Do It Again (1972)" and "Reelin' In The Years (1973)," but the bonus tracks on the LP were "Dirty Work," "Midnight Cruiser" and "Only A Fool Would Say That." They sounded every bit as good as Steely Dan's two hit singles and were often played on FM radio.

Pink Floyd's *Dark Side of the Moon* (1973) was an instant success and is one of the best-selling rock albums of all time. Its estimated sales have topped 45 million copies. Building on Roger Waters' admiration for *Sgt. Peppers'* coverage of some everyday life topics, *Dark Side of the Moon* themes included the passage of time, mental illness, greed and conflict.

In the first few years of the '70s, Motown could still claim to be "Hitsville, U.S.A." and "The Sound of Young America." It released a bounty of hit singles from The Jackson Five (12 Top 40 songs from 1970-73), Gladys Knight and The Pips, Marvin Gaye, Stevie Wonder, The Temptations, and Diana Ross. Stax Records still released some hit singles, but its sales dipped compared to the '60s, never able to rebound after Otis Redding's death. James Brown produced 14 Top 40 hits from 1970-73. Age was not slowing him down much in the studio and he was still a major force performing live shows. Other popular R&B/soul groups in the early '70s were The Stylistics, The Chi-Lites and The Spinners, each having five or more Top 40 songs.

47

Songs worthy of another or first time listen

♪

Many songs from the late '50s, '60s and early '70s, seldom receive airplay on stations like *Sirius*, *Pandora*, *Spotify* or the *Stingray* App. There were thousands of songs that reached the charts during that time, and many other popular songs appeared only on record albums. The total number of songs to choose from are too voluminous and unwieldy to include all of them along with songs released since then. Many songs made a brief appearance on the BB Hot 100 in the '60s, but never peaked in the Top 40, or even came close. Other songs, we never heard or heard only a few times, so we might or might not recognize them if we heard them for the first time in 40 or 50 years.

As I mentioned earlier in this book, we've all had our own unique playlist of songs we've heard during our lifetimes—the order and ages we were when we heard them, the impact they did or did not have because of surrounding circumstances, and the number of times we've heard them during our life. All these factors might affect whether a song sounds familiar to us so many years later after not having heard them in a long time. Van Morrison's "Tupelo Honey" and the Beach Boys' "Long Promised Road" are examples of two of my favorite songs that I heard often from my record albums, but they did not place high enough on the BB Hot 100 chart as hit singles to be played often on the radio. Many baby boomers might not know about them, unless they owned the LPs, *Tupelo Honey* and *Surf's Up*. Two slow dance songs that music fans of '60s music should sample are The Temptations' "You Can Depend On Me" and Otis Redding's "Send Me Some Lovin'."

My reel-to-reel tape lists from 50 years ago include songs I heard on the radio and on those tapes from 1966-68. Some of those songs are seldom, if ever played today on oldies stations or playlists for '60s music. They include songs that placed high on both the BB Hot 100 and the R&B chart: "The Marvelettes' "Don't Mess With Bill" and "The Hunter Gets Captured By The Game," The Isley Brothers' "This Old Heart Of Mine," and Martha and The Vandellas' "Jimmy Mack."

Songs on those lists I had forgotten about, until I played them on *iTunes* or *You Tube* recently are five from 1967: J. J. Jackson's "Four Walls (Three Windows And Two Doors)," the O'Jays" "I'll Be Sweeter Tomorrow (Than I Was Today)," Wilson Pickett's "Soul Dance Number Three," Jackie Wilson's "Since You Showed Me How To Be Happy" and James and Bobby Purify's "Shake A Tail Feather."

Many songs on those reel-to-reel tape lists that had success on the R&B chart, but only moderate success on the BB Hot 100 chart haven't received much airtime since the '60s. Examples include: Otis Redding's "I've Been Loving You Too Long," Shorty Long's "Function At The Junction," and Kim Weston's "Take Me In Your Arms (Rock Me A Little While)." Others include Martha and the Vandellas' "Love (Makes Me Do Foolish Things)," The Contours' "First I Look At The Purse," and Brenda Holloway's "Just Look What You've Done." If you love soul music from the '60s, but you have not heard these songs in a long time or don't remember some of them, you should check them out.

Conclusion

♪

WHEN I WAS A PRETEEN and early teen in the early '60s, it was the start of my hobby listening to music. It has carried me through life for more than 50 years since then. I "adopted" The Four Seasons in 1962, the Beach Boys in 1963, The Beatles, The Temptations and The Four Tops in '64, Otis Redding, The Rolling Stones and The Grassroots in '65. More artists kept coming, rounded out with The Doors in '67, Cream in '68, Chicago in '69, and The Doobie Brothers and Steely Dan in '72. More favorite musicians and songs have kept coming our way ever since. I've accumulated an enormous number of listening favorites beginning with many '60s songs. Millions of baby boomers nationwide (and even worldwide to some extent) adopted many of their favorite musicians and songs during this same era (late '50s through early '70s).

Our music was with us everywhere we were, even though we lacked the internet and social media that we have today. We had desk radios, transistor radios, jukeboxes in our school cafeterias and some eateries, record players at our houses and our friends' houses. We listened to music together in each other's houses to trade notes on what we liked and didn't like and heard many record albums for the first time on a friend's phonograph or turntable. We danced to live bands weekly at teen dance venues throughout the U. S., along with high school dances. We also had songs in our heads, maybe humming a tune as we walked down the street. We made frequent trips to record stores or 5 and 10 cent stores that sold records and grabbed copies of "this week's Top 40" list of hit songs. We did sing-along songs as we rode in our cars together listening to the radio or 8-track tape players.

AM radio was our chief source of listening to the current hit songs on the BB Hot 100, R&B, CW and AC charts in the '60s. We liked our music loud. In the late '60s and early '70s we started listening to psychedelic and hard rock on FM stereo stations. Along with FM stereo broadcasts, we switched to better quality music listening equipment—stereo receivers and large speakers. Now we liked our music loud with better quality.

R&B music in the U. S. heavily influenced the development of rock and roll both in the U. S. and Great Britain. Motown and Stax/Atlantic Records provided numerous soul love songs and fast dance songs that were catalysts for new dances or dance steps that teens and 20-year-olds did with a joy and swagger that sent their spirits soaring. Hank Ballard's original "The Twist" set the stage for Chubby Checker's cover that made the song a commercial sensation and national craze for teens and their parents, not once but twice—in 1960 and 1962.

The Beatles first appearance on *Ed Sullivan* on February 9, 1964, and their subsequent live appearances in the U. S from 1964-1966, made them the most popular recording group in the U. S. in the '60s. The British Invasion of popular music groups onto U. S. airwaves in 1964-65, ignited a bountiful exchange of popular music between the U. S. and U. K. that has occurred ever since then.

Popular music expanded into more genres in the '60s and musicians had more competition to reach hit single status on record charts. We music listeners were the lucky recipients of more choices of songs because musicians released albums more often and the LPs had less filler. R&B and rock and roll, country western and folk music in the late '50s and early '60s paved the way for more music from those genres in the '60s and new genres (or subgenres)—soul, garage rock, bubble gum, psychedelic rock, folk rock and psychedelic soul.

Our music in the '60s was a powerful antidote to the stress all around us from social unrest and upheaval. We often felt that our country was unraveling because of the assassinations of JFK, MLK and RFK. The Vietnam War caused a deep divide between protesters for and against it and their interpretation about what was patriotism and what defined support for our troops in Vietnam. We struggled as a nation in the '60s and early '70s to know what was the truth about what was happening there and was the War winnable? Likewise, The Civil Rights movement for better and fairer treatment of blacks and women was painfully slow in the face of Jim Crow laws. Many of our songs told the story of these social causes. Plenty of '60s songs also covered the generation gap between teens and their parents' age group. We welcomed other songs that simply fostered escape from daily woes and worries with a "let's live for today or the moment" approach—it's time to decompress with some easy going upbeat tunes.

By the mid-'60s instrumentation and technology in recording studios resulted in many new sounds on popular music records and experimentation by musicians expanded the different genres of music. The happy result for musicians and music buyers everywhere was a wide variety of music for our listening pleasure.

It's a rarity for recording artists to remain top hit-makers for five years or more for many reasons. If recording artists are not good songwriters themselves, it is often very difficult to keep finding new songs that are fodder for a hit record. Some recording artists have personal problems, tire of live performances or being in the same group, and a surprising number died at young age in the '60s and '70s. At the other extreme, popular music is strewn with a long list of one-hit wonders.

Some groups started out very strong on the BB Hot 100 and had short hit-making stints of one to three years before their hit-singles ended. Groups like The Lovin' Spoonful started strong, but they faded quickly in a few years. The Buckinghams had a strong one-year run in 1967, and then disappeared from the Top 40. Likewise, Gary Puckett And The Union Gap had a two-year string of six top 20 hits and four of them were million-sellers and The Classics IV had four hit records over two years and then faded away. Even The Mamas and Papas only had a two-year run of Top 40 hits.

Unless a musician died suddenly during that era, we did not find out why a musician or recording group fell off the music charts permanently, unless we were avid readers of *Rolling Stone* magazine that began publishing in 1967. In the '60s and early '70s, TV and radio news was brief rather than 24/7 coverage, and we had no internet, so we had no readily available search engine. There was no convenient method for asking a question about a musician through a computer and no way to gain instant answers about popular music and its musicians at home or at our local libraries.

Each listener has their own feel, their own interpretation, of what songs relate to each other within a few years or a decade, and across the decades. For me, songs that are direct descendants of the '60s and early '70s songs are scattered over many years. A few examples include: Hall and Oates' "She's Gone (1976)," "I Can't Go For That (No Can Do) (1981)," "Maneater (1982);" John Mellancamp's "Ain't Even Done With The Night (1981)," "Hurts So Good (1982)," and "Cherry Bomb (1987);" Aretha's "Freeway Of Love (1985);" Van Morrison's "Real Real Gone (1990)," Michael Bolton's "Love Is A Wonderful Thing (1991)," Matchbox Twenty's "If You're Gone (2000);" and Amy Winehouse's "Back To Black (2006)" and "Rehab (2006). " Most of these songs have an R&B soul sound reminiscent or stemming from '60s soul music.

While it may be primarily aimed at baby boomers, everyone hears '60s music today, whether they grew up in the '60s or not. Almost everywhere we went in 2016 and 2017, we still heard music from the '60s. We hear it in our drugstores and supermarkets, at the pump in gas stations, and in many restaurants and bars. Some popular music fans wonder, "How long will '60s music be played by music fans in the future, once most, or all baby boomers in the U. S. and around the world have passed away?

Many baby boomers and even younger music fans revel in the fact that some bands and music styles from the '60s have remained extremely popular. Anniversary tours and farewell tours by musicians and vocalists from the '60s and early '70s have been numerous throughout the U. S., even since 2010. *Motown: The Musical* based on Berry Gordy's life and the story of Motown Records thrived on tour from 2013-2017. The Broadway musical *Jersey Boys* about the 4 Seasons' lives and their musical career, thrilled 4 Seasons fans from 2005 through 2017. Chicago, often called "that rock and roll band with horns" continued to tour successfully in 2017 as did the Beach Boys, the Doobie Brothers and many other bands like The Eagles and James Taylor.

TV shows, movies, and TV and radio commercials have often used part, or all, of popular music songs from the '50s and '60s ever since that music was released. And it was still the case in 2017 and early 2018. In November 2017 alone, TV ads used a portion of Neil Diamond's "Sweet Caroline" for *Hyundai* cars, Joe Cocker's cover of "With A Little Help From My Friends" for *Volkswagen* with Woodstock Music festival-like video as the backdrop, and The Rascals' "Groovin'" for Subway sandwiches. For the 2017 Christmas season, Gabe's Department stores played The Temptations' "Get Ready" as the prompt for getting ready for the holidays and Big Lots played Three Dog

Night's "Joy To The World" during their holiday TV commercial. In early March 2018, *Applebees* was still advertising their quesadilla burger on TV with The Troggs "Wild Thing" playing in the background. Not only does it feel gratifying to baby boomers who see the ads and hear "our music" while watching them, but the lyrics fit well with the messages that companies are trying to convey, whether the TV viewer is a pre-baby boomer, baby boomer or someone born after 1964.

Notes

♪

Preface

p. xiv: **Tom Petty said in an interview for Soundbreaking**: Tom Petty, *Sound-breaking*, Episode 8, I Am My Music.

p. xv: **Phil Collins wrote in his liner notes**: Phil Collins. *The Essential Going Back* CD, 2016.

p. xv: **My high school classmate Jimmy Ulman recently said it best**: Jimmy Ulman, personal communication, email, 2017.

p. xvii: **"Day Tripper"**, *Wikipedia*, October 9, 2017; **"Good Vibrations"**, *Wikipedia*, October 9, 2017; **"Crimson and Clover"**, *Wikipedia*, October 9, 2017.

AM radio

p. 5: **The Beach Boys' Carl Wilson recalled**: *Time/Life History of Rock'N'Roll, Britain Invades, America Fights Back.*

Watching the top 40

p. 8: **You were conducting research**:": Stephen Rabin, personal conversation with Mark Millikin (hereafter, "author"): February 2018.

p. 9: **Paul McCartney recalled that his first 45-record was Gene Vincent's**: *Soundbreaking*, Episode 8, *I Am My Music.*

p. 9: **It was released in the U.S. on December 15, 1964:** *Beatles '65, Wikipedia,* April 16, 2018.

p. 9: ***Beatles '65* went on to sell more copies in 1965**: *Beatles '65, Wikipedia,* April 16, 2018.

p. 10: **Tommy James recalled**: *Soundbreaking,* Episode 8, *I Am My Music.*

p. 11: **A survey in the March 1966 issue of** *Newsweek*: Anonymous, *Newsweek,* March 21, 1966.

p. 11: **and an article in August 1966**: Louise Hickman, Baltimore *Sunday Sun,* August 14, 1966.

p. 11: **Whole 12-inch sub sandwiches were:** Tom Nicholson, phone conversation with author, December 3, 2014.

AM radio disc jockeys

p. 13: **"I shall return with 'Stop In The Name Of Love'**: *Soundbreaking,* Vol. 8, *I Am My Music.*

p. 13: **"You're gonna hear the whole 6-minute version here**: *Soundbreaking,* Vol. 8, *I Am My Music.*

p. 13: **A video exists of The Ronettes' Ronnie Spector**: *Beatles Anthology DVD.*

p. 14: **Fat Daddy, the "330-pound king of soul: 'Fat Daddy' was a voice in R&B:** Fredrick Rasmussen, Baltimore: *The Sun,* February 24, 2001.

p. 14: **Fat Daddy's intro was**: 'Fat Daddy' was a voice in R&B. Fredrick Rasmussen, Baltimore: *The Sun,* February 24, 2001.

p. 14: **When Fred Rockin' Robin" signed off in the mid – '60s**: Fred Rockin' Robinson, *Wikipedia,* April 8, 2018.

p. 15: **Baltimore's disc jockey Johnny Dark**: Kelly, Jacques and Frederick N. Rasmussen. Recalling Johnny Dark as a force in Baltimore rock radio. Baltimore: *The Sun,* September 16, 2016.

TV shows, movies and musicals

p. 18: **It's got a great beat and you can dance to it**: *Bandstand,* p. 49.

p. 18: **One future hit single flopped on** *Bandstand*'s **Rate-A-Record**: *Bandstand,* p. 84.

p. 20: **He caused a generation of baby boomer adolescents to rush home**: Michael Olesker, Baltimore *Sun,* 2003.

p. 21: **The Beatles was an animated cartoon show:** *The Beatles* (TV series): *Wikipedia*, November 14, 2017.

p. 21: **The Monkees sit-com TV show aired:** The Monkees, *Wikipedia*, November 14, 2017.

p. 22: **Two popular music/dance shows:** The Lloyd Thaxton Show, *Wikipedia*, November 14, 2017; Where The Action *Is*, *Wikipedia*, November 14, 2017.

p. 22: **Laugh In (1968-73) had "sketches with sexual innuendo":** *Laugh In*, *Wikipedia*, October 12, 2017.

p. 22: **The Smothers Brothers Comedy Hour:** *The Smothers Brothers Comedy Hour*, *Wikipedia*, December 6, 2017.

p. 23: **Hee Haw featured:** Bill C. Malone and Jocelyn R. Neal, Country Music, U.S.A., and *Hee Haw*, *Wikipedia*, April 17, 2018.

45-records and record albums

p. 26: **George Martin admitted to producer Jimmy Webb that "Hey Jude":** "Hey Jude", *Wikipedia*, October 12, 2017.

p. 27: **J. J. Jackson's "But It's Alright" was the projected B-side of "Boogaloo baby" in 1966:** J.J. Jackson, *Wikipedia*, February 10, 2018.

p. 27: **"The Horse" by Cliff Nobles was the projected B-side and instrumental:** "The Horse" by Cliff Nobles, *Wikipedia*, February 10, 2018.

p. 27: **Rod Stewart's "Maggie May" was released as the projected B-side of "Reason To Believe":** "Maggie May" by Rod Stewart, *Wikipedia*, February 10, 2018.

Listening to music with friends

p. 32: **"Upstairs in that room on Kendi Road, there was magic happening on the stereo:** Letter from Tom Douglass to the author, July 2, 2012.

Sing–along songs

p. 42: **On Just Right Radio in Raleigh:** Radio broadcast on *Just Right Radio*, 104.7 FM, August 19, 2017.

Music genres we like and our personality types

p. 44: **Genres can be defined as categories of music grouped together:** Alison E. Arnold and Jonathan C. Kramer, *What In The World Is Music*, 2016.

p. 44: **Styles are the sum totals:** Alison E. Arnold and Jonathan C. Kramer, *What In The World Is Music*, 2016.

p. 44: **Music psychologists divide music:** John Powell, Why You Love Music, 2016.

p. 45: **While our preferred music genres are usually formed:** John Powell, Why You Love Music, 2016.

Rock and roll before The Beatles – R&B and Elvis

p. 47: **Dick Clark asserted that Bill Haley was one of the originators of rock-abilly music:** *Time/Life History of Rock and Roll*, Disc One, Volume One, Rock and Roll Explodes.

p. 47: **The colored folks been singing it and playing just like I'm doing it now, man:** Andrew Grant Jackson, *Where's Elvis*.

p. 47: **R&B singer Ruth Brown said, "when Elvis came on the scene , he did it right:** *Time/Life History of Rock'N'Roll, Rock and Roll Explodes*.

p. 48: **Almost seven-years old, Bruce Springsteen recalled that after the show:** Bruce Springsteen, *Born To Run*, 2016.

p. 48: **Tom Petty said years later, "An entertainer [Elvis Presley] is really:** Tom Petty, *Time/Life History of Rock'N'Roll, Good Rockin' Tonight*.

p. 49: **He combined country and rhythm and blues to become one of rock and roll's biggest**: Mikal Gilmore, Chuck Berry, 1926-2017: Farewell to the Father of Rock and Roll. *Rolling Stone*, April 20, 2017.

p. 49: **Jackson Browne recalled: "Berry was a big influence:** *Time/Life History of Rock'N'Roll, Rock and Roll Explodes*.

The Twist breaks down the generation gap in music

p. 50: **The Twist was the most significant rock and roll record of all time:** Dick Clark, *Time/Life History of Rock'N'Roll, Good Rockin' Tonight*.

More rock and roll and soul in the early '60s

p. 53: **And that's why the bass singer would:** Ben E. King, *Time/Life History of Rock'N'Roll, Good Rockin' Tonight*.

The Beatles in the U.S. in 1964

p. 56: **Marsha gave the song's introduction:** *CNN '60s Special*, British Invasion, Episode 6.

p. 56: **One reporter asked, "What do you think of the comment:** *Time/Life History of Rock'N'Roll, Britain Invades, America Fights Back.*

p. 56: **Making fun of their long hair, another reported asked:** *Time/Life History of Rock'N'Roll, Britain Invades, America Fights Back.*

p. 57: **Middle-aged men were walking down Fifth Avenue:** George Martin, *History of Rock &Roll*, Disc 2, Vol. 1.

p. 58: **After their first Ed Sullivan appearance all the requests:** Bob Eubanks, *CNN '60s Special*: British Invasion: Episode 6.

p. 58: **The top five songs were:** Maher and Noonan, *Billboard Magazine*, 1964.

p. 59: **"When 'Hello Dolly' grabbed the top spot":** Bruce Springsteen, *Born To Run*, 2017.

p. 59: **"These girls were going nuts":** Jackson Browne, *Time/Life History of Rock-'N'Roll, Britain Invades, America Fights Back.*

p. 59: **"We knew it was a problem":** Ben E. King, *Time/Life History of Rock'N'Roll, Britain Invades, America Fights Back.*

p. 59: **"And I knew they were gonna be big"** Jerry Lee Lewis, *Time/Life History of Rock'N'Roll, Britain Invades, America Fights Back.*

p. 59: **"It was such a huge bonus that the music was the best":** Tom Petty, *Time/Life History of Rock'N'Roll, Britain Invades, America Fights Back.*

p. 59: **"We were completely jealous as hell":** Brian Wilson, *Time/Life History of Rock'N'Roll, Britain Invades, America Fights Back.*

The British Invasion of pop music

p. 63: **Just as important, the group's bad boy image:** John McMillian, *Beatles vs, Stones.*

p. 63: **"It was tough. America was very conservative in attitudes":** Mick Jagger, *Time/Life History of Rock'N'Roll, Britain Invades, America Fights Back.*

p. 63: **"What was more important was where you played":** Peter Townshend, *Time/Life History of Rock'N'Roll, Britain Invades, America Fights Back.*

p. 63: **"They took their name from Muddy Waters [presumably his 1950 song, Rollin' Stone]":** Peter Townshend, *Time/Life History of Rock'N'Roll, Britain Invades, America Fights Back.*

p. 64: **"But once you heard them sing:** Graham Nash, *Time/Life History of Rock'N'Roll, Britain Invades, America Fights Back.*

p. 64: **"I realized if you try to out-rock Chuck Berry":** Eric Burdon, *Time/Life History of Rock'N'Roll, Britain Invades, America Fights Back.*

p. 64: **"There was a great sense of brotherhood":** Eric Burdon, *Time/Life History of Rock'N'Roll, Britain Invades, America Fights Back.*

U.S. musicians respond in 1964-65

p. 67: **"We wore the same clothing: Dick Clark:** *Time/Life History of Rock'N'Roll, Britain Invades, America Fights Back.*

p. 68: **By 1966, clothing fads were influenced by The Byrds:** Anonymous. The Teen-Agers: A Newsweek survey of what they're really like. *Newsweek,* March 21, 1966.

p. 68: **The British Invasion was re-introducing American black R&B:** *CNN '60s Special, British Invasion,* Episode 6.

Less record album filler

p. 70: **George Martin recalled that he and Brian Epstein:** *Eight Days A Week* documentary, 2016.

p. 71: **I was surprised years later to learn that Beatles' producer George Martin said:** The Beatles, *The Beatles Anthology,* 2000.

Soul (R&B) music

p. 73: **Rhythm and blues has an African-American origin:** Rhythm and blues, *Wikipedia,* March 21, 2018.

p. 73: **Blues originated in the Deep South:** Blues music, *Wikipedia,* March 21, 2018.

p. 73: **Soul music developed in the late '50s and early '60s:** Soul music, *Wikipedia,* March 21, 2018.

p. 74: **"Motown brought my world into an abundance of color and soulfulness":** Annie Lenox, *Soundbreaking* Episode 5, Four On the Floor.

p. 74: **"Dancing In The Street – they would always kick off the night in any club":** Jeff Beck, *Soundbreaking,* Episode 5, Four on the Floor.

p. 75: **Tom Petty recalled, "I never saw a Hammond organ in my life until:** Tom Petty, *Time/Life History of Rock'N'Roll, Britain Invades, America Fights Back.*

p. 75: **"People don't realize the contribution the Rascals made:** John Sebastian, *Time/Life History of Rock'N'Roll, Britain Invades, America Fights Back.*

p. 77: **Other members of The Temptations:** Mark Ribowsky, *Ain't Too Proud To*

Beg.

p. 78: **George Harrison recorded "Pure Smokey:** Pure Smokey, *Wikipedia*, October 26, 2017.

At the dance with the teen center beat

p. 84: **Norma brought her portable wind up Victrola:** Norma Cronise, phone call with author, April 2018.

p. 88: **One article in the Baltimore** *Sunday Sun Magazine***:** Baltimore *Sunday Sun Magazine*

p. 88: **The Beatles recalled that in their early days:** *Eight Days of The Week* documentary, 2016.

p. 88: **For example, in Perry Hall High School:** Anonymous, *Hallmark*, Perry Hall High School, December 1968.

Folk music

p. 91: **Folk music in the late '50s and '60s was a direct outgrowth:** Folk music, *Wikipedia*, February 11, 2018.

p. 91: **The Carter family and the Almanac Singers:** *Dylan Goes Electric*, Elijah Wald, 2016

p. 91: **Folk music was traditional music handed down:** Folk music, *Wikipedia*, February 11, 2018.

p. 92: **There were young modern songwriters with bluegrass players;** John Sebastian, *Time/Life History of Rock'N'Roll, Plugging In*.

p. 92: **You had Bob Dylan singing – a great example of:** Judy Collins, *Time/Life History of Rock'N'Roll, Plugging In*.

p. 92: **He started getting attention from N.Y. critics:** Shelton, *New York Times*, September 29, 1961; Shelton, *New York Times*, July 29, 1963.

Folk rock music

p. 94: **Mark Knopfler of Dire Straits said in the mid- '90s:** *Time/Life History of Rock'N'Roll, Plugging In*.

Country (western) music

p. 99: **Country western music in the '60s grew out of hillbilly music:** Bill C. Malone and Jocelyn R. Neal; Notes from Dr. Marilyn Lynch's class, Radio Days: Music of the '40s, February 2018.

p. 99: **Starting on October 20, 1958: BB combined radio airplay:** Country western music, *Wikipedia*, February 11, 2018.

p. 100: **Country western songs appealed to many listeners who were proud:** Bill C. Malone and Jocelyn R. Neal.

Garage rock

p. 102: **It was based on a raw form of rock and roll coming from the perception:** Garage rock music, *Wikipedia*, October 28, 2017.

Bubblegum music

p. 104: **It had an upbeat sound and targeted preteens and teenagers:** Bubblegum music, *Wikipedia*, October 29, 2017.

Psychedelic rock music

p. 106: **"Psychedelic" was coined by English psychiatrist:** Richard Morton Jack, *Psychedelia*, 2017.

p. 107: **Britain's Pink Floyd's LP "Piper At The Gates of Dawn":** Pink Floyd, *Wikipedia*, February 12, 2018.

p. 108: **Vanilla Fudge specialized in "extended rock arrangements:** Vanilla Fudge, *Wikipedia*, January 9, 2018.

p. 108: **Carlos Santana said of Hendrix:** Carlos Santana, *Time/Life History of Rock-'N'Roll, My Generation.*

p. 109: **Ray Manzarek recalled; Jim was influenced by [writer] Jack Kerouac:** Ray Manzarek, *Time/Life History of Rock'N'Roll, My Generation.*

p. 109: **You could tell right away, well we got a writer (Jim) here:** Tom Petty, *Time/Life History of Rock'N'Roll, My Generation.*

p. 109: **Sometimes referred to as psychedelic rock or baroque pop:** Procul Harum, *Wikipedia*, October 29, 2017.

p. 112: **Led Zeppelin replaced The Beatles:** Anonymous, *New York Times*, September 16, 1970.

p. 112: **Their mega-hit song, "Stairway To Heaven:** Stairway To Heaven, *Wikipedia*, October 29, 2017.

Songs with a message

p. 120: **Scott McKenzie's "San Francisco:** Kaufman, *New York Times*, August 20, 2012.

p. 124: **Bill Douglass Sr. (a WWII veteran) told me in 2018:** Conversation with author at Mr. Douglass's house, March 21, 2018.

p. 127: **The First Edition's "Just Dropped In:** The First Edition, *Wikipedia*, October 6, 2017.

Instrumentals

p. 130: **It is believed to be the second most recorded song:** "The Girl From Ipanema", *Wikipedia*, March 7, 2018.

p. 131: **In an interview in mid-1966, Alpert characterized his sound as having "jazz, folk, rock, Dixie and a little mariachi or Mexican street band:** Bob Considine, Alpert's brassy sound of success. *News American*, August 25, 1966.

Vocals – the human instrument

p. 134: **They are personal and allow a truly authentic singer to resonate:** Annie Lenox, *Soundbreaking*, Episode 3, *The Human Instrument*.

p. 134: **The Rascals' Felix Cavalierre:** Felix Cavalierre, *Soundbreaking*, Episode 3, *The Human Instrument*.

p. 135: **Smokey Robinson recalled, "I used to call them the Five Deacons:** *Time/Life History of Rock'N'Roll, The Sounds of Soul*.

p. 136: **He and Ella Fitzgerald often used scat vocals:** Ken Burns Jazz CD Liner Notes, 2002.

p. 137: **Today's record producers often use Auto Tune:** Auto Tune, *Wikipedia*, January 31, 2018.

Vocal harmony at its best

p. 139: **The song's vocal layering inspired The Beach Boys:** "You Didn't Have To Be So Nice", *Wikipedia*, March 21, 2018.

Censorship of some songs

p. 158: **The Christian Anti-Communist crusade claimed:** The Sixties: Years of Hope, Days of Rage, Todd Gitlin.

p. 158: **Before Jim Morrison and The Doors appeared:** Richard Morton Jack, *Psychedelia*, 2017.

p. 158: **Some BBC stations banned "A Day In The Life":** George Martin, From The Beatles, *Beatles Anthology* DVD.

p. 158: **The Supremes pre-recorded "Stoned Love":** "Stoned Love", *Wikipedia*, November 7, 2017.

Rock and roll heaven and songs about death

p. 164: **The Drifters quickly brought back their former lead singer:** "Under The Boardwalk", *Wikipedia*, March 21, 2018.

Musicians competing and learning from each another

p. 178: **Keith Richards summed it up in a nutshell:** *Time/Life History of Rock-'N'Roll, Guitar Heroes.*

p. 178: **"Those records in those days were like gold [to us]:** Felix Cavalierre, *Time/Life History of Rock'N'Roll, Rock and Roll Explodes.*

p. 179: **In short order, Brian used some musicians:** Kent Hartmann, The Wrecking Crew, 2013.

p. 179: **Meanwhile, Mike Love based "Good Vibrations'" lyrics:** Good Vibrations: Mike Love, My Life As a Beach Boy, 2017.

p. 179: **"So we did Sgt. Peppers:** Paul McCartney, *Soundbreaking*, Episode 2, *Painting with Sound.*

p. 180: **"And I remember we just looked at each other:** Roger Waters, *Soundbreaking*, Episode 2, *Painting with Sound.*

p. 180: **"In that sense, it opened up Pandora's box:** Roger Daltrey, *Soundbreaking*, Episode 2, *Painting with Sound.*

p. 180: **"I Thought, where do we go from here?":** Roger Daltrey, *Soundbreaking*, Episode 2. *Painting with Sound.*

p. 180: **The sound of the orchestra in Hey Jude:** "You Can't Always Get What You Want, *Wikipedia*, November 14, 2017.

p. 181: **Love liked what he heard:** Mike Love, *Good Vibrations: My Life as a Beach Boy*, 2017.

p. 181: **Not long after, George Harrison used "Something in the way she moves":** Mark Ribowsky, Sweet Dreams and Flying Machines: The Life and Music of James Taylor, 2016.

p. 181: **Judge Richard Owen of the U.S. District Court:** "My Sweet Lord", *Wikipedia*, March 20, 2018.

p. 181: **And I think Eric Clapton was really shaken and I think we both wondered:** *Time/Life History of Rock'N'Roll, Guitar Heroes.*

p. 182: **A video of the Festival shows Cass sitting spellbound:** *Time/Life History of Rock'N'Roll, Plugging In.*

p. 182: **Likewise, Michelle Phillips watched Janis and said:** Brian Hiatt, Rock's first concert made stars of Hendrix and Joplin. So why did the Dead try to kill it? *Rolling Stone: The Fortieth Anniversary.* January 12-26, 2007.

p. 182: **A year later, a *New York Times* critic said:** Janis Joplin climbs the heady rock firmament, NY Times, February 19, 1968.

How did they make that sound?

p. 185: **Spector wanted records that were little symphonies:** Liner notes for *Phil Spector, 1961-1966* CD.

p. 186`: **The actual singer was Darlene Love:** The Wrecking Crew, Kent Hartmann.

p. 186: **"Have you ever heard it?" and Martin said, "No":** Paul McCartney, *Soundbreaking*, Episode 1, *The Art of Recording.*

p. 187: **"That's when The Stones became number the one rock and roll band":** Tommy James, *Soundbreaking*, Episode 4, *Going Electric.*

p. 187: **"That's the music for me":** Jeff Beck, *Soundbreaking*, Episode 2, *Painting with Sound.*

p. 188: **"You could put in backwards stuff":** George Martin, *Soundbreaking*, Episode 2. *Painting with Sound.*

p. 188: **George Martin recalled: "Tomorrow Never Knows" had no harmonies:** George Martin, *Soundbreaking*, Episode 2, *Painting with Sound.*

p. 188: **Engineer Geoff Emerick explained:** The Beatles made tape loops that sounded like seagulls": Geoff Emerick, *Soundbreaking*, Episode 2, *Painting with Sound.*

p. 188: **"Now we could use a symphony in 'A Day In The Life':** Paul McCartney, *Soundbreaking*, Episode 2, *Painting with Sound.*

p. 188: **The microphone was plugged into the Ampeg guitar with tremelo:** Crimson And Clover", *Wikipedia*, March 20, 2018.

Our popular music of the early '70s

p. 189: **By Mid–1971 classical music on many FM stations:** George Gent. Classical music dwindles on city's radio stations, *New York Times,* August 10, 1971.

p. 190: **At that point, it was estimated they had sold 250 million records:** Anthony Lewis. Lawsuit spells breakup for Beatles, *New York Times,* January 1, 1971.

p. 190: **Music critic Don Heckman wrote in September 1971:** Don Heckman. Survival of the hippest. *The New York Times,* September 9, 1971.

p. 194: **Pink Floyd's *Dark Side of the Moon* (1973 was an instant success:** *Dark Side of the Moon, Wikipedia,* December 23, 2017.

p. 194: **Building on Roger Waters' admiration of Sgt. Peppers' coverage of some everyday topics:** *Dark Side of the Moon, Wikipedia,* December 23, 2017.

Bibliography

Books

Arnold, Alison E. and Jonathan C. Kramer. *What in the World Is Music?* New York; Routledge (Taylor and Francis Group), 2016.

Beatles The. *The Beatles Anthology.* San Francisco: Chronicle Books, 2000.

Brokaw, Tom. *Boom! Talking About the Sixties.* New York: Random House, 2007.

Browne, David. *Fire and Rain: The Beatles, Simon and Garfunkel, James Taylor, CSNY and the Lost Story of 1970.* Boston: Da Capo Press, 2011.

Clark, Dick with Fred Bronson. *Dick Clark's American Bandstand.* New York: Collins Publishers, 1997.

Cohen, Rich. *The Sun & the Moon & the Rolling Stones.* New York: Spiegel and Grau, 2016.

Cross, Charles. 2005. *Room Full of Mirrors: A Biography of Jimi Hendrix.* New York: Hachette Books, 2005.

Davies, Hunter. *The Beatles.* New York: W. W. Norton Company, 2009 (original version 1968).

Fisher, Marc. *Something in the Air: Radio, Rock and the Revolution that Shaped a Generation.* New York: Random House, 2007.

Friedan, Betty. *The Feminine Mystique.* New York: W. W. Norton, 2013 (originally published in 1963).

Gitlin, Todd. *The Sixties: Years of Hope, Days of Rage.* New York: Bantam Books, 1993.

Gordon, Robert. *Respect Yourself: Stax Records and the Soul Explosion*. New York: Bloomsbury USA, 2013.

Gould, Jonathan. *Otis Redding: An Unfinished Life*. New York: Crown Archetype, 2017.

Guralnick, Peter. *Last Train to Memphis: The Rise of Elvis Presley*. Boston: Little, Brown and Company, 1994.

Guralnick, Peter. *Careless Love: The Unmaking of Elvis Presley*. Boston: Little, Brown and Company, 1999.

Guralnick, Peter. *Sweet Soul Music: Rhythm and Blues and Southern Dream of Freedom*. New York: Little, Brown and Company, 1999.

Guralnick, Peter. *Sam Phillips: The Man Who Invented Rock and Roll*. New York: Little, Brown and Company, 2015.

Hajdu, David. *Love for Sale*. New York: Farrar, Straus and Giroux, 2016.

Halberstam, David. *The Fifties*. New York: Fawcett Columbine, 1993.

Hartman, Kent. *The Wrecking Crew*. New York: Thomas Dunne Books, 2012.

Hepworth, David. *Never A Dull Moment – 1971: The Year that Rock Exploded*. New York: Henry Holt and Company, 2016.

Isbell, Dann. *Ranking the '60s: A Comprehensive Listing of the Top Songs and Acts from Pop's Golden Decade*. Jefrian Books, 2013.

Jack, Richard Morton. *Psychedelia 1966-1970. 101 Iconic Underground Rock Albums*. New York: Sterling, 2017.

Jackson, Andrew Grant. *Where's Ringo?* San Diego: Thunder Bay Press, 2014.

Jackson, Andrew Grant. *1965: The Most Revolutionary Year in Music*. New York: Thomas Dunne Books, St. Martin's Press, 2015.

Jackson, Andrew Grant. *Where's Elvis?* San Diego: Thunder Bay Press, 2016.

Kane, Larry. *Ticket to Ride: Inside The Beatles 1964 and 1965 Tours That Changed the World*. New York: Penguin Books, 2003.

King, Carole. *A Natural Woman*. New York: Grand Central Publishing, 2012.

Kubernik, Harvey. *1967: A Complete Rock Music History of the Summer of Love*. New York: Sterling, 2017.

Leonard, Candy. *Beatleness: How the Beatles and Their Fans Remade the World*. New York: Arcade, 2014.

Levine, Ken. *The Me Generation by Me: Growing Up in the '60s*. Self-published, 2012.

Love, Mike with James S. Hirsch. *Good Vibrations: My Life as a Beach Boy*. New York: Blue Rider Press, 2016.

Malone, Bill C. and Jocelyn R. Neal. 2010. *Country Music, U.S.A*. Austin: University of Texas Press. 2010 (third revised edition).

McMillian, John. *Beatles vs. Stones*. New York: Simon and Schuster Paperbacks, 2013.

Milner, Greg. *Perfecting Sound Forever: An Aural History of Recorded Music*. New York: Farrar, Straus, Giroux, 2009.

Powell, John. *Why You Love Music*. New York: Little Brown and Company, 2016.

Ribowsky, Mark. *Ain't Too Proud To Beg: The Troubled Lives and Enduring Soul of The Temptations*. New York: John Wiley & Sons, Inc., 2010.

Ribowsky, Mark. *Signed, Sealed, and Delivered: The Soulful Journey of Stevie Wonder*. New York: John Wiley and Sons, Inc., 2010.

Ribowsky, Mark. *Dreams to Remember: Otis Redding, Stax Records and the Transformation of Southern Soul*. New York: Liveright Publishing, 2015.

Ribowsky, Mark. *Sweet Dreams and Flying Machines: The Life and Music of James Taylor*. Chicago: Chicago Review Press, 2016.

Rowlands, Penelope (editor). *The Beatles Are Here: 50 Years after the Band Arrived in America, Writers, Musicians and Other Fans Remember*. Chapel Hill, NC: Algonquin Books, 2014.

Savage, Jon. *1966: The Year the Decade Exploded*. London: Faber and Faber, 2015.

Springsteen, Bruce. *Born to Run*. New York: Simon and Schuster, 2016.

Tolinski, Brad and Alan Di Perna. *Play it Loud: An Epic History of the Style, Sound, & Revolution of the Electric Guitar*. New York: Doubleday, 2016.

Wald, Elijah. *Dylan Goes Electric!: Newport, Seeger, Dylan, and the Night That Split the Sixties*. New York: Dey St, 2015.

Ward, Geoffrey C. and Ken Burns. *Jazz: A History of America's Music*. New York: Alfred A. Knopf, 2007 (paperback).

Ward, Geoffrey and Ken Burns. *The Vietnam War*. New York: Alfred A. Knopf, 2017.

Whitburn, Joel. *Joel Whitburn Presents Top 1000 Hits of the Rock Era: 1955-2005*. Milwaukee: Hal Leonard Corporation, 2005.

Whitburn, Joel. *Joel Whitburn Presents Across the Charts: The 1960s*. Menomonee Falls, Wisconsin: Record Research Inc., 2008.

Whitburn, Joel. *The Billboard Book of Top 40 Hits: Complete Chart Information About America's Most Popular Songs & Artists, 1955-2009 (Revised and Expanded Ninth Edition)*. New York: Billboard Books, 2010.

Articles

Anonymous. The Teen-Agers: A Newsweek survey of what they're really like. *Newsweek*, March 21, 1966.

Anonymous. Nat King Cole, 45, is dead of cancer. *The New York Times*, February 16, 1965.

Anonymous. Simon and Garfunkel sing their own compositions. *The New York Times*, May 2, 1966.

Anonymous. The Rolling Stones gather avid fans. *The New York Times*, July 4, 1966.

Anonymous. The White Album. *Rolling Stone*, October 26, 1968. (From *Rolling Stone: The Fortieth Anniversary*. January 12-26, 2007).

Anonymous. Led Zeppelin supplants Beatles in British poll. *The New York Times*, September 16, 1970.

Apple, Jr., R. W. The states ratify full vote at 18. *The New York Times*, July 1, 1971.

Arlen, Michael. Television's war. *The New Yorker*, May 27, 1967.

Aronowitz, Alfred G. The Doors seek nirvana note. *The New York Times*, November 25, 1967.

Baldwin, Mary Burt. Teenage girls show preference for bouffant. *The New York Times*, February 24, 1962.

Bart, Peter. 'California sound' dwells on crack-ups and danger. *The New York Times*, January 22, 1965.

Begley, Sharon. What the Beatles gave science. *Newsweek,* November 19, 2007.

Brackman, Jacob and Terrence Malick. Notes and comment. *The New Yorker*, April 13, 1968 [The assassination of Martin Luther King, Jr.].

Brackman, Jacob. Overdosing on life. *The New York Times*, October 27, 1970.

Braudy, Susan. James Taylor, a new troubadour. *The New York Times*, February 21, 1971. (from the book, New York Times: The Times of the Seventies, The Culture, politics, personalities that shaped the decade).

Carpenter, Ellen. 40 Years of Rock Style. *Rolling Stone: The Fortieth Anniversary*. January 12-26, 2007.

Christgau, Robert and David Fricke. 40 Essential Albums of 1967. *Rolling Stone: The Fortieth Anniversary*. January 12-26, 2007.

Cohn, Nik. The Who's pinball opera. *The New York Times*, May 18, 1969.

Considine, Bob. Alpert's brassy sound of success. Baltimore: *The News American*, August 25, 1966.

DeCurtis, Anthony. New York: As a counterpoint to the West coast scene, the city offered up an urbane, gritty radicalism all its own. *Rolling Stone: The Fortieth Anniversary*. January 12-26, 2007.

Dilts, James D. The Sound of Teen-Age Music in Baltimore. Baltimore: *The Sunday Sun Magazine*, August 28, 1966.

Farhi, Paul. A touch of brass: Herb Alpert hopes to get a second wind from his feel-good 'Tijuana' sound. Washington, D. C. : *Washington Post*, April 6, 2005.

Fricke, David. Detroit: The riots of 1967 left a permanent scar on the Motor City and shocked the nation. But the music scene refused to die. *Rolling Stone: The Fortieth Anniversary*. January 12-26, 2007.

Gardner, Paul. Beatles invade, fans scream. *The New York Times*, February 8, 1964.

Gates, David. Tuned In, Turned On. The Times They Were A-Changin', But in the Arts Only Music Kept Pace. *Newsweek*, November 2007.

Gelb, Arthur. Habitues of Meyer Davis Land, Dance the Twist. *The New York Times*, October 19, 1961.

Gent, George. Classical music dwindling on city's radio stations. *The New York Times*, August 10, 1971.

Gilmore, Mikal. San Francisco: How LSD, psychedelic rock and 75,000 hippie kids started a revolution. *Rolling Stone: The Fortieth Anniversary*. January 12-26, 2007.

Gilmore, Mikal. Making Sgt. Pepper. In 1976, the Beatles were at a crossroads—they quit touring, experimented with drugs and set out to change rock and roll forever. *Rolling Stone: The Fortieth Anniversary*. January 12-26, 2007.

Gilmore, Mikal. Chuck Berry, 1926-2017: Farewell to the Father of Rock and Roll. *Rolling Stone*, April 20, 2017.

Goldman, Albert. Aretha Franklin makes salvation seem erotic. *The New York Times*, March 31, 1968.

Goldstein Richard. We still need the Beatles, but… *The New York Times*, June 18, 1967.

Gould, Jack. Quartet continues to agitate the faithful. *The New York Times*, February 10, 1964.

Heckman, Don. Elton John: A new superstar? *The New York Times*, November 29, 1970.

Heckman, Don. Jim Morrison at the end, Joni at the crossroads. *The New York Times*, August 8, 1971.

Heckman, Don. Survival of the hippest. *The New York Times*, September 9, 1971 (1970s NYT book)

Heckman, Don. Rod Stewart a lasting rock star. *The New York Times*, November 28, 1971. (1970s NYT book)

Hentoff, Nat. The crackin' shakin' breakin'' sounds. *The New Yorker*, October 24, 1964 [subject: Bob Dylan].

Hertzberg, Hendrik. The Who. *The New Yorker*, November 15, 1969.

Hiatt, Brian. Los Angeles: High times in Laurel Canyon and on Sunset Strip. *Rolling Stone: The Fortieth Anniversary*. January 12-26, 2007.

Hiatt, Brian. Monterrey Pop. Rock's first concert made stars of Hendrix and Joplin. So why did the Dead try to kill it? *Rolling Stone: The Fortieth Anniversary*. January 12-26, 2007.

Hill, Michael. 1967: It was the year that rock came of age. Baltimore: *The Sun*, August 19, 2007.

Ivins, Molly. Obituary—Elvis Presley dies; rock singer was 42. *The New York Times*, August 17, 1977.

Jahn, Mike. Stones still exciting. *The New York Times*, November 28, 1969.

Jones, Steve. Chuck Berry: 1926-2017. Guitar Master Set Rock 'N' Roll Tone: Original Hall of Famer's Riffs Still Influence Music. *USA Today*, March 20, 2017.

Kaufman, Leslie. Scott McKenzie, singer known for 'San Francisco' dies at 73. *The New York Times*, August 20, 2012.

Kelly, Jacques and Frederick Rasmussen. An earth force for a generation of Baltimore teens. Baltimore: *The Sun*, July 17, 2003.

Kelly, Jacques and Frederick N. Rasmussen. Recalling Johnny Dark as a force in Baltimore rock radio. Baltimore: *The Sun*, September 16, 2016.

Keveney, Bill. Beach Boys in harmony on 50th anniversary: Discord in past as tour kicks off. *USA Today*, April 24, 2012.

Keveney, Bill. That's where they wanna go—back to the studio: Beach Boys set to release new album in June. *USA Today*, April 24, 2012.

Klemesrud, Judy. Rock fans play fashion game, too. *The New York Times*, December 26, 1969.

Lelyveld, Joseph. Ravi Shankar gives west a new old sound. *The New York Times*, July 20, 1966.

Levin, Gary. For always, Dick Clark, so long…*USA Today*, April 19, 2012.

Lewis, Anthony. Lawsuit spells breakup for Beatles. *New York Times*, January 1, 1971.

Light, Alan. London: Tightly knit, decadent and explosively creative, the scene was too good to last. *Rolling Stone: The Fortieth Anniversary*. January 12-26, 2007.

Light, Alan. Memphis. Harmony and dissension in the capital of soul. *Rolling Stone: The Fortieth Anniversary*. January 12-26, 2007.

Lingeman, Richard R. The big, happy, beating heart of the Detroit sound. *The New York Times*, November 27, 1966.

Lione, Louise Hickman. $15 Billion yearly spent by teenagers. Baltimore: *The Sunday Sun*, August 14, 1966.

Love, Robert. Celebrating the 50th Anniversary of the Summer of Love, 1967-2017. *AARP Magazine*, August-September 2017.

Lowe, D. and Thomas Whiteside. Brian Epstein. New York: *The New Yorker*, December 28, 1963.

Lydon, Patrick. Woodstock: 'A joyful confirmation that good things can happen there'. *The New York Times*, August 24, 1969.

Maher, Jack and Tom Noonan. Chart crawls with Beatles. *Billboard Magazine*, April 4, 1964.

Malcolm Donald, Lillian Ross, and E. B. White. [Notes and Comment]. *The New Yorker*, November 30, 1963 [The assassination of John F. Kennedy].

McGregor, Craig. Dylan: reluctant hero of the pop generation. *The New York Times,* May 7, 1972.

Miller, Jonathan. Views of a death. *The New Yorker*, December 28, 1963 [J. F. K.'s televised funeral].

Minzesheimer, Bob. Pete Seeger: He taught us to sing—and to think. *USA Today*, January 29, 2014.

Nash, Graham. I was there: The Climate, the people –It's meant to seduce. *Rolling Stone: The Fortieth Anniversary*. January 12-26, 2007.

Oldenburg, Ann and Gary Levin. Curtain may fall, but his legacy won't: Clark built an empire in front of camera, behind scenes. *USA Today*, April 19, 2012.

Olesker, Michael. AM fades with silencing of WCAO voices. Baltimore: *The Sun*, November 24, 1991.

Olesker, Michael. Deane helped define an era in Baltimore. *The Sun*, July 17, 2003.

Phillips, Tom. Rock speaks sweetly now. *The New York Times*, December 17, 1967.

Rasmussen, Frederick N. 'Fat Daddy' was a voice in R&B. Baltimore: *The Sun*, February 24, 2001.

Ross, Lillian. Sgt. Pepper. *The New Yorker*, June 24, 1967.

Rovere, Richard H. Letter from Washington. *The New Yorker*, June 15, 1968 [The assassination of Robert F. Kennedy].

Rowlands, Penelope. Love, Love, Love. : Remembering the blessed, fevered moment when America Met the Beatles. *AARP Magazine*, February–March 2014.

Shelton, Robert. 20-year-old Bob Dylan is bright new face. *The New York Times*, September 29, 1961.

Shelton, Robert. Folk-music fete called a success. *The New York Times*, July 29, 1963.

Shelton, Robert. Dylan conquers unruly audience. Folk singer offers works in 'new mood' at Forest Hills. *The New York Times*, August 30, 1965.

Shelton, Robert. The folk rock rage. *The New York Times*, January 30, 1966.

Shelton, Robert. Janis Joplin climbs the heady rock firmament. *The New York Times*, February 19, 1968.

Sloane, Leonard. Boots make a splash. *The New York Times*, May 12, 1963.

Stevenson, James. Simon and Garfunkel. New York: *The New Yorker*, September 2, 1967.

Stevenson, James and Faith McNulty. [From Notes and Comment]. *The New Yorker*, August 30, 1969 [Woodstock].

Stone, Judy. Two clean-cut heroes make waves. *The New York Times*, April 16, 1967.

Trillin, Calvin. March on Washington. *The New Yorker*, September 7, 1963.

Trilin, Calvin. [From] Letter from Berkeley. *The New Yorker*, March 13, 1965 [The Free Speech Movement].

Wallace, Kevin. Joan Baez. *The New Yorker*, October 7, 1967 ["non-violent soldier].

Wenner, Jann. Otis Redding, 1941-1967 (obituary). *Rolling Stone*, January 20, 1968 (From *Rolling Stone: The Fortieth Anniversary*. January 12-26, 2007).

Wenner, Jann. The Who Plot Rock "Opera. " *Rolling Stone*, September 14 and 28, 1968. (From *Rolling Stone: The Fortieth Anniversary*. January 12-26, 2007).

Wilentz, Sean. The Legacy of '67. *Rolling Stone: The Fortieth Anniversary*. January 12-26, 2007.

Willis, Ellen. Rock, Etc. *The New Yorker*, July 6, 1968 [Packaging Rock and Post-Rock].

Willis, Ellen. Rock, Etc. *The New Yorker*. September 6, 1969 [Woodstock].

Willis, Kim. The Beatles made it by going 'Eight Days a Week'. *USA Today*, September 12, 2016.

Wright, Robert A. 200,000 attend Altamont rock fete. *The New York Times*, December 7, 1969.

Movies/Documentaries—DVDs

The Beatles: The First U. S. Visit. Apple Corps Limited. 2003.

CNN's Sixties Special: The British Invasion (Episode 6). 2014.

CNN's Sixties Special: Sex, Drugs & Rock and Roll (Episode 10). 2014.

The Beatles' Eight Days A Week, The Touring Years: The Band You Know. The Story You Don't. A Ron Howard Film. Apple Corps Limited (White Horse Pictures and Imagine Entertainment). 2016.

Get On Up: The James Brown Story. Universal Studios Entertainment. 2015.

A Hard Day's Night: The Beatles (1964). The Criterion Collection. 2014.

Motown: The DVD. Definitive Performances. Hip-O Records, A Universal Music Company. 2009

Soundbreaking: Stories from the Cutting Edge of Recorded Music. Higher Ground LLC in association with Sir George Martin present a Show of Force Production. RLJ Entertainment, Inc. 2016 (Episodes 1 through 8). Episode 1: The Art of Recording. Episode 2: Painting with Sound. Episode 3: The Human Instrument. Episode 4: Going Electric. Episode 5: Four on the Floor. Episode 7: Sound and Vision. Episode 8: I Am My Music.

Standing in the Shadows of Motown. Artisan Entertainment. 2002.

T. A. M. I. Show: Teenage Awards Music International (October 29, 1964). Shout Factory/Dick Clark Productions. 2009.

Time/Life History of Rock and Roll DVD Series. Disc One, Volume One: "Rock and Roll Explodes." Disc One, Volume Two: "Good Rockin' Tonight." Disc Two, Volume One: "Britain Invades, America Fights Back." Disc Two, Volume Two: "The Sounds of Soul." Disc Three, Volume One: "Plugging In." Disc Three, Volume Two: "My Generation."

The Vietnam War. Ken Burns and Lynn Novick. Florentine Films Production. 2017.

Vinyl LPs

Allman Brothers. 1973. *Brothers and Sisters.* Capricorn Records.

The Beatles. 1964. *Beatles' 65.* Capitol Records.

The Beatles. 1967. *Sgt. Pepper's Lonely Hearts Club Band.* Capitol Records.

The Beatles. 1968. *Yellow Submarine.* Apple Records.

The Beatles. 1969. *Abbey Road.* Apple Records.

Blind Faith. 1969. *Blind Faith.* Atco Records.

Blood, Sweat and Tears. 1968. *Child Is Father To The Man.* Columbia Records.

Blood, Sweat and Tears. 1969. *Blood, Sweat and Tears.* Columbia Records.

The Chambers Brothers. 1967. *The Time Has Come.* Columbia Records.

Chicago Transit Authority. 1969. *Chicago Transit Authority.* Columbia Records.

Chicago. 1970. *Chicago.* Columbia Records.

Chicago. 1971. *Chicago III.* Columbia Records.

Chicago. 1974. *Chicago VII.* Columbia Records.

Clapton, Eric. 1972. *History of Eric Clapton.* Atco Records.

Clapton, Eric. 1972. *Eric Clapton At His Best.* Polydor Records.

Cream. 1966. *Fresh Cream.* Atco Records.

Cream. 1967. *Disraeli Gears.* Atco Records.

Doobie Brothers. 1972. *Toulose Street.* Warner Brothers Records, Inc.

Doobie Brothers. 1973. *The Captain and Me.* Warner Brothers Records, Inc.

The 4 Seasons. 1968. Edizione de Oro (The 4 Seasons Gold Edition). Philips Records.

The Four Tops. 1967. *Greatest Hits.* Motown Records.

The Four Tops. 1971. *Greatest Hits Volume 2.* Motown Records.

The Grassroots. 1971. *Their 16 Greatest Hits.* Dunhill Records.

Harrison, George. 1970. *All Things Must Pass.* Apple Records.

Kooper, Al. 1969. *You Never Know Who Your Friends Are.* Columbia Records.

The Lovin' Spoonful. 1967. *The Best of The Lovin' Spoonful.* Kama Sutra Records.

Morrison, Van. 1971. *Tupelo Honey.* Warner Brothers Records.

Pickett, Wilson. 1965. *The Exciting Wilson Pickett.* Atlantic Records.

Rare Earth. 1970. *Ecology.* Rare Earth Records (Motown).

Redding, Otis. 1967. *History of Otis Redding.* Volt Records.

Santana. 1969. *Santana.* Columbia Records.

Santana. 1970. *Abraxas.* Columbia Records.

Stewart, Rod. 1971. *Every Picture Tells A Story.* Mercury Records.

Stewart, Rod. 1972. *Never A Dull Moment.* Mercury Records.

The Temptations. 1965. *The Temptations Sing Smokey.* Gordy Records (Motown Records).

Three Dog Night. 1968. *Three Dog Night.* Dunhill Records.

Three Dog Night. 1969. *Suitable for Framing.* Dunhill Records.

Three Dog Night. 1970. *It Ain't Easy.* Dunhill Records.

The Turtles. 1967. *The Turtles! Golden Hits.* White Whale Records.

The Turtles. 1968. *The Turtles Present the Battle of the Bands.* White Whale Records.

Wonder, Stevie. 1968. *Greatest Hits.* Tamla Records (Motown).

Young Rascals. 1967. *Collections.* Atlantic Records.

Music CDs

Adams, Bryan. 2002. *The Best of Me.* A&M Records, Universal Music Company.

Adele. 2011. *Adele 21.* XL Recordings Ltd., Columbia Records, a Division of Columbia Records.

Allman Brothers. 2013. *Allman Brothers Band Icon.* Mercury Records, Universal Music Enterprises.

Herb Alpert & The Tijuana Brass. 2005 [originally 1966]. *SRO* [Standing Room Only]. Almo Properties, Distributed by Sony BMG Music Entertainment.

Herb Alpert and The Tijuana Brass. 2005 [originally 1965] *!!Going Places!!* Almo Properties, Distributed by Sony BMG Music Entertainment.

Herb Alpert's Tijuana Brass. 2005 [originally 1964]. *South of the Border.* Almo Properties, Distributed by Sony BMG Music Entertainment.

Herb Alpert & The Tijuana Brass. 2005 [originally 1966]. *What Now My Love.* Almo Properties, Distributed by Sony BMG Music Entertainment.

Herb Alpert & The Tijuana Brass. 2005 [originally 1968]. *The Beat of the Brass.* Almo Properties, Distributed by Sony BMG Music Entertainment.

Herb Alpert & The Tijuana Brass. 2005 [originally 1962]. *The Lonely Bull.* Almo Properties, Distributed by Sony BMG Music Entertainment.

Herb Alpert's Tijuana Brass. [originally 1965]. *Whipped Cream and Other Delights.* A&M Records.

The Beach Boys. 2003. *Sounds of Summer: The Very Best of The Beach Boys.* Capitol Records.

The Beach Boys. 2000. *Sunflower and Surf's Up.* Brother Records under license to Capitol Records,

The Beach Boys. 2006. *Pet Sounds 40th Anniversary.* Capitol Records. Music from EMI.

The Beach Boys. 2012. *That's Why God Made The Radio*. Brother Records, under exclusive license to Capitol Records.

The Beach Boys. 2012. *50 Fifty Big Ones*. Capitol Records.

The Beatles. 2009. *Please Please Me*. Capitol Records, EMI's Parlophone Records, Apple Corps Ltd.

The Beatles. 2009. *The Beatles For Sale*. Capitol Records, EMI's Parlophone Records, Apple Corps Ltd.

The Beatles. 2009. *With the Beatles*. Capitol Records, EMI's Parlophone Records, Apple Corps Ltd.

The Beatles. 2013. *Live at the BBC*. Apple Records, Capitol Records, Calderstone Productions Limited, a Division of Universal Music Group.

The Beatles. 2013. *On Air—Live at the BBC Volume 2*. Apple Records, Capitol Records, Calderstone Productions Limited, a Division of Universal Music Group.

The Beatles. 1964. *A Hard Day's Night*. Capitol Records, Parlophone Records, Apple Records.

The Beatles. 1965. *Help!* Capitol Records, Parlophone Records, Apple Records.

The Beatles. 1965. *Rubber Soul*. Capitol Records, Parlophone Records, Apple Records.

The Beatles. 1966. *Revolver*. Capitol Records, EMI Records Ltd., Apple Corps, Ltd.

The Beatles. 1967. *Sgt. Pepper's Lonely Hearts Club Band*. Capitol Records, EMI Records Ltd., Apple Corps, Ltd.

The Beatles. 1967. *Magical Mystery Tour*. Capitol Records, EMI Records Ltd., Apple Corps, Ltd.

The Beatles. 1968. *The Beatles* [often called The Beatles White Album]. Capitol Records, EMI Records Ltd., Apple Corps, Ltd.

The Beatles. 1969. *Abbey Road*. Capitol Records, EMI Records Ltd., Apple Corps, Ltd.

The Beatles. 2009. *Past Masters*. Capitol Records, EMI Records Ltd., Apple Corps, Ltd.

The Beatles. 2006. *Love*. Capitol Records, EMI Records, Ltd., Apple Corps Ltd.

The Beatles. 2016. *Live At The Hollywood Bowl from Eight Days A Week*. Capitol Records, Universal Music Group, Apple Corps, Ltd.

Berry Chuck. 2005. *Chuck Berry: The Definitive Collection*. Geffen Records, Chess Chronicles. A Universal Music Company.

Blood, Sweat and Tears. 1968. *Child Is Father To The Man*. Columbia Records.

Blood, Sweat and Tears. 1969. *Blood, Sweat and Tears*. Columbia Records, Sony Music Entertainment.

Booker T. & The MG's. 1994. *The Very Best of Booker T. & the MGs*. Atlantic Recording Co. and Fantasy Records. This compilation by Rhino Records.

The Box Tops. 1996. *The Best of The Box Tops: Soul Deep*. Arista Records.

Brown, James. 1991. *20 All-Time Greatest Hits*. Polygram Records, Inc.

Brown, James. 2014. *Get On Up. Original Motion Picture Soundtrack*. Polydor. Universal Records. A Universal Music Company.

Butler, Jerry. 1991. *Greatest Hits*. Curb Records.

The Byrds. 1996 [originally released 1965]. *Mr. Tambourine Man*. Columbia Records, Legacy.

The Byrds. 1996 [originally released 1967]. *Younger Than Yesterday*. Columbia Records. Legacy.

The Byrds. 1999 [originally released 1967]. *The Byrds Greatest Hits*. Columbia Records. Legacy.

Cash, Johnny. 2012. *Johnny Cash. The Greatest. The Number Ones*. Columbia Records. Legacy.

Charles, Ray. 2013. *Ray Charles: The Ultimate Collection*. Not Now Music Limited.

Chicago [originally named Chicago Transit Authority]. 1999 [originally 1969]. *Chicago Transit Authority*. Chicago Records, Inc. [Originally Columbia Records].

Chicago. 1971. *Chicago* [often referred to as *Chicago II*]. 1971. Chicago Records, Inc. [originally Columbia Records].

Chicago. *The Heart of Chicago, 1967-1997*. 1997. Chicago Records, Inc., Reprise Records.

Chicago. *The Very Best of: Only The Beginning*. The Rhino Entertainment Co., Warner Music Group.

Clapton, Eric. 1995. *The Cream of Clapton*. Polygram International Music, A&M Records.

Clapton, Eric. 2007. *Clapton: Complete Clapton*. Reprise Records, A Warner Music Group Company.

Cocker, Joe. 1970. *Joe Cocker Mad Dogs & Englishmen*. A&M Records.

Collins, Phil. 1998. *Phil Collins...Hits*. Atlantic Recording Corp. A Time Warner Company.

Collins, Phil. 2016. *Going Back*. Rhino Entertainment Company, a Warner Music Group Company.

Cooke, Sam. 1998. *Greatest Hits*. RCA, BMG Entertainment.

Cream. 1967. *Disraeli Gears*. Polydor Records, Polygram International Company.

Cream. 1968. *Wheels of Fire*. Polydor Records, Polygram International Company.

Creedence Clearwater Revival. 2008. *Bayou Country (40th Anniversary Edition)*. Fantasy records, Concord Music Group, Inc.

Crosby, Stills and Nash. 1969. *Crosby, Stills and Nash*. Atlantic Records, Rhino Entertainment group, A Warner Music Group Company.

Crosby, Stills, Nash and Young. 1970. *Déjà Vu*. Atlantic Records, Rhino Entertainment group, A Time Warner Company.

Curtis, King. 1998 [originally issued 1967]. *King Curtis Plays The Greatest Memphis Hits/King Size Soul*. Rhino Entertainment Company, Koch International, Ltd.

Derek and The Dominoes. 1970. *Layla and Assorted Other Love Songs*. Polydor Records, Polygram International Music.

Donovan. 1999. *Donovan's Greatest Hits*. Epic Records, Sony Music Entertainment, Inc., Legacy.

The Doobie Brothers. 1972. *Toulose Street*. Warner Brothers Records, Inc.

The Doobie Brothers. 1973. *The Captain and Me*. Warner Brothers Records, Inc.

The Doors. 2012 [originally recorded 1969]. *The Soft Parade*. Rhino Entertainment Company, a Warner Music Company.

The Doors. 1985. *The Best of The Doors*. Elektra/Asylum Records, A Division of Warner Communications, Inc.

Dylan, Bob. 2003 [originally issued 1963]. *The Freewheelin' Bob Dylan*. Sony Music Entertainment Inc., [originally Columbia Records].

Dylan, Bob. 2005 [originally issued 1964]. *The Times They Are A-Changin'*. Sony Music Entertainment Inc., [originally Columbia Records].

Dylan, Bob. 2004 [originally issued 1965]. *Highway 61 Revisited*. Sony Music Entertainment Inc., [originally Columbia Records].

Dylan, Bob. 2003 [originally issued 1965]. *Bringing It All Back Home*. Sony Music Entertainment Inc., [originally Columbia Records].

Dylan, Bob. 2004 [originally issued 1966]. *Blonde on Blonde*. Sony Music Entertainment Inc. [originally Columbia Records].

Dylan, Bob. 2003 [originally issued 1967]. *John Wesley Harding*. Sony Music Entertainment Inc. [originally Columbia Records].

Dylan, Bob. 2003 [originally issued 1969]. *Nashville Skyline*. Sony Music Entertainment Inc. [originally Columbia Records].

Eagles. 2003. *The Very Best Of The Eagles.* Warner Music Group.

5th Dimension. 2011. *The Essential 5th Dimension.* Arista Records, a unit of Sony Music Entertainment.

Fogerty, John. 2004. *The Long Road: The Ultimate John Fogerty/Creedence Collection.* Geffen Records, Concord Music Group.

Four Tops. 2008. *The Definitive Collection.* Motown Records, A Universal Music Company.

Frampton, Peter. 1996. *Greatest Hits.* A&M Records.

Franklin, Aretha. 1995 [originally issued 1967]. *I Never Loved A Man The Way I Love You.* Atlantic Recording Corporation, Rhino Records, Inc.

Franklin, Aretha. 1995. [originally issued 1967]. *Lady Soul.* Atlantic Recording Corporation, Rhino Records, Inc.

Franklin, Aretha. 2000 [originally released 1985]. *30 Greatest Hits.* Atlantic Recording Corporation, A Warner Music Group Company.

Friends of Distinction. 1996. *The Best of The Friends of Distinction.* RCA Records, BMG Entertainment.

Gaye, Marvin. 1999. *The Best of Marvin Gaye-Volume 1- The '60s. 20th Century Master: The Millennium Collection.* Motown Records., A Universal Music Company.

Gaye, Marvin. 2003. *Love Songs—Greatest Duets.* Motown Records, A Universal Music Company.

Gaye, Marvin. 2007. *Number 1's.* Motown Records., A Universal Music Company.

Gore, Leslie. 2000. *The Best of Leslie Gore. 20th Century Masters: The Millenium Collection.* The Island Def Jam Music Group, Universal Music and Video Distribution, Inc.

Grand Funk Railroad. 1988 [originally issued 1970]. *Closer To Home.* Capitol Records, Inc.

The Grassroots. 1994 [originally issued 1985]. *Temptation Eyes.* MCA Records.

Harrison, George. 2001 [originally issued 1970]. *All Things Must Pass.* EMI Records, Capitol Records, GN Records [originally issued on Apple Records].

The Jimi Hendrix Experience. 2000 [originally issued 1967]. *Are You Experienced.* Sony Music Entertainment, Legacy.

The Impressions. 1997. *The Very Best of The Impressions.* The Rhino Entertainment Company.

Iron Butterfly. 1968. *In-A-Gadda-Da-Vida.* Atco Records, A Division of Atlantic Recording Corporation.

The Isley Brothers. 2001. *The Best of The Motown Years. 20th Century Masters: The Mil-*

lenium Collection. Motown Records, A Division of UMG Recording.

Tommy James and The Shondells. 1993. *The Very Best of Tommy James and The Shondells*. Rhino Records, Inc., A Warner Music Group Company.

John, Elton. 2007. *Rocket Man: Number Ones*. Mercury Records, A Universal Music Company.

Jones, Tom. 1997. *The Best of Tom Jones*. The Decca Record Company, a Division of A&M records, Deram, A Polygram Company.

Joplin, Janis. 1999. *Janis Joplin's Greatest Hits*. Sony Music Entertainment Inc., Legacy.

King, Carole. 1977 [originally issued 1971]. *Tapestry*. Ode Records. Epic Records, A Division of Sony Music, Legacy.

Led Zeppelin. 2007. *Mothership*. Atlantic Recording Corporation, A Warner Music Group.

Lennon, John. 1997. *Lennon Legend*. EMI Records Ltd.

The Lovin' Spoonful. 2000. *Greatest Hits*. Buddha Records, BMG Entertainment.

The Mamas and The Papas. 1998. *Greatest Hits*. MCA records, A Universal Music Company.

Martha and The Vandellas. 1965. *Martha and The Vandellas Dance Party*. Motown Records.

Martha Reeves and The Vandellas. 1999. *The Best of Martha Reeves and The Vandellas. 20th Century Masters: The Millennium Collection*. Motown Records, A Universal Music Company.

The Marvelettes. 2000. *The Best of The Marvelettes. 20th Century Masters: The Millennium Collection*. Motown Records, A Universal Music Company.

McDonald, Michael. 2003. *Motown*. Motown Records under Universal Music International.

McDonald, Michael. 2004. *Motown Two*. Universal Records under Universal Music International.

Smokey Robinson and The Miracles. *The Ultimate Collection*. Motown Record Company L. P., A Polygram Company.

Morrison, Van. 1971. *Tupelo Honey*. Polydor, Polygram Records, Exile Productions, Inc.

Morrison, Van. 1990. *The Best of Van Morrison*. Polydor, Polygram Records Inc., Exile Productions, Inc.

Morrison, Van. 1993. *The Best of Van Morrison. Volume Two*. Polydor, Polygram Records Inc., Exile Productions, Inc.

Peter, Paul and Mary. 2005. *The Very Best of Peter, Paul and Mary*. Warner Bros. Records Inc., A Warner Music Group Company.

Pickett, Wilson. 2002. *The Exciting Wilson Pickett*. Rhino Entertainment Company under license from Atlantic Recording Corp.

Pickett, Wilson. 1987. *Wilson Pickett's Greatest Hits*. Atlantic Recording Corporation, A Warner Communications Company.

Pink Floyd. *Dark Side of the Moon*. 2016. Pink Floyd Music Ltd, Sony Music Entertainment.

Presley, Elvis. 2003. *Elvis 2ⁿᵈ To None*. RCA Records, BMG Music.

Presley, Elvis. 2002. *ELV1S 30 #1 Hits*. RCA Records, BMG Music.

Presley, Elvis. 2002. *Elvis 56*. RCA Records, BMG Music.

Springfield, Dusty. 1999. *The Best of Dusty Springfield. 20ᵗʰ Century Masters: The Millennium Collection*. Mercury Records, A Division of Polygram Records, A Universal Music Company.

Starr, Ringo. 2007. *Photograph: The Very Best of Ringo*. Capitol Records, Inc., Apple Records from EMI.

Rare Earth. 2001. *The Best of Rare Earth. 20ᵗʰ Century: The Millennium Collection:* Motown Records, a Division of UMG Recordings, A Universal Music Company.

The Rascals. 1993. *The Very Best of The Rascals*. Rhino Records Inc. Atlantic Recording Corporation.

Redding, Otis. [originally issued 1965]. *Otis Blue. Otis Sings Soul*. Atlantic and Atco Remasters. Atco records, A division of Atlantic Recording Corporation, A Time Warner Company.

Redding, Otis. [originally issued 1968]. *The Dock of the Bay*. Atlantic and Atco Remasters. Atco records, A division of Atlantic Recording Corporation, A Time Warner Company.

Redding, Otis. 1992. *Remember Me*. Stax Records.

Redding, Otis. 1992. *The Very Best of Otis Redding*. Atlantic Recording Corp., Rhino Records Inc.

Redding, Otis and Carla Thomas. [originally issued 1967]. *King and Queen*. Atlantic and Atco Remasters. Atco records, A division of Atlantic Recording Corporation, A Time Warner Company.

Rivers, Johnny. 1991. *Johnny Rivers Greatest Hits*. CEMA Special Markets, Capitol-EMI Music, Inc.

The Rolling Stones. 2002 [originally issued 1965]. *Out of Our Heads*. ABKCO Music and Records [originally issued by London Records].

The Rolling Stones. 2002 [originally issued 1969]. *Let It Bleed.* ABKCO Music and Records [originally issued by London Records].

The Rolling Stones. 2002. *Forty Licks.* ABKCO Music and Records.

The Rolling Stones. 2015 [originally issued 1971]. *Sticky Fingers.* Capitol Records, Universal Music Distribution.

The Rolling Stones. 2017. *On Air.* A Rolling Stones/Universal Music Enterprises Release. Promotone B.V. and ABKCO Music and Records, Universal Music Operations, Ltd.

Ryder, Mitch & The Detroit Wheels. 1997. *Devil with a Blue Dress On and Other Hits.* Flashback Records, A Division of Rhino Entertainment Company.

Sam and Dave. 1995. *The Very Best of Sam and Dave.* Atlantic Recording Corporation, Rhino Records Inc.

Santana. 1998. *The Best of Santana.* Sony Music Entertainment Inc., Columbia Records, Legacy.

Seger Bob and The Silver Bullet Band. 2011. *Ultimate Hits: Rock and Roll Never Forgets.* Hideout Records, Capitol Records.

Simon, Paul. 1988. *Negotiations and Love Songs. 1971-1986.* Warner Bros. Records.

Simon and Garfunkel. 1999. *The Best of Simon and Garfunkel.* Sony Music Entertainment Inc., Columbia Records. Legacy.

Sly and The Family Stone. 2007. *Greatest Hits.* Sony Music Entertainment, Sony BMG Music Entertainment.

The Spinners. 1993. *The Very Best of The Spinners.* Atlantic Recording Corp, Rhino records, Inc.

Steely Dan. 1972. *Can't Buy A Thrill.* MCA Records, Inc., A Universal Music Company.

Steely Dan. 1985. *A Decade of Steely Dan.* MCA Records, Inc.

Stewart, Rod. 1971. *Every Picture Tells A Story.* Mercury Records, A Polygram Company.

The Supremes. 2005. *The Supremes Gold.* Motown record, Chronicles, A Universal Music Company.

The Supremes. 2009. *Diana Ross & The Supremes: Number 1's.* Motown Records, A Universal Music Company.

Taylor, James. 1971. *Mud Slide Jim and The Blue Horizon.* Warner Bros. Records, A Warner Communications Company.

Taylor, James. 1970. *Sweet Baby James.* Warner Bros. Records, A Warner Communications Company.

Taylor, James. 2003. *The Best of James Taylor.* Warner Bros. Records, Warner Music Group, an AOL Time Warner Company.

Stewart, Rod. 2009. *Soulbook.* RCA/JIVE Label Group, a unit of Sony Music Entertainment.

The Temptations. 1998 [first released 1965]. *The Temptin' Temptations.* Motown record Company, A PolyGram Company.

The Temptations. 1998 [first released 1965]. *The Temptations Sing Smokey.* Motown Record Company, A PolyGram company.

The Temptations. 1999 [first released 1966]. *Gettin' Ready.* Motown Record Company, A Universal Music Group Company.

The Temptations. [first released 1967]. *With A Lot o' Soul.* Motown Records. USM japan, A Universal Music Company.

The Temptations. 2002. *The Temptations Gold.* Motown Records, Chronicles, A Universal Music Company.

Three Dog Night. 1982. *The Best of "3 Dog Night. "* MCA Records.

Three Dog Night. 2009 [first issued 1968/1969 on Dunhill Records]. *Three Dog Night/Suitable for Framing.* MCA Records. Beat Goes On records, A Universal Music Ltd.

Traffic. 2001 [originally issued 1970]. *John Barleycorn Must Die.* Universal Island Records, Ltd. The Island Def Jam Music Group.

Traffic. 2005. *Traffic Gold.* Universal Island Records Ltd., The Island Def Jam Music Group.

The Turtles. 1984. *20 Greatest Hits.* Rhino Records.

Vanilla Fudge. 1967. Vanilla Fudge. Atco Records. Atlantic Recording Corporation, A Warner Communications Company.

Various Artists. 1985. *Atlantic Soul Classics.* Warner Special Products. A Warner Communications Company.

Various Artists. 1988. *Top of The Stax: Twenty Greatest Hits.* Stax Records, Fantasy Inc.

Various Artists. 1992. *Hitsville U. S. A. The Motown Singles Collection*—Disc One. Record Company, L. P.

Various Artists. 1992. *Hitsville U. S. A. The Motown Singles Collection*—Disc Two. Record Company, L. P.

Various Artists. 1992. *Hitsville U. S. A. The Motown Singles Collection*—Disc Three. Record Company, L. P.

Various Artists. 1992. *Hitsville U. S. A. The Motown Singles Collection*—Disc Four.

Record Company, L. P.

Various Artists. 1999. *The Best of Bond…James Bond.* Capitol Records.

Various Artists. 2000. *Casey Kasem Presents America's Top Ten Through The Years: The '60s.* Top Sail Productions, Warner/Elektra/Atlantic Corporation, A Time Warner Company.

Various Artists. 2002. *Standing in the Shadows of Motown: Original Motion Picture Soundtrack.* Hip-O Records/Motown Records, Universal Music Group Recordings, Inc.

Various Artists. 2007. *'60s R&B Classics.* Rhino Custom Products, Compass Productions, A Warner Music Group Company.

Various Artists. 2007. *Monterrey International Pop Festival.* Razor and Tie Direct LLC, Starbucks Entertainment.

Various Artists. 2011. *Wall of Sound: The Very Best of Phil Spector 1961-66.* Phil Spector Records, Inc., Sony Music Entertainment. EMI, Legacy

Various Artists. 2011. *Teenage: Teenagers & Youth in Music, 1951—1960* (Compiled by Jon Savage). Bear Family Records (Made in Germany).

Various Artists. 2013. *Feelin' Groovy.* Mood Media Entertainment Ltd., Sony Music Entertainment.

Various Artists. 2013. *Motown The Musical: The Original Broadway Cast Recording.* Motown Records, A Universal Music Group Company.

Various Artists. 2015. *Jon Savage's 1966: The Year the Decade Exploded.* Ace Records, Ltd.

Various Artists. 2017. *Jon Savage's 1967: The Year Pop Divided.* Ace Records, Ltd.

Various Artists. 2018. *Jon Savage's 1965: The Year The Sixties Ignited.* Ace Records, Ltd.

Jr. Walker and The All Stars. 2000. *The Best of Jr. Walker & The All Stars. 20th Century Masters: The Millennium Collection.* Motown Record Company, A Universal Music Company.

The Who. 1971. *Who's Next.* MCA Records, Inc.

Wonder, Stevie. 1996. *Song Review: A Greatest Hits Collection.* Motown Record Company, EMI records.

Wonder, Stevie. 2005. *The Best of Stevie Wonder. The 20th Century Masters: The Millennium Collection.* Motown Records, Chronicles. A Universal Music Company.

Wilson, Jackie. 1987. *The Very Best of Jackie Wilson.* Brunswick/Ace Records. Made in the U. K.

Young, Neil. 2004. *Greatest Hits.* Reprise Records, A Warner Music Group Company.

Index